Japan
A CONCISE HISTORY

Japan
A CONCISE HISTORY

MILTON W. MEYER
California State University, Los Angeles

1976

LITTLEFIELD, ADAMS & CO.
Totowa, New Jersey

Library of Congress Cataloging in Publication Data

Meyer, Milton Walter
   Japan: A Concise History

   (A Littlefield, Adams Quality Paperback No. 318)
   Bibliography: p.
   Includes index.
   1.   Japan—History.
DS835.M4   1976   952   76-9045
ISBN 0-8226-0318-7

For Shogo, Motoko, Junichi, and Akio

PREFACE

The purpose of this book is to provide an introduction to the history of Japan. Approximately half of the material deals with pre-Meiji Japan, the period before 1868. The other half narrates domestic and relevant foreign events since that epochal date, a watershed in Japanese history that may be considered the transition between traditional and modern Japan.

I am indebted to many for help in the formulation of this volume. Sir George Sansom, through his lectures at Columbia University and lucid books, early opened vistas on fundamental aspects of Japanese life and culture. Further studies at Stanford University and travels to Japan broadened the horizons, while my students at California State University, Los Angeles, in Japanese and Asian history courses over the years helped to focus the presentation and organization of the oral and written material.

MILTON W. MEYER

CONTENTS

PART THREE
MODERN JAPAN

PART FOUR

POSTWAR JAPAN

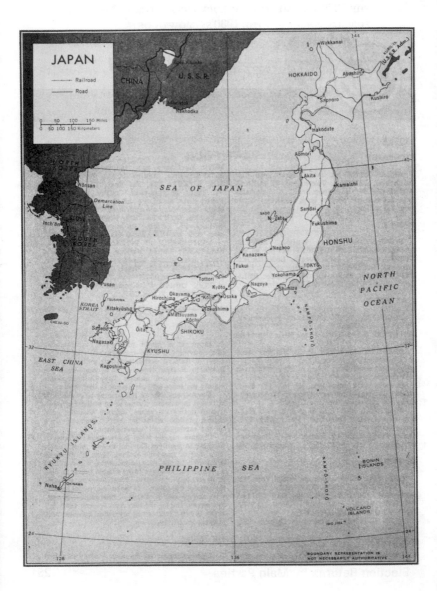

INTRODUCING JAPAN

The emergence of Japan as a world power has been one of the success stories of the modern age. Though small in geographic area, the archipelago is the sixth most populous country today;[1] its one hundred million people cram themselves into an area the size of the state of California. Its natural resources are almost nonexistent, yet today it ranks as the third most highly industrialized nation.[2] Drawing on a century of modernization as historical precedent, despite the catastrophe of World War II, the Japanese have developed over the decades an expert base for technological know-how.

But the amazing record is of recent vintage. Although now involved in, and helping shape, international political and economic trends, Japan was traditionally more self-contained and semi-isolated in its archipelago off the Asian mainland. Over the premodern centuries, never a world power, it pursued its own historical path on the fringes of a great Chinese civilization. Although they borrowed from China periodically but extensively into the mid-nineteenth century, the Japanese adopted and adapted such imported ideas

1. After the Peoples Republic of China, India, the Soviet Union, the United States, and Indonesia.
2. After the United States and the Soviet Union.

1

with modifications and rejected others. This selective reception from other countries was repeated after the mid-1850's when the West helped to open Japan to modern ways, and again it was evidenced a century later when the American occupation ended.

Despite cultural accretions from East and West, the Japanese maintained an inner resistant core of traditional values. Agriculture constituted the primary occupation; land was the chief source of wealth. Group loyalties predominated, for the individual was subordinated to the family, village, region, and country. At the apex of the national Japanese family was the imperial line, one of the oldest continuous traditions in history, that provided an ideological focus for the people. Left alone in their process of historical development, rarely experiencing disastrous invasions at home and only fitfully engaging in campaigns abroad, Japan coursed its own way over the centuries. Internally, it experienced a plethora of civil wars but no major revolutions that implied drastic change. Over time, events superimposed themselves on one another in an ongoing process. Changes, whether induced internally or externally, tended not to occur in cyclical fashion but rather fused themselves into a cumulatively linear pattern.

And so continuity of indigenous cultural patterns, made possible through geographic protection of the people in their close-knit islands, coexisted with selectively imported elements. Hence contradictory stereotypes of Japan have persisted into contemporary times; traditional arts, food, and architecture appear alongside with frenetic manifestations of modern life styles. As a repository for traditional and foreign ideas, Japan not only was of itself but also of both East and West. In the Eastern tradition, it has maintained a unique historical process; in the Western context, it is the most modern of all Asian countries.

The Geographic Setting

Japan consists of some four thousand islands strung out in an extended arc off the coast of northeastern Asia. Only a handful of islands are of adequate size to sustain human activity. The thousand-mile long archipelago, if superimposed on the same latitude in the western hemisphere, would stretch from Montreal in Canada to Tallahassee in Florida. The country lies chiefly in the temperate zone. It receives good rainfall, it has fairly fertile soil, and it is located near China and Korea from whom the Japanese early adopted some of their basic cultural concepts. In area, Japan is similar to the state of California or to that of Montana, though in terms of terrain, climate, and productivity, a more appropriate comparison would be with the Middle Atlantic states of New York, Pennsylvania, Maryland, and Virginia. Less than 150,000 square miles in area, the country could be fitted into the United States more than twenty times. Japan is smaller than France or prewar Germany, but it is larger than Italy or Great Britain. Comparisons with Great Britain seem natural. Both are insular countries lying off continental land masses. Both have been traditionally free from armed invasions. Both have developed distinct cultures that have been exposed, nonetheless, to neighboring mainland cultural influences.

Within the Japanese archipelago, there are only four principal islands. The northernmost is Yezo or Hokkaido (the Northern Sea Circuit, an old administrative designation). It lies in the latitude of the New England states and is cold and underpopulated, and has remained outside the mainstream of Japanese history. Honshu, the main island, is the largest and the most populated. Containing huge cities and the chief agricultural areas, it has been the stage for important events in Japanese national life. To its south, across the beautiful Inland Sea, lie the two islands of Shikoku, traditionally known as the Four Provinces, and Kyushu, the Nine Provinces. Kyushu, in the latitude of the state of Georgia but with a subtropical climate, has played an important role in Japanese cultural history as the nearest and the most receptive of the four chief islands to early Chinese and Western influences. For administrative purposes, Japan is divided into forty-six prefectures or provinces, an arrangement dating in present form to the late nineteenth century. All of Hokkaido counts as one prefecture but three large cities of Japan are enumerated separately: Tokyo, the country's largest city with over ten million inhabitants; Osaka with three and a half million; and Kyoto with over a million.

As mentioned, Japan's climate is temperate. It is determined in part by its closeness to the Asian mainland. Winter winds from the continent bring cold dry air, but sometimes they pick up precipitation over the Japan Sea to drop rain or snow on western coastal and mountainous areas, such as the Japanese Alps. Summer winds from the southwest seas bring warm and heavy rains as well as late summer or early autumn hurricanes, known in northeast Asia as typhoons (from a transliteration of the Chinese meaning "big wind"). The climate is additionally conditioned by two gulf streams—the Japan Current, known also as the Black Current or Kuroshio, which brings a warm ocean stream up from the tropics northward along the Pacific coast, and the Oyashio or Okhotsk stream, which is a cold current from the north sweeping southward in the Japan Sea.

Japanese topography is marked by extensive mountain areas. Almost all of the country is hilly or mountainous, with several distinct ranges and many high peaks. Over five hundred volcanoes are numbered, of which sixty have been active in historic times. The most famous of these is Mt. Fuji, over 12,000 feet high and a popular subject in Japanese art. It last erupted in 1707. Two-mile high coastal mountain ranges coexist with nearby ocean depths that plummet five miles into the Pacific Ocean off the eastern Honshu coast. These great elevation differentials within short longitudes have produced stresses on the earth's crust, and earthquakes are common in Japan. Up to fifteen hundred shocks a year are recorded. Abetted by extensive fires, the most disastrous Japanese earthquake in modern times occurred in September, 1923, in the Tokyo-Yokohama area.

Less than a fifth of Japan's land mass is level. But an important fifth it is, since it produces most of the food. The chief Japanese plains lie in east-central Honshu. The largest and the most famous of these is the five-thousand-square-mile Kanto plain, where Tokyo is situated. This area has been a main source of national economic, military, and political power. To its west is the Nobi plain, six hundred square miles, where Nagoya, one of Japan's main cities and a ceramics center, is located. Another traditional historic center is the Kinki, Kinai ("Home Provinces"), or Kansai plain, five hundred square miles in area situated at the eastern end of the Inland Sea, where Japan's old capital cities of Nara and Kyoto and the more recent commercial urban centers of Osaka and Kobe are located. With these plains and lesser ones supporting great cities and providing most of the available farmland, the further expansion of cultivable land, already encroaching upon hillsides in neat terraces, is limited to a possible 10 per cent. Reclamation schemes, swallowing up some of the country's inland bays or extending its coastline, are projected.

Limitations in the extent of arable land are matched by deficits in natural resources. Japan has sufficient copper but is handicapped by meager coal deposits and negligible oil or iron reserves. Japan's annual oil output is equalled in the United States every six hours, and Japan's known iron reserves would last only three months in the United States. Probably its most important natural resource is water. Plentiful rainfall makes possible a lush countryside. Vegetation abounds, forest products are harvested, and wood provides a main ingredient of the country's homes and buildings. Agriculture is based on wet farming, and rice, the main crop, is grown in most parts of the country. Though irrigation is practiced, the short rivers of Japan require no large-scale works or flood control projects. Streams are rushing and short (the longest is less than three hundred miles), but they provide much hydroelectric power. With no broad, meandering rivers in the land, a riverine tradition is not prominent in Japanese literature, which has no counterparts to the Swanee, the quiet-flowing Don, or the "sweet Thames." Counterbalancing this lack of rivers, however, is the accessibility of coastal transportation. Prominent among the clustered islands are protected bays, straits, the Inland Sea, the lack of open ocean gaps between islands as in Hawaii, and the 17,000 mile coastline (the United States has under 13,000 miles), which provides many good harbors.

The Effects of Geography

These diverse geographic factors have helped to shape Japanese historic life. Because of its insular nature, Japan developed in relative political isolation, for it lay a hundred miles across the straits from Korea and five times that distance over open seas from China. Never occupied and never having experienced a successful invasion before 1945 (the Mongols were twice driven back in the thirteenth century), the Japanese, in spite of cultural borrowing, developed in their psychology a nationalistic, patriotic, "we are different" spirit.

In economic life, geography affected human activity in basic ways. The country was beautiful, but the rugged terrain caused many hardships. Poverty hid behind an agreeable topographic mask, for crops could not grow on mountains and rains leached the soil. Yet, while water was destructive, it also gave. Rain and climate favored rice production, so paramount in Japanese as in most Asian diets. A nutritious cereal, it gave the highest yield of any grain for the area cultivated. Surrounded by water, the Japanese also pursued coastal and deep sea fishing. Fish provided high protein food sources, in lieu of relatively scarce dairy and meat products. The wide-ranging Japanese quest for adequate fish supplies in international waters and the many multilateral arrangements regulating the catch constituted a major part of the diplomatic history of the country.

But in its historic domestic agrarian economy, land was the traditional source of wealth. Ruling classes lived off land revenue in the form of rents or of taxes. Civil wars prior to the modernization of the country reflected in no small way attempts to control productive rice lands. Ruling families built up their estates and attempted to keep them off the government's tax rolls. Because of the geographical limitations imposed on the extent of arable acreage, intensive, rather than extensive, agricultural patterns were practiced. Many men and women cultivated little land. A vast expenditure of muscle power went into the cultivation of rice, which was traditionally planted and harvested by hand. Because of the high ratio of people to productive land, population problems and food supplies became acute considerations in modern times. After having remained comparatively static for some time prior to the mid-nineteenth century, in the course of the past hundred years Japan's population skyrocketed more than three-fold, from thirty million in the 1860's to one hundred million in the 1970's.

Besides political and economic ramifications, geographic factors also have had social and cultural effects. The length of the island chain helped to account for early and differing racial strains in the Japanese people, whose forebears migrated into the country from a variety of neighboring overseas areas, including Sakhalin Island off Siberia to the north, Korea and China to the west, and Formosa to the south. Early subjected to Asian migrations and cultures, the Japanese again much later, because of their location as the closest of Asian peoples in spite of the vast Pacific Ocean to the United States, played the reverse role as the first interpreters of occidental culture and its ways to East Asians. Whereas the United States through Perry in the mid-1850's helped to open Japan, Japan in turn two decades later helped to end Korean isolation.

Yet Japan continued to retain many of its traditions, and its semi-isolation helped to maintain a degree of cultural conservatism. Foreign pressures did not brush aside all old ways, which were retained alongside newer importations. Japan could simultaneously record various religious stages into modern times, among them animism, Buddhism, Shintoism, Confucianism, and Christianity. Major historical phases of the theater were superimposed on each other, as the thirteenth-century, Buddhist-inspired *No* dramas, the later Kabuki and puppet plays, and the contemporary Western dramatic forms. Partial isolation made the Japanese cognizant of their cultural borrowings. Whether or not they fully understood the content of foreign ideas borrowed, they were at least aware of the aspects in imported ideas which departed from indigenous patterns. Concepts that came via sea rather than by land routes were easily identifiable. Imported ideas, such as Buddhism, the Chinese script, and centralized Chinese political and administrative patterns, left their noticeable marks, but the Japanese retained much that was uniquely theirs. This was reflected particularly in their own architectural forms and furnishings, as the *tatami* or straw floor mats, the *shoji* or sliding paper wall panels, the airy home structures, the *tokonoma* or alcove for art objects, the *hibachi* or charcoal-heating braziers, and the wooden and iron bathtubs. If the Japanese borrowed, they also exported and traded abroad; their maritime trade as early as the fourteenth and fifteenth centuries was extensive in east and south Asia.

Despite the human pressures on the geographic landscape, it infused a love of beauty among the Japanese, who early developed a sense of aesthetics with regard to nature. They took pleasure in reflecting on the countryside. They wrote poems on it, they enjoyed picnics, and they held spring cherry-blossom viewing parties. Their attitude toward nature was one of awe or appreciation, rather than fear. Mountains were the homes of gods and of saints rather than of evil spirits. On high peaks monasteries were built. Yet on high ground or low, traditional structures blended into the landscape. Readily available wood was the most common material; little stone and almost no brick were used.

A final comment on the effects of geography on Japanese society and culture would indicate the dominance in Japanese life of the coastal areas, in an axis ranging from northwestern Kyushu along the Inland Sea and its plains up to the Tokyo area. This was the country's richest historical vein, the home of the greatest cultural achievements, the most productive area in commerce, industry, and agriculture, and the site of the best climate. The story of Japanese history is centered here.

Historic Periods and Records

Japanese call their country Nippon or Nihon. These are transliterations of the Chinese characters *jih-pen*, roughly pronounced *urban* in northern China, which means "the land of the rising sun." A phonetic variation of this Chinese-derived term also crept into Western use. Marco Polo, who served in China under Mongol rulers in the thirteenth century, heard of this designation for the country that lay across the sea, a country that the Venetian never visited. In a later transcription of his memoirs in Europe, an approximation of this terminology was translated as Chipango or Zipango. In time these became latinized as Japan. From the Chinese original, both East and West adapted their respective nomenclatures of Japan.

Japanese history may be divided into some half-dozen convenient periods. These are generally designated after geographic centers of political power or after families that wielded the power in the name of the relatively impotent imperial line. Early native culture flourished from prehistoric times to about 400 A.D. Then, for approximately three centuries, continental influences, mainly Chinese, filtered into ancient Japan, which sought out and welcomed them. Next, from about 700 A.D. to 1200 A.D., a synthesis of foreign and native ideas and institutions took place, resulting in the first major definable political eras of history, with centralized capitals located first at Nara and subsequently at what is now Kyoto. In the ensuing four centuries, characterized by the growth of militant groups, the political divisions in the country, and civil wars, Japan experienced what has been termed a period of military feudalism. By the turn of the seventeenth century, chiefly through the efforts of three successive outstanding leaders, Japan was politically reunified for two and a half centuries under the Tokugawa shogunate. With the advent of Perry and other men and forces from the Western world in the mid-1850's, Japan entered its modern phase. The cliché "Japan between East and West" has sometimes been used to describe Japan's modern century.

The Japanese themselves have written extensively of their history over the centuries. Though Japan was mentioned in Chinese annals as early as the first century A.D., the first Japanese to order an official history was Japan's first great statesman, Prince Shotoku Taishi (d. 621). This work has been lost, but within a century two official general histories, derived from the Chinese in language and in concept, were compiled. The earliest history still extant, the *Kojiki*, or *Record of Ancient Matters*, was compiled in 712 but dates in origin to 628. It consists mainly of legendary tales preserved by bards attached to the leading families of early Japan. Within eight years another compilation, the *Nihon Shoki* or *Nihongi*, or the *History of Japan*, was drawn up, and this constituted the first volume of the so-called Six National Histories, which subsequently brought the story down to 887. Augmenting these early official general works were *fudoki* or local histories of various provinces, composed by order of the central government. Only one of these, compiled in 733, has survived intact. Others survive in part, and one is an abstract contained in another work. In addition to the official tradition of compiling general or local chronicles, early native or Shinto ritualistic texts were written.

In these eighth- to tenth-century works that constituted the first period of historical literature, there was a conscious imitation of the millenium-old principles of Chinese historiography. The writing of historical annals as it developed in China and as it was borrowed by Japan consisted of four parts. First came the records of the imperial family; second, the genealogical tables and lists of officials and the bureaucracy; third, the essays and commentaries, such as those on Confucian ceremonies, religion, economic development, and literature; and, lastly, the biographies of prominent officials and military figures, as well as resumés of foreign relations. This structure, which emphasized emperors, courts, and officialdom, was adopted by the Japanese, but without the full range of lives and treatises that were found in a standard Chinese history. Probably this was due in part initially to the lack of biographies and monographic material. In their adaptations, Japanese historians were also faced with another problem of history. Traditional Chinese histories were dynastic in nature (China was ruled by some two dozen dynasties between the eighteenth century B.C. and the twentieth century A.D.), but since Japan had the tradition of only one unbroken imperial dynasty established in 660 B.C., historians usually chose for their texts the reign of a single emperor or an arbitrarily chosen group of successive reigns.

In the course of the second period of Japanese historiography, roughly from the eleventh to the fourteenth centuries, a vernacular tradition in writing arose, which used Japanese phonetics based on Chinese scripts. In this period family histories, known as *kagami* or mirrors and *monogatari* or narratives, abounded. These works, of which half a dozen are the most prominent, related the numerous civil wars and the fortunes of the military factions in these campaigns. Some of the works embodied causal principles in order to justify certain actions or to advance the biases of the protagonists involved. A Buddhist historical tradition also became evident in these centuries. One of the most outstanding works was *Gukanshu* or *Fool's Miscellany* (1224?), composed by the priest Fujiwara Jien. This might be considered as the first Japanese attempt to survey and to interpret Japanese history within the Buddhist context. Since political anarchy prevailed in these centuries, cloisters became a refuge of learning and of writing, as had the Christian monasteries in medieval Europe.

With the reunification of Japan in the Tokugawa period in the sixteenth century and with the restoration of law and order after decades of intermittent civil war, the strong central authority again officially encouraged works along Chinese models in the Chinese language. One branch of the official Tokugawa family at Mito began an exhaustive general history of Japan in 1657 (it was not completed until 1906), to cover events from Japanese origins to 1393. Stressing the paramount role of the imperial family, the first part of 100 volumes (with 146 volumes to go) was finished in 1709, and it was presented to the emperor in 1810. A subsequent edition of seventeen volumes covered the years 660 B.C. to 1412 A.D. Other individual historians, with or without official Tokugawa patronage, also drew up multi-volume projects. The growth of printing encouraged the writing of history, and the rise of modern libraries, including that of the imperial family, helped to preserve records.

After the reopening of Japan in the mid-nineteenth century, historical scholarship borrowed techniques from the West. The Japanese erected national libraries, founded universities, established professorships, started scholarly journals, and promoted research institutes. In 1869 the government called for another edition of Japanese history. Eight years later a Bureau of Historical Compilation was founded. Within another decade this agency was moved to the newly created Imperial University of Tokyo, which became the country's leading center of historical studies. The first modern historical efforts, official and otherwise, continued to stress political events, though with the advent of the twentieth century, cultural, social, and economic topics were also elaborated. Pre-World War II studies not only reflected a diversity of approaches, but the growth of monographic literature, reference works, and primary source materials. With the rebirth of militarism in the 1930's and with the Pacific War, historical writing was diverted into other channels, but in the postwar period the varieties of Japanese historical scholarship sprouted anew. Compendia in the language were produced; the *Dictionary of Japanese History* reached twenty volumes; an *Encyclopedia of World History* ran to twenty-five volumes; the *Illustrated Compendium of Japanese Cultural History* covered 114 volumes. The output was noticeably smaller in foreign languages, including English.

Problems of Understanding

Though the Japanese produced voluminous works relating to their own history, less study in this area was accomplished by Western authors. Before World War II, few specialized texts on Japan were written by occidentals. A few Englishmen, resident in Japan, though nonprofessionals in the historical discipline, made the first attempts. James Murdoch authored a three-volume *History of Japan* (1903–1926), and his compatriot Sir George Sansom published in 1931 the first edition of the classic *Japan: A Short Cultural History.* American scholarship was even more restricted in scope. William E. Griffis, a science teacher in Japan, wrote *The Mikado's Empire* (1876), in popular use prior to World War I. Later American historians, some concentrating on diplomatic affairs with relation to the United States, worked mainly in Western sources. Few scholars knew Japanese; prior to 1941 in the United States probably only a dozen universities taught Japanese.

The Pacific War stimulated the study of Japanese language and history, and the ranks of professionally trained American historians of Japan swelled with additions of postwar students. University centers at Yale, Columbia, Michigan, Washington, California, and Stanford promoted Japanese studies. Specialized monographs were published; library holdings relating to Japan zoomed nine-fold from 90,000 volumes in 1940 to over 800,000 in 1958. The need to study Japan had suddenly become imperative. The country's early modernization, its rise to world power, World War II, and the Occupation provided immediate impetus, and Japan's contemporary importance in Asian and world affairs, particularly in economic matters, necessitated continued close study.

The short period of United States relations with Japan—only a little over a century—contributed to difficulties in mutual understanding. American interpretations and images of Japan varied in this period, swinging between extremes of depicting Japanese either as passive imitators or as land-hungry barbarians. During the first decades of Japanese-American contact, or in that period between the advent of Perry in 1853 and the Russo-Japanese War of 1904–05, there was general approval and approbation of Japan by those Americans who studied the country at all. Since the Japanese had adapted to Western ways, at least on the surface, they had become in culture more like Westerners, and hence more understandable and likeable, a simplistic argument ran. On political grounds, Japan was not yet to be feared, for there was little conflict with United States interests in Asia. On aesthetic grounds, Japan and Japanese were considered quaint, beautiful, and slightly ludicrous. Gilbert and Sullivan's *The Mikado,* composed in 1885, enjoyed great vogue with its stock Japanese theatrical types. Puccini's opera, *Madame Butterfly,* adapted from a play which in turn was based on a novel, portrayed a classic story of love cutting across racial lines. Western writers living in Japan also contributed to exotic images. Born of Irish-Greek parentage, Lafcadio Hearn went to live in Japan in 1890. There he became a Buddhist, lived in a Japanese house, and took a Japanese name and a Japanese wife. He wrote widely read books of stylistic excellence, including *Japan: An Attempt at Interpretation,* which portrayed traditional and modernized aspects of Japanese life.

With the establishment of Japan as an Asian power of considerable importance after the Russo-Japanese War of 1904-05, relations with the United States took a turn for the worse. Japanese territorial expansion in Asia particularly affected United States treaty rights in China, as well as the security of the Philippines, acquired by Americans from Spain in 1898. Rivalry also developed in naval and commercial matters. American immigration exclusion laws acerbated Japanese sensitivity. Friendship turned into enmity, which finally erupted in the Pacific War.

Yet after the maelstrom of war and the resulting Occupation, a defeated Japan was again characterized as a friend, a "bastion of democracy," and an "ally"—which were seldom defined and loosely used terms advanced by Americans. In the United States another craze for things Japanese developed. Japanese architectural landscapes blossomed in American gardens; department store bargain basements promoted shoji screens and electric hibachis; the study of what was taken to be Zen Buddhism flourished. Americans borrowed many outward forms from Japan, as the Japanese themselves had done for centuries from both East and West, but American appreciation and understanding of Japanese substance and content proved more difficult to acquire.

PART ONE

TRADITIONAL JAPAN

Traditional Japan developed from both indigenous and imported patterns. The Japanese in prehistoric and recorded eras evolved certain peculiar characteristics. A divine imperial family reigned but did not rule, for the political direction was provided by other families who operated behind the imperial facade. Pronounced hierarchical patterns characterized society; the economy was overwhelmingly agrarian. Embryonic art and architectural forms were crystallized in early abstractions. Native Shinto was formulated; imported Buddhism provided theological and cultural dimensions to life. The Chinese script was adopted, and ancient literary models were moulded by proto-historians borrowing Chinese concepts. By grafting compatible alien ideas onto native concepts, the early Japanese achieved a higher degree of cultural sophistication.

II

ANCIENT JAPAN (TO CA. 400 A.D.)

Sources of early Japanese history consist of both unwritten and written records. Archaeology has uncovered a variety of artifacts, tombs, sea shell mounds, physical remains, and human skeletal forms scattered all over Japan. Chinese dynastic histories, with information dating to the first century A.D., corroborate some of these archaeological finds, and these foreign Asian annals help to fill some of the physical gaps. In subsequent centuries, Japanese began to compose their own histories, but their works tended to confuse facts with myths and emperors with gods. Yet these works do contain germs of historical accuracy, for they chronicle in allegorical form the foundations of the ancient Japanese state. In subsequent times, more and more detailed information relating to early Japan came to light, but knowledge remained conjectural about Japan prior to the fifth century A.D., when Chinese writing was adopted by the Japanese, who possessed no native script. Despite projections back to antiquity, recorded Japanese history, bolstered by the tradition of one long continuous imperial dynasty, is comparatively recent, as major civilizations go. The Roman empire was falling apart as the Japanese commenced patterns of recognizable historical development. And over the previous two millenia, neighboring China had long since evolved major, definable cultural traits.

Archaeological Periods

Little is known of the racial origins of the Japanese. The oldest present inhabitants are the Ainu, once spread out over Japan but now restricted chiefly to government reservations in Hokkaido. Probably related to the earliest culture, they are proto-Caucasians, for they are relatively hairy, fair-skinned, and sometimes blue-eyed. Later immigration waves from northern and southern Asian regions either absorbed them or pushed them farther north. Earlier and more important, the northern Asian strain fashioned Japanese life. Artifacts related to those uncovered in Mongolia, Korea, and Manchuria have been found in early Japan. Similarities in language have enhanced cultural connections between the Japanese and northeastern Asians, for the Japanese language is one of the Altaic group, which includes Korean. Since Japan is nearest to the Asian mainland at points opposite Korea, the geographical propinquity lends support to the theory that ancient cultural and racial invasions emanated from that direction.

A lesser southern strain came later, probably up from south and east China and southeast Asia. Physical anthropology reveals that many Japanese, smaller in stature and darker in complexion than northeast Asians, resemble Malayans, who live closer to the equator. Cultural anthropology discloses some similarities in language, in the propagation of the wet rice culture so pronounced in tropical Asia, in the architectural trait of highly slanted house roofs and eaves, in a diet that includes raw fish, and in the existence of a matriarchy in early times (still noticeable in certain parts of Burma and the large island of Sumatra in Indonesia). Though of mixed origins, these diverse and ancient Japanese racial elements blended together, so that by historic times, around 400 A.D., the Japanese had become a racially homogeneous people, unified by common language and culture.

Archaeological records note several successive cultures in prehistoric Japan. These records consist entirely of artifacts, for none of the ancient records include written symbols or primitive hieroglyphics. Paleolithic, or Old Stone Age, finds were unearthed in at least three different strata at Iwajuku in the Kanto plain, but few conclusions have yet been drawn from the extant evidence. Possibly the first Paleolithic culture waves entered the islands as early as 200,000 B.C. Stone implements uncovered from excavations are roughly flaked; some of the larger specimens resemble chopper instruments found elsewhere in Asia. A later culture wave produced similar tools but smaller in size. No skeletal evidence, however, has as yet come to light, but such recent finds indicate that man existed in Japan prior to the inception of the later pottery cultures.

The first major Japanese culture dates to the Mesolithic, or Middle Stone Age, and lasted roughly from 3000 B.C. to 300 B.C. It is termed Jomon from a Japanese word meaning "cord pattern," because most of the pottery discovered had such a pattern pressed into external surfaces. Several hundred Jomon sites have been uncovered throughout Japan as well as in the Ryukyus. Most of the remains have been unearthed in eastern and northern Japan, where the culture lasted the longest. Artifacts include shell mounds, stone weapons, pottery in over seventy shapes and forms, and *dogu* or clay figures, representing simplified abstractions of men and animals, which have been found near the shell mounds or in graves. Stone implements and pottery were used for ceremonial purposes or for cooking.

The Jomon were not a settled agricultural people, but were nomads who hunted, gathered roots and nuts, and ate fresh and salt water shell fish, the remains of which were left scattered about near home sites. These early people lived in primitive semi-sunken rectangular or round houses of thatch and bark that was stretched over wood frames. Floors were dug into the ground about two feet. Usually the floors were earthen, but sometimes they were stone-paved. A central hearth provided heat and cooking. In religion the Jomon people were animists worshipping natural objects out of reverence rather than fear. Important natural sites became centers of religious worship.

The next culture phase has been called the Yayoi, derived from a Tokyo street where a more advanced type of pottery was first discovered. Lasting approximately 300 B.C. to 300 A.D., Yayoi culture spread over Japan from its origins in Kyushu, extending north and displacing the Jomon. The Yayoi, a Neolithic, or New Stone Age people, practiced rice cultivation to augment hunting and fishing. They continued to live in pit dwellings, but in the latter stages of their culture they cast iron and bronze implements, including mirrors, swords, spears, and bells. Yayoi pottery, more delicate and more advanced in technique than that of the Jomon, is found in more than three dozen types and was created by the potter's wheel. Some of it has scenes incised on the surfaces. Most interesting artifacts are the bronze bells or *dotaku*, some four to five feet in height, but too thin to ring. Many of them have geometric designs or depict scenes from life. Not found everywhere in Japan, the bells are concentrated in the Kinki plain of central Honshu.

Sometimes considered as the last phase of the Yayoi, the tomb culture (ca. 300 to 600 A.D.) was superimposed on the existing inhabitants by new waves of immigrants from Korea. Like the previous cultures, it spread from Kyushu northwards. These newcomers were a militant and aristocratic people, whose invading warriors rode horses, wore helmets and armor, and used iron swords. The tumuli or period name derives from remains of high earth tombs or stone burial chambers, similar to those erected in ancient Korea and in northeast Asia. Some of the earth tombs above ground are quite large; one ranges 1500 feet in length and 120 feet in height, surrounded by moats. Some are round, some are square, and others are shaped like a keyhole in three tiers. Inside the tombs are hollow clay figures or *haniwa*. Ranged in concentric circles, they consist of pottery cylinders surmounted by figures of red-painted men and women, animals, warriors, and houses. Other entombed items include curved jewels, mirrors, and swords, similar in nature to Korean ornaments and weapons. These tombs, the burial sites of early Japanese priest-kings, are found mostly in the ancient capital district of Nara and Kyoto in the Kinki plain.

Chinese and Japanese Annals

Early Chinese historical annals complement these ancient Japanese archaeological finds of successive cultures. Chinese historians viewed Japan, as they did all other surrounding areas, simply in a subordinate and inferior relation to China, Chinese interests, and Chinese prestige. They called Japan *Wa*, a derogatory term meaning "dwarf." As narrated by a mid-fifth century Chinese history, the first recorded contact between China and Japan took place in 57 A.D., when a Japanese envoy came from the Wa state of Nu, possibly in Kyushu, to the Chinese capital of the great Han dynasty, which at the time was located at Loyang in north China. The Japanese ambassador received a gold seal from the Chinese emperor; such a gold seal was found in 1789 in north Kyushu which seems to read "King of Nu of Wa, (Vassal of) Han."

Another and earlier Chinese dynastic history, compiled around 300 A.D., incorporated a fairly authentic account of Japanese life as it was evolving from Yayoi to tomb culture. The history recorded the existence in Japan of a hundred states, or more properly tribes, thirty of which had relations with China. The political units varied in size, and they were headed by kings or queens, of whom the most remarkable was a Queen Himiko or Pimiko, an archaic Japanese term meaning "Sun Daughter." The Chinese annal pictured a law-abiding, liquor-loving society that followed the arts of agriculture, spinning, weaving, and fishing. It described very marked social differences among the Japanese, and, as indicated by haniwa dating from the period, it confirmed tatooing and bodymarking practices in Japan. Later Chinese histories, compiled after the fifth century A.D., portrayed the growing unification of Japan under the imperial clan, a story by then also being chronicled by the Japanese themselves.

The two main Japanese sources of ancient history, the compilations of the *Kojiki* and the *Nihon Shoki* of the early eighth century, are often inaccurate and contradictory. But their creation myths, their story of the Sun Goddess, their concept of the divinity of the emperor and of the uniqueness of the Japanese race reflected beliefs held by the Japanese until very recently (not until New Year's Day of 1946 did an imperial rescript disclaim the doctrine of imperial divinity). The two works reshaped Japanese mythology and history to enhance the prestige of the ruling family clan in the Kinki plain. They created through their reconstructed genealogical studies a false picture of antiquity and centralized rule in order to bolster the imperial claims to legitimacy. Yet in these allegorical studies of gods, goddesses, and heavenly events, the mythology paralleled some possible historical men and events. And in their chronologies and their reporting the latter sections of the histories became more credible than the earlier portions.

Naive and crude, the creation myths were concerned mainly with the procreation of a multitude of deities and creation of the islands of Japan. Among the first of the heavenly host were the brother and sister, Izanagi and Izanami, who between them produced some fourteen islands of Japan and three dozen deities, the last of which was the Fire God. Consumed by the birth of this final child, Izanami died. She descended to the nether world, where Izanagi visited her, only to be driven away because of the putrefied state of her body. Cleansing himself, Izanagi, by discarding his clothes and washing away various parts of his body, created another group of Japanese islands and gods. Included this time were the Sun Goddess or Amaterasu, the Moon God, and Susa-no-o, who, as a destructive force, embodied the enemies of the imperial family. In turn, Amaterasu and Susa-no-o produced more progeny but argued, after which Susa-no-o was banished to Izumo on the north coast of west Honshu. Archaeology does not show the Izumo area to be a major center of early Japanese culture, but the great shrine there is the oldest and second most important one in Japan.

The two Japanese chronicles continue to relate that Ninigi, a grandson of the Sun Goddess, descended from heaven to Kyushu. More myths center about his activities on that island, which, as noted, was a major cultural region and chief point of contact with the continent. Ninigi brought with him the three imperial regalia, all of which were plentiful in the tomb culture. These were a bronze mirror to represent the sun, a curved jewel the moon, and an iron sword a lightning flash. In turn, Ninigi's grandson, Jimmu Tenno, moved up from southeast Kyushu via the Inland Sea to the eastern shores in the Yamato area in the Kinki plain. There he ascended the throne and founded the Japanese state on February 11, 660 B.C.

Such an arbitrary date is suspect. It was arrived at in the early seventh century A.D. by Japanese rulers, who were then adopting Chinese time concepts by counting back 1260 years, which was a major cycle of historical time according to the Chinese. The reigns of the Yamato rulers after 660 B.C. proceeded on an uneven course. According to the chronicles, the first seventeen priest-kings after Jimmu ruled an improbable 1060 years. Three of these rulers are credited with reigns of a century or more, but the last seventeen rulers, some of whom are historical, reigned only for a total of 126 years. Whatever its claim to legitimacy, the imperial clan and the Yamato state on the Nara plain emerged as the strongest in Japan by historic times (400 A.D.).

The story of Jimmu Tenno's conquest eastward follows the archaeological record, but its actual date is probably a millenium later than recorded in legend, occurring sometime in the first half of the fourth century A.D. The state of Yamato grew in size and power during the next two centuries, until its rulers could claim suzerainty over 121 political units in Japan alone. Probably members of a solar cult strains of which recur throughout these early Japanese histories, these rulers set up their chief shrine to the Sun Goddess at Ise, on the east coast of central Honshu facing the rising sun. This became the most important shrine in Japan. Into the twentieth century members of the imperial family regularly visited Ise to report important events to their grand ancestor of the sun line.

Expanding outward from their base, the early Yamato rulers won control over their neighbors, in part because of the strategic central location of the area, and in part because of the strong economic base provided by fairly widespread but low-lying fertile rice lands. Yamato kings ruled north to the Kanto plain and south to Kyushu and for a time across the straights into Korea. Political ties with Korea were close. In the fourth century A.D., Japanese rulers sent military expeditions to the peninsula, where the Japanese established themselves in the state of Mimana on the southern Korean coast until 562 A.D. One early major invasion from Kyushu was credited to the empress-regent Jingo, whose son was later deified as Hachiman, the god of war. Japanese also interfered in intra-Korean affairs, for that country was divided at the time into the three warring states of Paekche, Silla, and Koguryo.

Accompanying military contact were closer cultural ties. Some scholars with Chinese learning were dispatched to Yamato (for by then Chinese colonies and culture had existed in Korea for some five centuries). These and later Koreans and Chinese immigrants were literate, highly skilled, and in great demand in early Japan. They were given noble rank and honored. One-third of the entries listed in a seventh-century who's who of Japan were descendants of Koreans or Chinese. The scholars who were installed at Yamato around 400 A.D. kept records in Chinese, and the two earliest Japanese histories drew upon them. With these first cultural impulses from the mainland, Japan commenced its historic life.

CHRONOLOGY

B.C.

200,000	First possible Paleolithic cultural waves
ca. 3000 to ca. 300	Jomon culture
660, February 11	Traditional date for founding of Yamato state by Jimmu Tenno
ca. 300 to 300 A.D.	Yayoi culture

A.D.

57	First recorded Japanese contact with China
ca. 300 to 600	Tomb or Kofun culture
ca. 300	Chinese dynastic history relating Japanese events
ca. 400	Yamato state emerges; historic Japan commences.

III

YAMATO JAPAN (CA. 400–710)

By the advent of the fifth century, with both Japanese and Chinese annals recording events, a clear historical focus centers on the imperial family. Its location in the Yamato plain was propitious for economic and security reasons. The region, though small in area, was agriculturally productive, with easy access to the Inland Sea. In this favored spot the core of the early Japanese state was fashioned. The kings initially exercised authority indirectly through clans, but with the gradual rise of clans other than the imperial one to greater real power, the Yamato monarchs were relegated to secondary political influence. The kings lost power, though they were kept on the throne and maintained their claim to divine status. They reigned but did not rule. This form of monarchy was an aspect of Japanese political history that persisted into the twentieth century. Yet however great the dissatisfaction might have been from time to time with the royal order, never in history was the imperial family overthrown or replaced. Rather, political struggles centered around great families who endeavored to control the imperial line and by so doing sought to direct the destinies of Japan. The system from early times of kings who were theoretically absolute and divine but subject to indirect rulers with actual power constituted a basic Japanese political phenomenon.

Society

Yamato society was aristocratic, hereditary, and closed. It revolved around a loose federation of extended families or clans called *uji*. The uji were a later and smaller social unit than the "hundred tribes" mentioned in early Chinese chronicles. They consisted of hereditary members who claimed descent from a common god and who worshipped this deity (*ujigami*) under the patriarchal chief (*uji no kami*). As first among equals, the imperial uji traced its descent from the Sun Goddess. Other aristocratic clans claimed the ancestry of lesser gods, who later joined the sun line or who were descendants of earth gods who had submitted to Jimmu. Some uji were grouped according to occupations, and these concerned themselves with primary functions in military, literary, or religious matters. Among the more prominent were the Mononobe or Armorers, and the Nakatomi or Court Ritualists.

As clan structure became more complex, subsidiary attendants, termed *be* (or *tomo*) were attached to the uji. In reality acting as labor forces, these were also hereditary groups, organized like the clans under their own chiefs. The be provided necessary economic and agricultural support services. Most grew rice which fed not only themselves but their overlords; other groups specialized in certain forms of livelihood such as fishing, weaving, or ceramic making. Skilled foreigners were grouped in this category, for through adoption by Japanese families they could be assimilated into the existing social structure.

Lowest on the social and economic scale were the slaves, few and of little economic importance. Within the larger clan groupings, the immediate family was the basic unit. In it, generally the eldest male presided over family matters. Monogamy usually prevailed, but those who could afford concubines or secondary wives kept them.

Yamato religion was early Shinto. Nameless at first, this primitive religion received a Chinese appellation, loosely translated as the "way of the gods" to differentiate it from Buddhism and from Chinese Confucian beliefs that later entered Japan. Shinto was brought to Japan by those early Japanese who emigrated to the islands from other regions of Asia. In time Shinto became indelibly regarded as the Japanese national religion. Early Shinto embraced cults of diverse origins: animism, fertility rites, ancestor worship, nature worship, and the complex of heroes, gods, and goddesses, among whom the Sun Goddess was paramount. Despite the existence of many cults and shrines, of which at least three thousand existed by the eighth century, all cults acknowledged the divinity of the emperor. Shinto worshippers believed in *kami*, a superior thing or person. In animistic fashion, anything and anyone could be kami, including beautiful sites, great trees, unusually shaped stones, and deceased warriors. An expression of the most intimate Japanese sentiments, Shinto possessed no founder, no inspired sacred book, no teachers, no saints, and no martyrs.

A Shinto shrine was usually a simple affair. Constructed of wood, it consisted of a single room, sometimes partitioned, raised from the ground, with steps at the side or in front. Rarely containing imagery or icons, it enshrined symbolic articles such as mirrors or swords representing kami. A *torii* or gateway stood outside, as well as a water basin to cleanse the mouth and the hands of worshippers. Acts of worship were simple. They involved clapping the hands, bowing, and making modest offerings of food, drink, cloth, or money. Ceremonial dances were performed, and shrine festivals were usually gay. Shinto possessed neither moral code nor philosophy; it had no sense of sin or guilt. Rather, emphasis was placed on cleanliness, a feature adumbrated in the creation myths. Ritual impurity could be caused by a number of events or conditions, including physical dirtiness, sexual intercourse, menstruation, childbirth, wounds, or death. The main point was to wash these impurities away. Essentially a cheerful and sunny religion, elementary and primitive Shinto remained part of Japanese culture until modern times.

Sinification, The First Phase:
Asuka or Suiko Period (552-645)

To this indigenous, primitive heritage of Yamato, the Japanese added an element of sinification, or Chinese influence. Long in contact with Chinese culture, the Japanese first borrowed from their neighbor slowly and unconsciously. Not until the mid-sixth century did some of the Japanese become aware of the advantages of the great continental culture and of the desirability of learning more about it. The result was a sudden acceleration around 550 A.D. in the rate of importation of Chinese concepts in religion, politics, economics, and language, initiating a period of conscious and voluntary cultural borrowing that persisted for about three hundred years.

During this period China exerted great power, for this was

the era of the Sui dynasty (589–618) and its successor the T'ang (618–907), the greatest of all China's two dozen dynasties and largest empire in the world at the time. Through her great prestige and strength, China attracted not only the Japanese but other Asian peoples and states into her periphery. For their part, Japanese ruling classes experimented with Chinese ideas. By the sixth century, they had acquired a higher degree of culture but recognized the desirability of importing certain concepts to strengthen the centralized government in order to manage more efficiently the loose clan system. Nothing was forced on them from the mainland. The Chinese (contrasted with the Mongols) were never interested in the physical conquest of Japan, so in their semi-isolation the Japanese were free to adapt Chinese importations as they desired.

Buddhism was the first major conscious borrowing from China. Its adoption in Japan, to the point of becoming the state religion for a time, was a remarkable story. The mainland conducted neither holy wars nor proselytizing campaigns. The religion came to Japan from China and Korea, but it had originated in India a millenium earlier. Its founder, whose traditional dates are 567–487 B.C., had several names, the personal ones of Gautama or Siddhartha as well as the appellations of Sakyamuni (Sage of the Sakya tribe) and the Buddha (Enlightened One). Born the son and heir of a king ruling over part of present Nepal, Gautama was brought up in luxury, received a good education, married, and fathered a son. A sensitive man, however, he brooded continually over the mysteries of human life and the problems of suffering, sickness, calamities, and death. He renounced his riches and royal succession to find answers to these problems.

After subjecting himself to various experiences to find the truth, Gautama finally reached enlightenment after long meditation under a fig tree. He concluded that life consisted of four truths. These truths were that life equalled suffering, that suffering was caused by desire, that to rid oneself of suffering one had to eliminate desire, and that desire was eradicated through the eight-fold path. The eight-fold path in turn, he declared, consisted of right views, resolve, speech, conduct, livelihood, effort, mindfulness, and concentration. For further guidance, he also gave his disciples ten commandments, similar in nature to those of the Old Testament. He stated that through these precepts each individual must find the path to salvation, which he termed nirvana, or the annihilation of self. The Buddha never claimed to be divine himself, and he set up no gods or religious pantheon.

After his death, his disciples propagated the faith that in time gave rise to differing interpretations. To help preserve doctrinal unity, councils were periodically called in India, but by the fourth council, around 100 A.D., two basic branches of Buddhism had developed. The earlier and purer form was termed Hinayana or Lesser Vehicle, because it rejected all later accretions. It is known also as Theravada, its main and only surviving sect. Drawing from the Buddha's sayings and doctrine, Hinayana emphasized self-salvation. Though monastic orders grew in this branch, emphasis was placed on the layman's activity to gain merit through the performance of ritual acts. Hinayana became widespread in Ceylon and the southeast Asian countries of Burma, Thailand, Cambodia, and Laos.

The later, amended Buddhistic thought was called Mahayana or the Greater Vehicle. First formulated in north India, it spread into China, Korea, and then on to Japan. This branch posited fundamental differences from Hinayana. Over the centuries, nebulously and anonymously, Mahayana developed the concept of salvation by faith in a plethora of buddhas, including the historical Buddha, who was venerated as only one of many. In this exalted buddha rank (*nyorai* in Japanese) came to be included Amida, the buddha of the western world or paradise, Dainichi, the universal buddha, and Yakushi, the buddha of medicine and healing.

Mahayana adherents also revered compassionate *bodhisattvas,* or beings of wisdom, who postponed their own salvation, though qualified for it, until they could save others. The main bodhisattvas that were revered in Japan (as they had been earlier, along with the buddhas, in China) included Kannon, the goddess of mercy and handmaiden of Amida, and Miroku, the saint of the future coming or millenium. A host of popular gods and holy men were also embraced in the wide-ranging theological field of Mahayana adherents. Moreover, to substitute for a "nothingness" nirvana, Mahayana advanced the reality of an afterlife. The idea of a western paradise arose, as well as a hierarchy of heavens and hells to reward believers or punish unbelievers. In simpler and more understandable form, Mahayana took hold in northeast Asian countries.

Differing in basic respects, both major streams of Buddhism adopted the canonical categories of the *Tripitaka* ("Three baskets"): that for conduct, which were rules for monks and nuns; that for discourses, which consisted of the Buddha's sayings or sutras; and that for supplementary doctrines, which were works of Buddhist psychology and metaphysics. With nothing comparable to one book considered holy as the Bible or the Koran, the Tripitaka was elastic in content and scope, not only between Hinayana and Mahayana but among the Mahayana sects themselves. A specific, orthodox canon in the Tripitaka was never crystallized, and national and regional variations remained great. A recent compilation of the Mahayana texts as utilized by the various Japanese Buddhist sects required several dozen volumes.

Originating in India and transmitted by China and Korea, the new alien faith appealed to the Japanese for several reasons. It filled a religious vacuum, for Shinto had no moral teachings. Through the concept of reincarnation, Buddhism buttressed not only ancestor worship but the continuity of Japanese "national" life. It compromised with Shinto for it admitted Shinto gods as buddhas or bodhisattvas. The Sun Goddess, progenitress of the sun line, was equated with the universal Buddha, called Dainichi or Vairocana. Moreover, the adoption of Buddhism was meshed with Japanese domestic and foreign politics.

According to the traditional account as contained in the *Nihon Shoki*, in 552 Paekche, an ally of Japan and probably the Korean state most subject of the several to Chinese culture, sent a Buddhist image and scriptures to Yamato. The message stated that Buddhism had come from China, and that great prestige lay behind it. It urged the Japanese to adopt Buddhism as the true religion, and at the same time it implied that the Korean ally could use Yamato help in its military campaigns then progressing against neighboring Silla. This traditional date of the introduction of Buddhism inaugurated the so-called Asuka epoch, after a capital site location in the Yamato plain, or the Suiko period, after the reign period (593–628) of a prominent empress of the time.

The uji in Yamato split over the issues of aiding Paekche and of adopting Buddhism. The military and religious clans, the latter dominated by the Nakatomi who were Shinto ritualists, opposed continental and religious involvements. Advancing a contrary position was a rising clan, the Soga, who wanted to enhance their position at court. Though the emperor sent no material aid to the Korean supplicants, he permitted the Soga to worship the image in private, at least until an epidemic broke out. Blamed for the pestilence, the image was thrown into a moat, and the Soga family temple was razed. Nothing much is then heard about the story until 584, when another member of the Soga clan was given two images from Korea. He erected a temple to enshrine them, and a Korean priest living in Japan at the time ordained three girls as nuns. After another plague, the images were again thrown into a moat, and the nuns were defrocked. But the disease continued to spread, and the emperor agreed to allow the Soga to follow Buddhism.

The nuns' robes were restored, and more Korean priests arrived. At court the Soga grew in influence until they reached their height under Shotoku Taishi, an outstanding individual, who might be called Japan's first statesman.

As regent (593–622) for his aunt the empress, Shotoku was a scholar and a devout Buddhist who composed three commentaries on Buddhist texts, still preserved today. He promoted the new faith as well as a centralized government focused on the imperial clan. He realized these ideas through the so-called Seventeen-Article Constitution of 604. This document, ascribed to Shotoku, was probably a later work dedicated to him a generation or more after his death. At any rate, the declaration represented his ideas, for it consisted of a set of injunctions to the uji to adopt Buddhism and to support the emperor. The articles emphasized the highly centralized Chinese governmental structure as it existed in Sui dynastic politics, which were based on Confucian virtues of sincerity, love, goodness, form and ritual, and the validity of Buddhism as a peaceful, unifying religious force. The theme was set in the first article, which advanced a plea for unity in words directly taken from the *Analects* of Confucius, "Harmony is to be valued, and an avoidance of wanton opposition to be honored." In this statement of principles, the prince endeavored to unite the loosely federated uji, subject to Soga guidance, under imperial rule.

Shotoku and his Soga colleagues constructed some of the earliest Buddhist temples and monasteries in Japan. Although few of the originals exist today, they or their reconstructed versions are priceless works of art. The most ancient of these, commenced in 593, was the Shitennoji ("Four Heavenly Kings" Temple; the suffix *ji* means a temple) in Naniwa, present-day Osaka. Another contemporaneous temple, begun the same year, was the Hokoji or Asukadera, farther inland. The most famous is the Horyuji temple complex, also in the Nara area, built in 607 by Shotoku. It was destroyed by fire within the century and rebuilt around 700. The Horyuji is a Buddhistic architectural prototype. The grounds are surrounded by a covered colonnade (*horo* or *kairo*) with a prominent middle gate (*chumon*) guarded by likenesses of deities. Inside the compound are located a five-storied pagoda, a golden hall (the *kondo*, probably the oldest wooden building in the world) to house principal paintings and imagery, and a lecture hall (*kodo*).

These temples contained early sculptural representations of Buddhist gods as well. The oldest native image is the bronze Asuka Buddha in the Angu-in near Nara. The Horyuji itself is rich in statuary. In its buildings are contained a bronze Yakushi buddha (607) and a bronze Shaka trinity (623) with the historical Buddha flanked by two bodhisattvas, attributed to the famous Tori Bushi, grandson of a Chinese immigrant. It also houses a larger-than-life standing wooden statue of the Kudara (Paekche) Kannon. The nearby nunnery, Chuguji, contains a charming seated contemplative Miroku. Another Miroku is at the Koryuji in Kyoto, which is identical to Korean models of the time.

The Imperial Household Collection has a colored portrait on paper of Shotoku Taishi and his two sons (or a son and a brother?), but few paintings of the Asuka period exist. The sides of the Tamamushi shrine, also in the Horyuji, execute scenes from the life and earlier manifestations of the Buddha done in a mixture of lacquer and oil. The temple also preserves fragments of textiles from the times, while the Chuguji has a tapestry showing Prince Shotoku in paradise.

Shotoku and his colleagues borrowed other Chinese ideas. The Chinese calendar was adopted at the turn of the seventh century (and so the 660 B.C. dating of Jimmu Tenno's founding of Yamato). Chinese hierarchical patterns were grafted onto the imperial family and the court bureaucracy, both of which were graded and ranked. To get word of the latest developments on the continent, Shotoku sent three embassies to Sui China. He addressed his letters on the basis of equality from the emperor of the rising sun (the concept of Nippon) to that of the setting sun. The Chinese emperor, accustomed to subservience from foreign rulers, was not amused. After Shotoku, thirteen more official missions were sent to China between 630 and 838. The cost, size, and perils of these missions were great. Generally they consisted of several ships carrying between five to six hundred men. To avoid being captured by hostile Koreans, they usually sailed across five hundred miles of open sea to ports on the central Chinese coast. The missions were successful in bringing to Japan the latest Chinese cultural and technological advances. Students and Buddhist monks mingled with official Yamato emissaries and spread Chinese ideas and customs on their return to Japan.

Sinification, The Second Phase: Hakuho (645–710)

After the death of Shotoku Taishi, the Soga line gradually weakened. One of the Nakatomi uji, together with a prince later to become the Emperor Tenchi, seized power and reorganized the government. In recognition of services rendered the emperor rewarded the Nakatomi with the new surname of Fujiwara, which has survived into contemporary Japan as the name of one of the oldest, most continuous aristocratic families in the world. After the accession of these new parties to power, the Fujiwara retained Buddhism, which was a complete change, since the Nakatomi had previously been the guardians of the Shinto faith. This development was a tribute to the groundwork that Shotoku had laid, for in the second overall attempt at sinification through the Taika (Great Transformation) reforms of 645–650, the Fujiwara and the Emperor Tenchi preserved Buddhism and further strengthened centralized imperial rule. These reforms presaged the so-called Hakuho period after the reign name of the Emperor Temmu (673–86), a prominent monarch of the time.

With ideas borrowed whole from China, the Taika reforms sought to transform Yamato economically and politically. They posited long-range and ambitious goals, which, had they been fully realized, would have had far-reaching impact. Private ownership of land was abolished. All land was nationalized in the name of the emperor, who redistributed it on the basis of households. To effect this policy, periodical censuses were taken. Three main types of taxes were imposed on individuals in the households: a grain tax in kind, usually rice; a tax on products other than cereals, such as textiles and handicrafts; and a labor or corvée tax, which might involve military duties for the state but which might be commuted by payment of other taxes. Under the central government, provincial (*kuni*), district (*gun*), and village (*ri*) administrations were organized. Peasant communities were blocked into groups of five families each, and these groups were held mutually responsible for the implementation of official directives.

Toward the end of the period, in 702, the Taiho (Great Treasure) code was promulgated. It elaborated the general laws of political conduct for the people and defined the specific bureaucratic ranks for the rulers. A council of state was created to advise the emperor, with a prime minister and ministers of the left and right. Then came eight ministries and in turn scores of lesser offices and bureaus. Servicing the structure was a bureaucracy that was eventually divided into twenty-six ranks, each subdivided again into "senior" and "junior" classes, and the latter into "upper" and "lower" grades.

The effects of such wide-ranging policies, which included the implied destruction of the uji and the reorganization of land patterns, could have been severe. Actually, as often occurred in Japanese practice, only nominal changes took place. New forms were merely imposed on existing patterns; otherwise the procedures would have been too bloody and too revolutionary. In the provinces, the local aristocracy simply received new titles, and the same persons carried on in new paper positions. As holder of crown land, the cultivator was to pay the taxes directly to the state in order to eliminate the creation of a class of tax-exempt and privileged landowners. But in time, tax-exempt estates grew with impunity as the central government was unable to effect its Taika tax policies. The reforms, never fully implemented, gradually broke down because the Japanese could not totally absorb the Chinese ideas. Even in T'ang China, as in other Chinese dynasties, this highly centralized economic and political system itself had operated on an effective basis only irregularly and only under strong emperors and strong regimes. It was too much to expect that such grandiose experiments, which were difficult enough to operate in China, would work more efficiently in Japan.

As ambitious political and economic structures were imported and grafted onto the Japanese systems, Buddhism grew in imperial favor. While previous rulers and aristocrats individually had espoused the faith, it was elevated to court status under Emperor Temmu and his successors. With official aegis, the religion grew in imperial favor and disposition. Few physical remains, however, date from the Hakuho period. The east pagoda of the Yakushiji near Nara, with its three sets of double-tiered eaves, provide an insight not only into Japanese architectural styles of the time but into T'ang China, where original prototypes have long since disappeared because of civil wars and the attrition of time.

In the same temple compound is now kept a bronze trinity of Yakushi and two bodhisattvas. The incomparable Horyuji, with its storehouse of Buddhist treasures, includes a Miroku in meditation (645) and the Lady Tachibana's shrine, with painted panels and a small sculpted Amida trinity inside. The walls of the kondo were decorated with frescoes of Mahayana Buddhist scenes, including Amida trinities in T'ang style, but regrettably in 1949 faulty electrical wiring destroyed many of these priceless wall paintings. Yet from what was left behind from this remarkably creative period in both religious and secular spheres, much can be learned about the advancing sophistication of the Japanese.

CHRONOLOGY

ca. 400	Chinese writing introduced into Japan
552	Traditional date for introduction of Buddhism into Japan from Paekche
552–645	Asuka or Suiko period
562	Japanese withdrawal from Mimana state in Korea
574–622	Shotoku Taishi
589–618	Sui dynasty in China
593	Construction of Shitennoji and Hokoji (Asuka-dera)
593–622	Shotoku Taishi as regent for Empress Suiko
593–628	Empress Suiko reign
604	Traditional date for Seventeen-Article Constitution
607	First construction of Horyuji
607, 608, 614	Shotoku Taishi's three embassies to Sui China
618–907	T'ang dynasty in China
630–838	Thirteen Japanese official missions to T'ang China
645–650	Taika (Great Transformation) reforms
645–710	Hakuho epoch
673–686	Rule of Emperor Temmu
ca. 700	Horyuji rebuilt
702	Taiho code

IV

NARA JAPAN (710–794)

Continuing to borrow basic Chinese concepts, the Japanese at Nara on the fertile Yamato plain planned a centralized capital city to house the imperial family. Previously, kings had resided on their personal estates scattered about in the Yamato area. The political capital moved according to the location of the new monarch's residence. Perhaps the chief reason for this continual movement was the concept of ritual impurity caused by sickness and death of the rulers, which precluded their successors' remaining in the same residence as their predecessors. Primitive architectural styles of palaces and homes facilitated the many moves. But in 710, after extended planning, Nara became the site of a permanent Japanese capital. It provided a headquarters and focus for both centralized government and the Buddhist religion. Nara was chosen in part because Buddhist temples already existed there and in part because of its propitious natural geographical setting as interpreted by geomancers.

Nara was designed on the model of the T'ang Chinese capital of Ch'ang-an, which was a great walled metropolis measuring some five by six miles and embracing about two million inhabitants. The new Japanese capital, similarly shaped in a rectangular pattern but considerably smaller, measured two and two-thirds miles by three. It was laid out at the northern end of the Yamato plain. The palace was located in the northern section of the city, which lacked walls. The western half was never developed. The city in time withered away when the capital was relocated in Kyoto, and the Nara of today developed from a medieval town that later grew up around the old Buddhist monasteries and Shinto shrines at the edge of the eastern hills. But in the eighth century, Nara was Japan's only urban center. Commercial centers, like those in China, had not yet developed in Japan. The main focus of Japanese life continued to be principally religious and political and was concentrated at the capital, a city of some 200,000 in a country with an estimated population of six million.

Politics and Society

Nara politics revolved around the sovereign and court life. In theory the concept persisted of a strong monarch, designated as *tenno* as in Jimmu Tenno, a Chinese term that implied an omnipotent, divine ruler. But the kings, already having lost effective rule, were actually quite weak. They were subject to manipulation at court by powerful families, notably the Fujiwara. And the monarchs remained weak through the practice of royal abdication that arose in the eighth century. The emperors, because of either devout religious calling or strong pressure from powers behind the throne, became cloistered in Buddhist monasteries or took up other duties. Removed from the political scene, the ex-emperors confined themselves to religious rituals and works, though a few of them in later times tried vainly to reassert their imperial influence and rule.

The *kuge*, or court nobility, concerned itself with much ritual and ceremony. Orchestral music and dances were imported from China. *Gagaku*, the imperial musical tradition, though it died out in China after the T'ang, persisted in Japan into contemporary times, to become one of the oldest authenticated music and dance traditions in the world. The Japanese borrowed other concepts as well. Chinese-derived administrative codes formalized an elaborate bureaucracy that was based on birth and family connections. These codes followed T'ang models to a great extent but were somewhat modified to allow for conditions in Japan.

No longer extant, the Taiho code of 702 provided the base for a revised version of the Yoro code of 718 that embraced both penal laws and administrative practices. The latter code confirmed the Japanese concept of the emperor's divinity; the Chinese, on the other hand, had always held that the monarch, as a temporary adjudicator of the will of heaven, held office by virtue and good behavior through a "mandate of heaven." To help administer central political affairs, the Yoro code also provided for a department of religion. This was unique to Japan, for there was no counterpart to this organ in China. The code also provided for a department of government that consisted of a supreme council of state, a chancellor, ministers of left and of right as high administrative officers, councillors, and eight ministries. Six of these ministries were based on Chinese prototypes—rites, civil office, treasury, punishments, war, and home affairs. The other two, the imperial household and its treasury, were uniquely Japanese.

The local government structure confirmed the three tiers of provinces, districts, and town or village units.

The emperor appointed provincial governors. As men of high rank, who included princes, the governors received as income some twenty-four acres of land for their rank and about five additional acres for their office. Some officials grew rich on these economic emoluments. Many spent their time in the capital and delegated their administrative duties to subordinates, who were the district officials. District magistrates were also imperial appointees, usually ranking members of local clans. They collected the taxes, and they also amassed fortunes. District appointments were often made for life, but the office in time became hereditary, a tendency in Japanese political affairs.

Commoners, at the bottom of the political and social structure, either were held in bondage or enjoyed free status. In the former category were serfs and slaves; the latter group consisted chiefly of farmers, who had been the beneficiaries of land redistribution policies during the Taika. A free man received about one-half an acre of land, while a woman received two-thirds as much. An entire family probably averaged holdings of two to three acres in size. They paid the land or grain tax amounting to about 5 per cent of total yields in kind.

Land was distributed on the basis of a rice production, with adjusted scales for sex, age, and the status for each member of the household. The Taika reforms had provided for the reallotment of land every few years to keep it in the hands of the free farmers. This policy proved difficult to implement, and large land holdings were accumulated, particularly by aristocrats and monastic orders. Theoretically all lands were taxable, but increasingly the nobility and the monasteries, through court connections, received fiscal immunity. With the growth of these nontaxable estates, those peasants who had to bear the burden of taxation grew worse off. Life became harder for them, and some escaped to frontier areas, became vagrants, or put themselves under the protection of higher and more powerful persons.

Realizing the problem, the Nara government promulgated a policy of replacing state control by private proprietorship as early as 743, when private ownership of rice land was made legally possible. It also embarked on a program of expanding and of reclaiming arable land areas which for incentive purposes were made nontaxable for a number of years. But since the reclamation projects required capital outlays, most schemes were undertaken by monasteries or the nobility, which had the means and which were already exempt from taxes. The newly acquired lands remained free from taxation. The common people continued to assume increased tax burdens, and agrarian poverty was widespread. The central government lost interest in the estates that provided no income, a tendency that helped lay a basis for the later economic and political decentralization of Japan.

Religion

While time-sanctioned economic and political patterns atrophied in the Nara period, Buddhism grew. Half a dozen sects flourished, of which a few emerged as the more prominent at the time. Their philosophies, partially influenced by Hinayana, arising in India, changed by China, and transmitted directly or indirectly to Japan, were difficult to understand. The main philosophical features of Nara Buddhism were concerned with the problems of negation and of the illusion of the material world, with the attainment of enlightment through the mental powers (because the only reality was man's own consciousness), and with the doctrine of the harmonious whole that emphasized a cosmological harmony under the universal Buddha. Buddhism in the Nara period tended to be aristocratic and exclusive, for the peasant in the field lacked the time to appreciate and the will to understand the complex religious doctrines.

First in point of time, the Sanron ("Three Treatises") sect was introduced in 625 by a Korean monk. Its idealistic philosophy stressed the unreality of material phenomena. The Jojitsu, with a similar doctrine, soon merged with the senior group. The Kusha also dealt with the metaphysical. Its origin is unclear and it might not have existed as a separate corporate entity. The Ritsu sect, emphasizing ritual, was founded by the blind Chinese monk Ganjin (688–763). After five unsuccessful attempts to reach Japan, he finally located in Nara at the Toshodaiji temple in 759. His likeness in a dry lacquer sculpture at the site is the oldest surviving representation of a historic person in Japan. The temple buildings themselves are pure copies of T'ang architecture, most of which have long since disappeared on the mainland. The Hosso sect, the leading one of the time, had been introduced into Japan around 650, and its main temple came to be the Horyuji. Like the others, it tended to stress the unreality of the physical world and the reality of consciousness.

Another major sect, the Kegon, was introduced by a Chinese monk. In the art of this sect, the universal Buddha of the harmonious whole, equated with the Japanese Sun Goddess, is portrayed on a lotus throne of a thousand petals, each of which is a universe containing millions of worlds. The best example of such a Buddha image is in the Todaiji, or the Great Eastern Temple, in Nara itself. In 735, following a pestilence, as a devout Buddhist, Emperor Shomu (who ruled 724 to 749) ordered the construction of the image and its encasing temple. It took fourteen years to complete the bronze figure, which is fifty-three feet high, sits on a lotus throne sixty-eight feet in diameter, and is surrounded by lesser figures. Vast amounts of material went into its construction: 1 million pounds of copper; 17,000 pounds of tin and lead; 2000 pounds of mercury; and 500 pounds of gold gilding (gold was fortuitously discovered in 749). Bronze segments for the image of ten feet by twelve feet and six inches thick were cast. The huge Buddha figure was housed in the Great Hall, 284 by 166 by 152 feet high. The present hall was rebuilt nine centuries later, but it remains as the largest wooden building in the world. In 752, at the dedication of the image and the hall, an international assembly gathered that included two Indian monks, a Brahman, a Cambodian monk, and a Chinese scholar, who was the president of the University of Nara. Emperior Shomu gave the temple tax-free lands, and he promulgated Buddhism as the state cult by ordering branch monasteries and nunneries to be constructed throughout the provinces. Late in life he abdicated and retired to the cloisters.

The Emperor Shomu's widow gave to the monastery a log cabin warehouse, the Shosoin. Still extant, the warehouse contained many of the personal belongings of the imperial family. Some items apparently had traveled long distances, such as Byzantine marble, Roman-inspired glass and pottery, and Persian articles. The emperor's daughter, the Empress Shotoku (who ruled 764 to 770, in the second of two short reigns), was also a devout Buddhist. She fell in love with a Buddhist monk, Dokyo, a master of the Hosso sect, whom she promoted to be chief minister. Dokyo wanted to be emperor, but he was ousted from office by the powerful Fujiwara family after the death of the empress. So important were the Emperor Shomu and his family to the development of Buddhism that the Nara period is alternately designated as Tempyo, after his reign.

After 770 the influence of Buddhism at court waned slightly. Subsequent to the unfortunate experience of mixing religion with politics, Japan had no more women rulers of any consequence after the Empress Shotoku. There were only two empresses after her but both were insignificant, although prior to Shotoku's rule, between 592 and 770, half the rulers of Japan had been female. The Empress Shotoku is important in Japanese Buddhism for another reason. She had a million Buddhist charms printed, many of which remain today as the earliest examples of wood block printing in the world. This art had developed earlier in China and was adopted by the Japanese.

Thanks to the copying of Chinese models, not only in religious ideas but also in visible architectural and art forms, the Japanese preserved for history a better understanding of the contemporaneous T'ang, and Chinese, culture. Nara abounded with temples and monasteries. Some of the temples were family sponsored; others were official. The imperial court under Emperor Shomu made the Todaiji the national temple, as it were, of Japan, of the time. Protective attributes were bestowed on the structures; they were believed capable of warding off evil and disasters. Complementing structures from the times, later reproductions faithful to the period were fashioned. Temple complexes that reflect the flavor of the Nara era include the Yofukuji, the Saidaiji ("Great Western Temple"), and other minor structures in the Horyuji. These include the octagonal Yumedono ("Hall of Dreams"), erected at the site of Prince Shotoku's private chapel, and the nearby Dempodo, originally Lady Tachibana's residence.

Beautiful statuary filled the halls. The chief works in the earlier decades of the Nara period were executed in bronze. In later years the dry lacquer medium was preferred. The statue would be executed either on a solid wooden core or over a hollowed center replaced by a wooden skeleton. In this manner were sculpted the Eight Guardian Devas (734), now in the Nara museum, of which the most famous is the Ashura, who before his conversion was a Hindu demon king. Clay statues were also shaped. The Shosoin contains objects of the Nara period with either religious or secular motifs.

Although Buddhism took hold of the arts and crafts, it did not supplant completely the native Shinto, which affected the daily lives of the common folk. Both faiths operated at differing levels of religion and philosophy. Moreover, even at the sophisticated level, the imported religion could be simply grafted on to indigenous belief; Shinto deities became equated with Buddhist gods; each group reinforced the other in the religious hierarchy. This fused result became known as Dual Shinto (Ryubu Shinto). As the leading family, the Fujiwara built both Buddhist and Shinto temples; the latter family shrine in Nara is the Kasuga. Unaffected by the complex theology and ramifications of the alien faith, the commoners continued in their simple acts of faith performed before local shrines and kami. And since Shinto transcended formal forms of religious worship as a state of mind or attitude, it would have been difficult to eliminate or to replace.

Literature and Language

Literature flourished during the Nara period. The *Kojiki* history and the *Nihon Shoki* were compiled in this period. The former was written partly in the difficult Chinese script and partly in Chinese characters used phonetically to represent Japanese syllables of similar pronunciation. The latter is written in pure Chinese, and it is quite detailed and involved. It not only incorporates the mythology relating to the evolution of the sun line, but it includes some metaphysical explanations for the creation of the world according to popular Chinese intellectual thought and philosophy of the day. This outlook emphasized harmonious relations between heaven, earth, and man. Such harmony, it taught, was to be sought in convenient groupings of a duality—the *yang* (the positive, male, bright element) and the *yin* (the negative, female, and dark element). This school of thought affected later Japanese historical writing. The *Nihon Shoki* commenced with a story of genesis in which heaven and earth had not yet been separated and the yang and the yin not yet divided. The universe was a chaotic mass, likened in a simile to an egg of indefinite proportions. Through time, the purer and clearer part of the egg became drawn out and formed heaven, while the yolk was transformed into the earth.

In addition to histories, collections of poetry were edited at Nara. Compiled in 751, the anthology *Kaifuso* (*Fond Recollections of Poetry*), with a preface, contains 120 poems written in Chinese. This collection includes works composed over a previous seventy-five-year period. Among its authors were emperors. Some poems sound quite stilted, for they resemble copybook exercises of Chinese literary forms. Other poems, reflecting Japanese attitudes, reach a keen level of indigenous expression. Another poetry collection, the *Manyoshu* (*Collection of Ten Thousand Leaves*), compiled in 760, contains 4516 poems composed over the previous century. The compilation borrows from Chinese characters which are utilized in a phonetic sense in most cases. Though some of the poems are long, the majority of them are *tanka* or short poems consisting of five lines with thirty-one Japanese syllables in a 5-7-5-7-7 arrangement. Some tanka have impressionistic themes, such as the emptiness of human life or the beauties of nature. Others deal with a wide-ranging variety of topics as loyalty to the sovereign, reverence for national deities, the weariness of frontier life, and clandestine village love.

The basis for written Nara literature was Chinese characters, which had been introduced into Japan around the turn of the fifth century. Because of the great prestige of Chinese learning and the lack of any native Japanese script, the imported forms were utilized by Japanese scholars. Inherent in this cultural borrowing were basic problems. Oral Chinese, which is basically monosyllabic, is quite different from the Japanese, which is polysyllabic and with different sounds and pronunciations. Written Chinese hardly reflects the Japanese style of phonetics. One Chinese character stands for one sound in Chinese, but since there were up to some 40,000 Chinese characters and only several hundred sounds or vocables, many characters are pronounced by the same sound and in different tones. On the other hand, agglutinative Japanese words, like polysyllabic English, required several Chinese characters used in a phonetic sense to spell out every separate syllable to approximate the single Japanese word. And while some Chinese characters were adopted for their similarity to Japanese sound, other characters were utilized for their ideas. *Kanji* are formal Chinese characters used for their meaning, and *kana* (of which there are two versions) are Chinese characters utilized for their approximate sounds. The Japanese grappled with these linguistic issues. The *Manyoshu* used the phonetic approach to Chinese characters in order to introduce Japanese words and expressions, but since there was no standardization of forms at this time, one Japanese sound could be expressed by a number of similarly spoken Chinese characters.

The End of Nara

After having settled in Nara for seven and a half decades, the court moved again. The Emperor Kammu (who ruled 781–806), championed by the Fujiwara, wanted to rule effectively and to free himself from the insubordination of the great monasteries, whose growth his royal predecessors had encouraged. In 784 he transferred his court to nearby Nagaoka where, over a five-month period, with 300,000 men working day and night, a palace and royal center were erected. To defray the costs of this expensive undertaking, the peasantry was heavily taxed. Their suffering increased, and available clothing and food proved inadequate.

Within a decade, the emperor undertook a second move. Bad omens had plagued Nagaoka, epidemics were frequent, and the heir to the throne, who had been exiled after palace intrigues, had died and his vengeful spirit had to be placated. In 794 the transfer was made to Heian, the city of "peace and tranquility." There the imperial capital stayed until 1868, when it was relocated at Tokyo.

The Nara epoch saw the peak and the beginning of the decline in borrowing from the Chinese. Now encompassing all Kyushu and Honshu as far north as present Sendai, the central government zealously promoted Buddhist religion and art, which existed in concrete, recognizable, and vivid forms. The transplantation of the more complex, detailed, and less vivid Chinese political and economic concepts proved more difficult. Those Chinese ideas that could be pragmatically adopted or those that were similar or understandable to Japanese concepts persisted, such as the notions of hierarchy, titles, and court rituals. Those ideas that proved impractical or unassimilable died out, such as the concept of a strong state based on extended and well-structured economic, political, and administrative forms.

While the Japanese borrowed wholesale, they also insisted on retaining their own traditions. Bureaucracy was maintained through hereditary aristocracy and not through the Chinese Confucian system of education and examination. The Japanese continued to emphasize the divinity of the emperor. They never accepted the Chinese idea of the mandate of heaven, which implied the right to revolt. As propounded in China by Confucian philosophers the mandate could be used against "evil" emperors, who, because of their immorality and injustices, became unfit for their office, which required, in theory, virtuous men to perform virtuous functions. The Japanese retained their emperors and only changed their ruling families behind the throne. Despite a heavy dose of sinification, Nara traveled its own cultural path.

CHRONOLOGY

710–784	Nara (or Tempyo) period
712	*Kojiki* compiled
718	Yoro code
720	*Nihon Shoki* or *Nihongi* compiled
724–749	Rule of Emperor Shomu
743	Private ownership of rice lands permitted
751	*Kaifuso* compiled
752	Dedication of Todaiji temple
760	*Manyoshu* compiled
764–770	Second rule of Empress Shotoku
781–806	Rule of Emperor Kammu

V

HEIAN JAPAN (794–1185)

In new surroundings the city of Heian took shape. Its geographic location was propitious; convenient access lay to the Inland Sea by river and to the eastern provinces by the principal land route of the Tokaido. Like Nara, the new capital was laid out on the Chinese model but on a larger scale that roughly measured three miles by three and one-third. No walls were erected, but a moat surrounded the city. Broad roads divided the city into squares, and the imperial residence, with fourteen gates, was located in the northern sector. Most structures in the city were of wood. Here classical Japan reached its height during the four-odd centuries of imperial rule, principally through regents of the notable Fujiwara family. Although the de facto capitals of Japan were later to be removed twice from the Heian area, the emperors located there until 1868, when the royal capital moved to Tokyo.

Politics and Economics

Though the Emperor Kammu had tried to re-exert imperial rule, the imperial position at Heian continued to be weak. Great families exerted indirect control over the monarchs. The first three sons to succeed the emperor on the throne were more interested in learning than in ruling. The most influential of the families, the Fujiwara, promoted their own cause diligently. They capitalized on their past affiliations with emperors. They cornered a monopoly on the interpretation and performances of the intricate court ceremonies. They arranged marriages between their daughters and imperial heirs. Under Fujiwara tutelage, the practice of emperors retiring or withdrawing to a monastery became pronounced. Of the thirty-three emperors who reigned during the almost four centuries of the Heian period, nineteen abdicated (six between 809 and 876), one was deposed, and thirteen ruled until their death. Sometimes because of the early age of imperial retirement, there were two ex-emperors living at the same time as the titular emperor.

Court life was concerned with much form and elaborate ritual. Like a miniature Versailles, the court assembled daily. Social behavior and costumes were regulated to the minutest point. Solemn edicts fixed the color of official robes, the length of swords, and the nature of salutations. Women could wear no more than six skirts. The emperor and his ministers paid their greatest attention to these rites and were left with little time for pressing political and economic questions, a state of affairs that was encouraged by the Fujiwara.

So influential did the Fujiwara become that the latter part of the Heian era has been designated as the Fujiwara period. In 858, Yoshifusa, a sixth-generation Fujiwara, assigned himself as regent for a nine-year-old grandson whom he placed on the throne. This was the first time that a minor had been put on the throne and the first time that anyone outside of the imperial line had acted as regent (*sessho*). The Fujiwara went a step further and in 884 Mototsune assumed the post of regent for adult emperors (*kampaku* or civil dictator). The tide was temporarily checked by Emperor Daigo, in whose reign (897–930) the regency was temporarily suspended. The Fujiwara family bounced back to reach its height under Michinaga (966–1027), who as its titular head (995–1027) married four daughters to emperors and placed two nephews and three grandsons on the throne. His son Yorimichi (992–1074) acted as regent for another fifty years, and so for eight decades two Fujiwara in effect constituted the ruling power behind the reigning monarchs.

Respecting hereditary authority, the Fujiwara never usurped the throne, which enjoyed a theoretical yet special religious aura. By the thirteenth century the family had so proliferated that its branches were known by inherited titular posts or by streets on which its palaces were located. Until the nineteenth century, regents and civil dictators were traditionally chosen from its five main branches. Despite the appropriation of honorific titles by the Fujiwara, the family declined in political power after the Heian. Their eclipse came with the rise of other families and with the weakening of the powers of the central government, where the Fujiwara had concentrated their efforts.

Because of the changing nature of the Japanese political scene, the Heian period experienced modifications in the operations of the central government. The Chinese-styled offices established by Shotoku Taishi and his successors continued in form but they lost actual power. Such offices as the ministers of the right and of the left, the prime minister, and the councillors continued into the nineteenth century, but they had become hereditary and had lost political significance. A pragmatic realignment of political duties had become necessary because of the growth of important families, the overall rise in population, and the accumulation of wealth and prestige outside the capital.

By the early ninth century three organs emerged which simplified and streamlined the central government. In 790 an audit office was established to audit accounts of local retiring bureaucrats. In time this office branched out to regulate taxation matters, whatever was left of them, between the central administration and the provinces. In 810, to regulate court procedures, a bureau of archivists was created to draft imperial decrees and to arrange interviews with the emperor. About a decade later, to insure law and order, police commissioners were instituted. They replaced the palace guards and the draft conscripts. From their original base in the capital, they issued laws and made arrests; later they established offices in the provinces.

The tax-land structure continued to weaken during the Heian. As tax exemption increased, the central government received less revenue. More and heavier taxes fell upon fewer peasants. Akin to arrangements that developed in the Middle Ages in Europe, for self-protection the taxable peasants commended their lands to a tax-free lord or monastery, and through this process of commendation they received immunity. Similarly, in the reverse process of benefice, the peasant received certain rights or benefits for the protection guaranteed to him. The arrangements did not necessarily involve a change in land ownership. These mutual rights of the holders in regard to land were known as *shiki*. The tax-exempt private holdings of manor and field, dating to Nara times, were termed *shoen*. The central government tried to arrest the trend. In 902 it forbade false claims to tax-free status, and in 1069 the emperor decreed that all shoen without charters attesting to fiscal immunity would be abolished. However, the decrees were of little effect because the chief offenders included the high ranking court officials themselves. Tax-free holdings of nobles and monasteries remained extensive. In 850 the Todaiji monastery controlled some 30,000 acres of rice lands, or 1 per cent of all cultivated land in Japan at the time.

These divisive trends in Japan led to the growth of feudalism. A tricky word capable of varying definitions in varying ideologies, *feudalism* denotes economic, political, and social structures resulting from rights and privileges based on land arrangements. In a broader sense, feudalism implies a breakdown of central authority and the growth of small, divided units. By the latter half of the Heian, both definitions could be applied to the Japanese situation. An economic base for feudalism was shaped through the presence of several phenomena. The continued growth of tax-free estates created economically autonomous units. Provincial landowners furthered their own interests by increasing their own holdings. Estate managers, representing absentee court or monastic landowners, administered lands, and they passed on to the proprietors a share of their income. Court members, themselves in exile or voluntarily seeking to enhance their position, built up their fortunes in the provinces. From this fluid situation, new economic and social forces emerged.

The latter half of the Heian also experienced the growth of military institutions in Japan. In the vacuum left by the decline of central authority in the provinces, local chieftains raised havoc on their own. Mounted and armed soldiers calling themselves *bushi*, or warrior gentlemen, roamed the countryside to prey on travelers and farmers. Pirates operated on the Inland Sea and along coastal areas. The Ainu proved troublesome, and the Emperor Kammu levied thousands of troops from various parts of the kingdom to suppress them. He gave command of the troops to the first significant military leader in Japanese history, Sakanoue Tamuramaro, who received the title of *Sei-i-tai-shogun* (abbreviated as *shogun*), or Great Barbarian-Subduing General. The Ainu were defeated, but the temporary military commission became permanent, to evolve as the power behind the throne in later centuries.

Clerical wars added to military confusion. Strong and militant Buddhist temples, maintaining their own guards for self-protection, fought against each other, against the nobles, and against the court. Clans rival to the Fujiwara, which faded to the background in the national scene, began to contest for power behind the throne. Two such families, the Taira and the Minamoto, who had become strong in the provinces, clashed with each other in the latter half of the twelfth century. In the course of what amounted to a thirty-years war, the Taira in 1160 first emerged victorious, only to be defeated in 1185 by the Minamoto, who commenced a new political period in Japanese history known as the Kamakura, after their capital located near present-day Tokyo.

Buddhism

Amidst political and economic confusion, Buddhism grew. Continuing the process begun in pre-Nara times, the religion absorbed native cults. It conditioned Heian art, literature, politics, language, and culture. As it became more and more a popular religion, it spread from the capital into the provinces with the establishment of more monasteries, particularly in Kyushu and in the Kanto plain. It introduced innovations in Japanese society, such as the practice of cremation to replace the custom of mound burial. It somewhat softened life, at least in the first centuries of the period. Banishment rather than execution was the recourse of justice, though the banished parties often suffered violent deaths. The faith proscribed meat-eating, but in Japan the vegetarian Buddhists allowed the eating of fish, a major dietary staple.

While Buddhism did affect Japan in basic ways, Japan in turn affected Buddhism. Shinto absorbed buddhas and bodhisattvas, and the strands of the two religions were not separated until the nineteenth century. Buddhist egalitarianism was changed to fit Japanese hierarchical patterns in monastic organizations and in doctrines that emphasized stages of enlightenment. There was a general relaxation of beliefs marked by a trend away from the Hinayana-inspired Nara Buddhist sects, in which each believer was to achieve his own salvation, toward the more popular Mahayana forms, which advanced the doctrine of salvation by faith through which he could let the saints lead him to salvation. More sects were founded, and in this era of institutional expansion and easing of doctrinal rigidity, two schools particularly dominated Heian Buddhism.

One was the Tendai sect, founded by the monk Saicho (767–822). A few years before the court moved to Heian, he had established a little temple at Mt. Hiei to the northeast of the town. This was an auspicious location because that direction was traditionally considered as a source of danger and evil. The monastery gained the favor of the Emperor Kammu, who may have relocated his new capital near Heian partly because of the monastery. Unlike the independent Nara Buddhist sects, the Tendai remained subservient to the court. In 804–805 Saicho was sent to China by the court to study the latest Buddhist doctrines. Upon his return he established at his temple the new school which borrowed heavily from the Chinese Buddhist T'ien-t'ai (in Japanese transliterated to Tendai) sect.

As in Nara, the doctrine continued to emphasize the universal Buddha, but it declared that one could achieve salvation through moral perfection, which was attained through meditation, virtue, good work, and scripture reading. Deriding the Nara scriptures as derivative and secondary, Saicho championed the Lotus sutra as the one that contained the Buddha's own words. A strict moralist, organizer, and disciplinarian, he established three classes of monks at his monastery. The first rank, as the "treasures of the nation" and the most exemplary ones, stayed at Mt. Hiei. The second and the third ranks went out to the court and into the countryside to lecture and to preach. His monastery grew to a complex of three thousand buildings by the late sixteenth century, when many of them were destroyed in civil wars.

The second chief Heian Buddhist school was the Shingon or True Word, derived from another Chinese Buddhist sect, called Chen-yen. Its founder was Kukai (774–835). An extraordinary genius, he was a poet, artist, calligrapher, philosopher, and a prodigious writer. Many miracles were attributed to him. A light shone at his birth, he could cause rain and he could stop it, and he was credited with the introduction of tea and of kana into Japan. Known as Kobo Daishi or Great Teacher, he was probably Japan's most beloved and best-known Buddhist saint. He came from a great aristocratic family who had opposed the move from Nara and so was disgraced. Kukai decided to become a Buddhist monk, though he read widely in other doctrines. At the age of seventeen he composed a book on the tenets of Confucianism, Buddhism, and the Chinese philosophic system of Taoism. In it he proclaimed the supremacy of Buddhism which incorporated, he declared, ideas of the other two schools. In 804 he sailed to China in the same mission as Saicho but on a different ship. He studied at the T'ang capital of Ch'ang-an for two years and returned to Japan in 806. The Emperor Kammu's son favored him, and he was well received by the court. A decade later he built his monastery on Mount Koya near Osaka, some distance from Heian. However, Kukai spent most of his time at the capital and after the death of Saicho, who was first a friend and then a rival, he became the abbot of the temple that commanded the main entrance to the capital.

The doctrine of the True Word maintained the unity of the universal Buddha, the idea that the whole universe was his manifestation and that all action centered in him. But the path to salvation, Kukai claimed, was through the true word, or the final ultimate secrets which the master of the sect would impart orally just before his death to one outstanding disciple. Full of mysteries, formulas, incantations, and oral transmissions, the doctrine emphasized the importance of speech as one of the three mysteries, the others being those of the body and of the mind. The mysteries of the body included ways of holding the hands and postures of meditation known as *mudra*. The mysteries of the mind referred to the methods of perceiving truths. The mysteries of speech included the true words and secret formulas. These truths of esoteric or secret Buddhism were absolute and independent of place and of time. Only the thoroughly initiated could aspire to understand them. Some of this doctrine was written out, and Kukai himself composed the "Ten Stages of Religious Consciousness," which ranged from animal life through Shingon (he placed Tendai eighth on the list). The True Word doctrine was expressed in great artistic and aesthetic works. Vivid paintings of *mandala* or inscription-filled halos and many-armed gods indicated the schematic arrangements of its philosophic ideas.

Some doctrinal amalgamation between the two main Heian sects of Tendai and Shingon was effected. The monk Ennin of the Tendai monastery of Enryakuji on Mt. Hiei, who traveled in T'ang China between 838 and 847, left behind a detailed and fascinating diary of these years. He combined esoteric with exoteric or popular Buddhism, to release the secret doctrines to all. Also of the Enryakuji, Genshin (942–1017) in his work, *The Essentials of Salvation*, portrayed the horrors of hell and the beauties of paradise. Forerunners of later popular sects that stressed salvation by faith, these monks propagated the new doctrine stressing divine love and compassion. They claimed that buddhas and bodhisattvas could help one achieve salvation simply by invoking their names. The invocation of faith was termed *nembutsu*. This more popular approach fit in with the politically fluid times of the later Heian, and the promise of easy salvation won many converts among the optimistic Japanese in subsequent centuries.

As the Nara region had been, the Kyoto area soon became dotted with temples, including the large compound of the Toji (Great Eastern Temple), the main Shingon shrine. Other Shingon temples located themselves in more remote hilly areas, away from the distractions of court or city life. By their distance from the political center, with its ever-increasing involvement in factional and civil strife, they managed to preserve their physical grounds and theological independence. A few buildings remain from the Heian period, which has been subdivided into two parts—the first century known as Jogan or Konin (794–894) after two of the more illustrious reign periods, and the latter period the Fujiwara (895–1185) because of the dominance of that family in political and cultural affairs. From these epochs date the golden hall and the pagoda of the Muroji, a Shingon temple located some forty miles from Kyoto in a beautiful sylvan setting, and the Jingoji and Kozanji, also in wooded areas but nearer the capital. Religious sculpture continued to be fashioned in bronze, clay, and dry lacquer, but wood grew in favor in later decades. The humanitarian Buddhism gave impetus to representation of the gentle Amida but the fierce Fudo, a protector of the Buddhist world, was also portrayed.

Culture

While Buddhism flourished and expanded, the Shinto cult, though relegated to the background, also prospered. Shrines were erected throughout the country; a list at the beginning of the tenth century enumerated more than 2800 of them, both local and official. The Ise imperial shrine remained the focal point of worship but there were innumerable private and village places of worship. At least half a dozen different types of shrine architecture flourished in Heian times.

Art and architecture flourished at the Heian court. The so-called Fujiwara style of structure provided for light, airy pavilions connected by covered passageways, surrounded by subdued landscapes and quiet ponds. Most representative of this type was the Phoenix Hall of the Byodoin, with an Amida carved by Jocho, a Fujiwara temple erected at Uji south of Kyoto.

In painting, in addition to Buddhist art, secular themes expressed themselves in *Yamato-e*, or pictures of Yamato, that illustrated on scrolls scenes from court or selections from novels. One such scroll, the work of several court painters in the 1120's, depicts episodes from *The Tale of Genji*, Japan's first lengthy novel. Another, the Toba scroll, is a satire on court life and portrays humans as animals playfully cavorting. The aristocratic culture immersed itself in such art forms and sought a new sophistication in ceremonies, food habits, and dress. Native tastes were reasserted in arts and letters, and cultural missions to China, of which the last had returned in 838, were officially terminated in 894.

Heian crafts were of varied nature. Lacquer and mother-of-pearl were used for decorative media on sutra boxes, chests, tables, and other items of furniture. Pottery and stoneware continued to be made, but with the Chinese contact lessening, no new strides were recorded. Metal works included bronze mirrors. Although few textiles have been preserved from this time, literary accounts described the elaborate court habits of men and women, as noted above.

In Heian literature, the Japanese continued to adapt Chinese characters for their own use. Pure Chinese was used for Buddhist and official literature, while kana as the phonetic variations of Chinese developed for use in general secular literature. Two forms of kana were formulated—*katakana,* a syllabary of some fifty sounds in which part of a Chinese character was adopted for a Japanese sound, and *hiragana,* wherein a whole Chinese character was abbreviated for the sound. A book of poetry, the *Kokinshu (Ancient and Modern Collection),* was compiled in 950 on imperial order by a Chinese scholar and chief of the court library. Almost all of its 1100 poems are tanka, but it contains a preface, the Tosa diary, an early form of Japanese prose, written by the author who narrated a trip home to Heian from Tosa in Shikoku where he had been a governor. Family chronicles, including those of the Fujiwara, were also composed. Glorifying that family were the *Eiga Monogatari (Tale of Splendor)* of the late eleventh century, and the *Okagami (Great Mirror)* of the early twelfth century.

In the tenth century two early novels were written. One was the *Bamboo Gathering Stories* which told of a three-inch maiden found in a bamboo tree, her development into a beautiful woman, and her subsequent love affairs. The other, *Tales of Ise,* revolved around the love affairs of young court nobles. The latter theme again was taken up by Sei Shonagon, a woman of remarkable talent and wit at court, in her *Pillow Book,* composed about 1002. If lacking in great depth, it was filled with impressionistic accounts, delicate nuances, and moments of comedy as they related to aristocratic court life.

In a class by itself was Lady Murasaki Shikibu's *The Tale of Genji (Genji Monogatari).* Probably written during the first years of the eleventh century, it is the great masterpiece of Japanese literature. A historical novel of complexity, magnitude, and broad scope, it dealt mainly with the life and loves of Prince Genji, the son of an emperor by a concubine, who was the composite of all commendable manly characteristics. Underneath, however, lay the themes of subtle pathos, the transience of life, and the impermanence of human relationships. *The Tale of Genji,* as well as most other literary works of the Heian, though sensitive to beauty and to life, portrayed but one aspect of Japanese affairs, that of the luxurious and shallow ways of nobility. More virile and realistic life and leadership were emerging from areas beyond the effete capital.

Aristocratic Japan of the Heian period had initially focussed official affairs in definite geographical centers of power. Continuing to borrow concepts from China but shaping them to native needs, the Japanese evolved a system of government that met their requirements. The phenomenon of indirect rule by families through an emperor claiming divine status persisted, although the governmental structure became more complex with the custom of royal abdications and the cloistering of former monarchs. But after the first centuries of governmental centralization, divisive factors became noticeable in the land. Trends toward growing economic, military, and political decentralization resulted in the greater importance of provincial areas. Yet this very decentralization helped to round out Japan's geographical borders. And in spite of factors favoring regionalism, general cultural advances were made. Buddhism became more popular, architectural styles reflected refined tastes, art flourished, and indigenous literature enjoyed a golden age. The course of Japanese history proceeded unevenly along its variegated path.

CHRONOLOGY

758–811	Shogun Sakanoue Tamuramaro
767–822	Saicho and Tendai sect
774–835	Kukai and Shingon sect
794–894	Jogan or Konin period
804–805	Saicho in China
804–806	Kukai in China
838–847	Ennin in China
858	Fujiwara Yoshifusa becomes regent for minor emperor
884	Fujiwara Mototsune becomes regent for adult emperor
894	Official missions to China terminated
895–1185	Fujiwara epoch
897–930	Reign of Emperor Daigo
942–1017	Genshin
950	*Kokinshu* compiled, with Tosa diary
966–1027	Fujiwara height under Michinaga (from 995)

992–1074	Fujiwara Yorimichi
ca. 1000	Writings of Sei Shonagon and Lady Murasaki (*Tale of Genji*)
1118–1181	Taira Kiyomori
1147–1199	Minamoto Yoritomo
1158–1189	Minamoto Yoshitsune
1160–1185	Taira dominance

PART TWO

FEUDAL JAPAN

In feudal Japan, patterns of political, economic, and social life rearranged themselves. Particularly important was the role of the military in local and central leadership. Civilian families, such as the Fujiwara, lost ground to military ones, who, however, continued to exercise indirect authority through the imperial line at Kyoto. Mounted warriors and their foot retainers grew in stature. The Minamoto at first managed to retain political control over most of Japan, but in the latter decades of their epoch, and particularly in the ensuing shogunal rule of the Ashikaga, the country fell apart politically. Yet commercial activity at home, and with China, improved, and Buddhism reached its popular apex. After Japan experienced its political low point, in the latter half of the sixteenth century three strong-willed men managed to reunite the country.

The Tokugawa, who emerged on top in this successive country-welding process, ruled the land with an iron hand. To preserve political stability, they tried to freeze society at home and forbade contacts with or from abroad. Yet try as they might, the shogunal rulers could not prevent changes as the decades progressed. By the mid-nineteenth century, when the West was knocking on Japan's doors most persistently, the domestic situation favored the opening up and modernization of Japan. This led to the Tokugawa downfall by 1868 and the "restoration" of power to the new young emperor, who, with his advisers, embarked Japan on a new course of action.

VI

KAMAKURA JAPAN (1185–1333)

The Kamakura era initiated what has been called the feudal period of Japan. While some anachronistic features of Japanese culture persisted, these years were not a dark age between more glorious preceding and succeeding eras. Far from being static, society registered the growth of new classes. Rule was decentralized but effective. Culture spread, and Buddhism became the popular faith. The noticeable social and economic gaps that had existed between court and country, aristocrat and commoner, were reduced. Agricultural acreage increased, roads were extended, and domestic and foreign trade flourished. Peripheral areas of the country became important, yet in these years strife was endemic, and life could be violent. In this age of feudalism, militarism became a pronounced aspect of Japanese civilization. The bushi, or warrior lords, and military retainers assumed predominance in national life. As rearrangements of social and economic life proceeded, new forces came into prominence in Japanese history.

The Minamoto Shogunate

After overcoming the Taira family and the opposing court factions in 1185, Yoritomo of the Minamoto family devised a form of government which with only some later modifications persisted well into the nineteenth century. He located his political center at Kamakura, a pleasant town south of Tokyo, which had been his base of power. For the first time in Japanese history, the de facto or effective capital was located in the provinces apart from the court and emperor. But Yoritomo retained much of the traditional political and administrative structure of the central government that he had inherited. He retained the imperial house, and he continued to issue decrees in the name of the reigning monarch. He did not exterminate the Fujiwara, who continued as regents at Heian, nor did he circumscribe the estates or ritualistic duties of the other court families, over whose political affairs he kept close control. He maintained the provincial and local administrators in civil functions, and in 1192 he received from the cloistered emperor, who had endorsed his cause, the title of shogun or generalissimo. He transformed the shogunate for the first time in its three-hundred-year history into the effective organ of indirect rule.

Onto the existing national administrative system, Yoritomo added his own family administrative structure, a pattern which was followed throughout the land by his military retainers. The country became a patchwork of theoretically decentralized units that were controlled only through a combination of strong shogunal rule and loyal vassal allegiance to it. This system of government presumed some elements of a feudal system, such as those of hereditary military groups who pledged personal allegiance and loyalty to the lord and received their lands from him. Yorimoto did not technically endow his retainers with the fiefs as was the case in European feudalism, because his warriors, as the owners or managers of the estates, continued to derive their titles to the property from Kyoto rather than from Kamakura. However, the distinction was negligible, because the shogun rewarded or redistributed estates as he saw fit, even if he did not assign the titles.

Yoritomo attempted to systematize land distribution by appointing to each estate stewards or overseers responsible directly to him. Earlier, the Taira had utilized to a limited extent the steward system, but Yoritomo sought to perpetuate it throughout the whole country. Previously the estate managers had been appointees of the owners; now they became the self-supporting personal retainers of Yoritomo. Stewards were supported by shiki, or their share of the estate produce. They maintained peace and order on their property, they performed the various functions of the local government, and they collected taxes whether or not the estates had been previously exempted from taxes, for Yoritomo did away with the shoen. Unlike the estates of Europe, those in Japan generally consisted of scattered irrigated rice fields. In this sense they resembled the agrarian holdings of the earlier uji, yet they were also different because the communities on the estates were grouped less by blood or common ancestry than by a complex of shiki, feudal rights, and privileges. The steward emerged as an important figure in late twelfth-century provincial society, and the position, like most others, became hereditary. Yoritomo designated himself the Steward General. In time, there arose from the ranks of the stewards some of the later lesser gentry and *samurai* or retainers.

To give some cohesiveness to the decentralized steward pattern, in 1185 Yoritomo appointed one retainer in each province to a managerial rank that came to be known as protector or constable. These were in essence military governors who were responsible for maintaining peace and order in their provinces and for commanding the local retainers in wartime. The system again was not new, but Yoritomo endeavored to make it lasting and uniform. The post of military governor also became hereditary and the holder sometimes doubled as the civil governor of the province. Yoritomo was the Constable General. There were some irregularities and regional variations in the pattern, but the system worked fairly well, and it persisted after Yoritomo's death. From the constable ranks evolved the *daimyo* or great lords, so important in the late feudal period and in the Tokugawa era.

The title of shogun gave Yoritomo control of all the military forces of the land. The administration to which he gave form was known as the shogunate or *bakufu* ("tent government"). At Kamakura he created three central boards: an administrative board to act as a central policy making body; a board of retainers to regulate the affairs of his followers; and a board of inquiry that served as an appelate court of final jurisdiction in the administration of customary family law. His courts developed careful and exact judicial procedures, and the judges appeared ready to implement an even-handed justice, at least as it was defined by the military of the time. All boards arrived at unanimous decisions, which gave impetus to a Japanese predilection for collective responsibility and for collective leadership.

As a result of the newly improved Minamoto family system upon traditional political forms, complex groupings of administrative rights arose during the Kamakura period. Many of Yoritomo's retainers acted in several official capacities. As a more extreme example, one Yoritomo follower in southern Kyushu, in the area that later came under the famous Satsuma family, was the steward of an estate and the constable over three provinces. But he was not the civil governor, and under the old Taika code still on the books he was responsible to that officer. Since he had the effective military authority, he could keep all civil officials off his estate. He also enjoyed court rank, and he had obligations to the emperor and to Kyoto. Yet as vassal of Yoritomo, he could not present himself at court without the permission of the bakufu. The multiple loyalties imposed by court, Taika, and feudal laws were not easily handled, but the feudal obligations in the early Kamakura period proved the most overriding.

This emerging dominance of the military over the civilian authority had continuing significance in Japanese national life. Japan turned its back upon the Chinese example of the supremacy of the educated civilian bureaucrat in political affairs. In the Japanese tradition of a ruling, hereditary, and landed aristocracy that stressed military strength, Japan was more nearly like Western Europe than China. Perhaps this was one reason why the Japanese adjusted more readily to Western stimuli in the nineteenth and twentieth centuries than did China, and why the military could have dominated Japan by World War II. In theory, the military organization continued to rest on a drafted peasant army and an elite corps of capital guards, but in fact the provinces and estates through local defense groups carried on effective military institutions.

As a descendant of the ancient mounted warrior of the tumuli period and the aristocratic armored knight, the retainer of Yoritomo re-emerged in the twelfth century as a man of military prowess. Armed with bows and arrows, the mounted warrior wore armor consisting of small strips of steel held together by leather thongs. He fostered ideals of bravery and of loyalty, and the extra-family ties that existed between him and his lord ranked higher than family bonds (quite unlike China where the family remained the strongest social unit). By the later twelfth century his tactics included suicide through a process of disembowelment, known in the West as *harakiri* ("belly slitting"), probably arising from a fear of capture, torture, and beheading by the enemy.

The Hojo Regency

After Yoritomo died in 1199, his family did not hold power for very long. His line constituted essentially a one man's rule. Yoritomo himself contributed to the premature decline of his family, because he was very jealous of his close relations, including especially the position and military successes of one brother, Yoshitsune, with whom he refused to deal. He did away with an uncle, and he had another brother put to death. When he himself died, the only remaining close family members were two immature sons. Actual power passed to the hands of the Hojo, a family ironically related to the Taira and from whose ranks came Yoritomo's widow, the strong-willed Lady Masa. The Hojo proved to be astute advisers, and Lady Masa's father became regent for the young sons of Yoritomo, who in turn became shoguns. Both sons met with early and untimely deaths, and as the Minamoto faded out, three successive generations of the Hojo family helped to consolidate strong Kamakura rule.

After 1252, the Hojo, who chose not to accede as shoguns but in effect continued as the real power in the shogunate in the role of regents, set up imperial princes as shoguns. During the remainder of the Kamakura period a confusing pattern of political power persisted. In Kyoto an emperor resided, but he had long since lost his power to a Fujiwara regent, who in turn, by the late eleventh century, through court intrigues and factional strife had lost his own power over the court to cloistered emperors. All these royal factions in Kyoto were controlled from Kamakura by a titular shogun, who, however, had been supplanted by a Hojo regent. Thirteenth-century Japan experienced the height of indirect political rule.

The court was weak and divided, but in 1221 one cloistered ex-emperor, Toba II, tried to reassert his power. He had strengthened his own military forces from the imperial estates over the years, and in the uncertain times that prevailed between the end of the Minamoto family and the consolidation of the Hojo, a showdown occurred between the troops of the retired emperor and those of the shogunal regent. The Kamakura army quickly put down the rebellion, and Toba II was sent into exile. A more amenable brother was put into the position of retired emperor, although he had never been enthroned. Shogunal deputies were stationed at Kyoto to tighten control, and the court was more closely watched than ever. The Hojo confiscated royal and court lands and redistributed them to their followers. But they continued to show the traditional respect for the imperial position as the source of all legitimate, orthodox power.

For some decades afterwards the bakufu through the Hojo regents ruled Japan efficiently and ably. In 1232 the central administrative board drew up a written code, based on the preceding half-century of Minamoto experience, to regularize the conduct of the warrior classes. Based on customary family law, this Joei code, named after the year period of the emperor's reign, crystallized and epitomized military relationships. Not meant for the people, the code consisted in essence of a set of judges' rules. Unanimity continued to be the rule for arriving at decisions. Written in difficult Chinese, it included a solemn oath to be taken by the shogun and all his advisers, who were to be fair and uniform in dealing out justice.

The code consisted of fifty-one sections. The first few articles dealt with the proper maintenance of Shinto and Buddhist shrines and observance of religious rituals. Some nine or ten articles then outlined the duties of stewards and constables. Several articles related to the tenure of fiefs and rights of succession. Property was to remain in the holder's hand, which meant the practical retention of land by military men since they occupied most of it. Rights were granted to women, who had begun managing estates while their husbands were away at war. They could adopt heirs, hold fiefs, and even obtain divorces. Some articles outlined contractual relations; others regulated personal relationships. Punishments were prescribed for breaches of the peace. Grounded in practical experience, the code recognized the actual conditions of feudalism. Unlike earlier imperial codes, this was not a Chinese importation but rather a pragmatic response to existing situations.

In the countryside peasant life continued much the same. Little was written about the farmers or their unglamorous lives. The lowest classes were tillers of the land and workers in corporations and guilds. Some peasants had minimal property rights, but there was no real improvement in their status. The distinction between the farmer and the foot soldier was not very clear in this period, for often the two were identical. In the time of peace the farmer was a cultivator; in time of war he became a soldier. The line between commoner and foot warrior, as differentiated from the mounted warrior, blurred. But the lower classes, because of the economic and military necessities of the time, were incorporated into a leavening society to a greater degree than they had been previously. For the first time, their life and activities were portrayed in the picture scrolls of the period.

Religion and Culture

The Kamakura era was marked by striking developments in Japanese Buddhism. Originally the faith had been the property of aristocrats in the capital and of the great monasteries, but in the course of time Buddhism spread to the provinces, and it began to penetrate the lower social strata. Buddhism was becoming a popular religion, and it was taking on distinctively Japanese forms. The leaders of the new sects were chiefly of humble origin, and they wrote in simple Japanese. More Buddhist schools were founded and more of their doctrines became intelligible to the common man. Both the masses and the military responded to the new versions. Some converts looked for escape from the endemic warfare of the age; others sought easier paths to salvation. For some Buddhism filled a void, for others it offered a consolation of, or a discipline for, the spirit.

One central feature of some of the new schools that appealed to the ordinary Japanese was the concept of salvation by faith. This belief had found earlier expression, but not until the Kamakura did it give rise to distinct schools. In 1175 Honen (1133–1212), a monk from Mt. Hiei, founded the Jodo or Pure Land sect, which emphasized faith in the pure land, or the western paradise, of the buddha Amida. A derivative of a similar Chinese Buddhist school called the Ch'ing Tu, it maintained that salvation would be achieved simply by a repetitious invocation or *nembutsu* of Amida's name. The faith was simple, for it involved no temples, no priesthood, and no ritual. The simplicity elicited violent reaction from the older sects. Honen was sent into temporary exile by the court, which marked an unusual instance of persecution and intolerance in the annals of Japanese Buddhism.

One of Honen's followers, Shinran (1173–1262), carried the idea further in his True Pure Land sect or Jodo Shinshu, sometimes designated simply as the True sect. Discarding the idea of a repetitious cycle of Amida's name, he maintained that only one wholehearted and sincere invocation of Amida was sufficient to insure salvation in the western paradise. Carrying further the element of simplicity, he discarded monastic church organization and most of the Buddhist scriptures. He preached the faith to the masses through evangelical messages. He permitted his priests to marry, to lead normal lives, and to mix with believers in congregational groupings. His disciples were to live as members of lower ranks of society and to be teachers rather than monks. Egalitarian at first, Jodo Shinshu grew in popularity but later developed strict hierarchical patterns. Later centered in Kyoto in the Temples of the Original Vow (the Eastern and Western *Honganji*), it attracted more adherents than any other Buddhist sect in the country.

A third major school of the popular faith movement took the name of its originator, Nichiren (1222–1282), a descendant of humble fishermen from the Kanto area. He found the way to salvation in the Lotus sutra, rather than in Amida, and he taught his followers to chant the formula, "Hail to the Sutra of the Lotus of the Wonderful Law." Accordingly, this sect also became known as the Lotus sect. A dominating personality, Nichiren was aggressive, passionate, and highly intolerant of other Buddhist schools. His teachings were quite nationalistic in tenor. He argued that Japan was the center of the Buddhist faith and that his doctrine was the one true one. He damned his religious rivals. He predicted national calamities, and the Mongol invasions of Kyushu in his later years seemed to bear out his pessimistic predictions. Buddhist concepts in feudal Japan as advanced by Honen, Shinran, and Nichiren that stressed salvation by faith, a paradise, and a highly monotheistic concept of one Buddha or of one sutra, plus the use of vernacular in scriptures, paralleled in certain respects the development of Christianity in medieval Europe.

The other aspect to the religious revival was the rise of Zen, the meditation school. Originating in India and termed *dhyana* in Sanskrit, it was transmitted to China, where it was known as Ch'an. Dhyana was adopted into Japanese phonetics in two characters pronounced *zenna*, a term later shortened to *zen*. Its tenets had been known previously in Japan, but again it was not until the Kamakura that it gained status as a separate school. It existed in two main branches. In 1191, Eisei (1141–1215) brought the Rinzai variation of Zen back from China, and in 1227, his disciple Dogen (1200–1253) introduced the Soto also from the mainland. Eisei established his headquarters at Kamakura, where in later times one of the chief Zen temples, the Enkakuji, was constructed. Eisei also brought back tea from China. Known for some time in Japan, tea did not become popular until it was praised by the monk for its therapeutic values, later becoming the national drink of the country. Dogen, a more rugged individualist, located on the isolated west coast of Honshu. Both Zen variants adopted the posture of *zazen*, or sitting in meditation, which the Soto emphasized, and *koan*, or the intellectual riddle, on which the Rinzai focused. Eschewing dogma, Zen declared that enlightenment came through sudden inner experience. Its antischolasticism, simplicity, austerity, discipline, and close relationship between master and disciple appealed particularly to the military.

The Buddhist fervor reflected itself in Buddhist art. There was a great spurt of temple building. Monasteries throughout Japan became repositories of art and learning, just as Christian monasteries had been in feudal Europe. The great fifty-two-foot bronze Great Buddha or Daibutsu representing Amida at Kamakura was one of the more grandiose efforts at monumental art. Multistoried architecture patterned after Chinese Sung dynasty (960–1279) models were reflected in pagodas and towering main temple gates. Although few extant examples remain from the age, there are the Shariden, a small scriptural depository in the Enkakuji at Kamakura, the Sanjusangendo (Hall of the Thirty-three Bays) in Kyoto, and the Tahoto shrine (near Otsu), a unique architectural blend of an Indian rounded stupa on a tiered pagoda.

Many of the larger temples were decorated with picture scrolls illustrating their histories, their leaders, and their religious ideas. The *Hungry Ghosts* scrolls are one of the more representative types that illustrate vividly the tortures of the damned in Buddhist hells. These picture scrolls or *nise-e* (likenesses) also depicted secular life, and they provide us with data on feudal life and times. Historical themes and personages are portrayed, as in the portrait of Yoritomo in the Jingoji. Tea drinking became the fashion among Zen adherents as an aid in meditative vigils. Religious urges promoted carving and lacquer making, and artistic items were offered as gifts to the buddhas. Tea drinking gave rise to the ceramic industry, which turned out beautiful but simple cups and pots to contain the hot liquid.

The Kamakura age made no outstanding contributions to literature. At court, anthologies of poetry continued to be compiled, of which the most prominent was the *Shin Kokinshu (The New Ancient and Modern Collection)*, completed in 1205. Travel diaries were composed, as well as court miscellanies and records. In contrast were the realistic military tales that began to appear at this time. These war stories recounted chiefly the struggles between the Taira and Minamoto. One of the more important of these literary endeavors is the *Heike Monogatari (Tale of the House of Taira)*. A true Japanese epic, it not only relates feats of arms, but deals with the theme of evanescence of glory. Even military men felt the transience of power and life, which was symbolized by the falling petal blossom tossed about by the wind. Emotional and sentimental, the poetical prose was chanted to the accompaniment of a lute, and it became the source of many popular ballads. Two shorter volumes also dealt with episodes in the interclan struggle: the *Hogen Monogatari (Tale of the Hogen War*, of 1156), and the *Heiji Monogatari (Tale of the Heiji War*, of 1159–1160). In the mid-thirteenth century, the entire narrative was reconstructed as the *Gempei Seisuki*

(*Rise and Fall of the Minamoto and Taira*). Legal documents from the time also survive.

Kamakura Decline

Though the Kamakura system of Yoritomo and the Hojo regents weathered the challenges of change for a century or so, in its latter decades it encountered serious difficulties. Internal circumstances helped to weaken the ruling line, whose drive and vigor dissipated in ensuing generations. Succession quarrels at court plagued the shogunate, for through the last will and testament of an early monarch the imperial title, often contested, was to alternate between the descendants of two heirs, from whom derived the senior and the junior lines. While the shogunate endeavored to remain neutral, it could not help becoming embroiled in these court squabbles. Factional discord became acute, and the rapid turnover of occupants of the throne resulted at one time in five living ex-emperors in Kyoto.

Moreover, the initial emphasis of warriors on simplicity and economy vanished with their exposure to court and town luxuries. With the passage of time, their loyalty, which had at first been given unstintingly to Yoritomo, wore thin to the figurehead successors. They gave only lip-service to military codes and ethics and many found it easy to switch allegiances. Rewards and spoils for their service in the forms of offices and estates became scarce. Retainers fell into debt, and the financial situation became so desperate for the warriors that in 1297 the Kamakura government issued a general cancellation or postponement of debts and mortgages of its followers. After four or five generations of Minamoto and Hojo rule, confidence in the government had broken down.

An external factor, the Mongol invasions, helped to hasten the end of Kamakura rule. The Mongols, who had overthrown the Sung dynasty in North China, under Kublai Khan established a new ruling house in Peking. Consolidating his rule at home as well as expanding into the weak peripheral areas of China, as early as 1266 Kublai sent envoys to demand tribute from Japan. The Hojo regent refused to bow. After sending several more unsuccessful missions, the Mongol ruler resorted to force. In November, 1274, he launched from southern Korea a force of some 25,000 Koreans and Mongols, which landed at Hakata Bay (Fukuoka) in northern Kyushu. The Kamakura government dispatched forces to counteract the invasion, but the brunt of the fighting fell upon its retainers in the area. The first encounter turned out to be only a one-night stand, for in the face of foul weather and heavy winds, the invaders re-embarked and retired to the mainland.

After this initial defeat, Kublai sent more messengers to demand submission, but the Hojo regent twice executed the Mongol's envoys. Busy with the subjugation of South China, Kublai did not return his forces until mid-summer of 1281. Numbering now about 140,000 Chinese, Mongols, and Koreans, the expeditions proceeded from both Chinese and Korean ports to rendezvous in Kyushu, where the bulk of the troops landed again at Hakata. In the interim years the Japanese had erected a wall around the bay, and the enemy forces were restricted to a narrow beachhead. For some two months the Mongols were held at bay, until a hurricane struck. A large number of the vessels were destroyed and many of the troops were stranded. Probably only half of the invading forces returned to China.

The Japanese maintained the Kyushu defenses for another twenty years, but the Mongols did not return. Not until 1945, at the end of World War II, was there another penetration of foreigners into Japan, this time a peaceful occupation by American troops. Japanese valor, geography, and climate factors helped to defeat the Mongols. The Japanese themselves usually ascribed their successes to their insularity and uniqueness, buttressed by the notion that the hurricane called *kamikaze* or divine wind destroyed the enemy. The invasions were vividly and impressionistically recorded in the so-called Mongol Scroll, which, composed by an artist who witnessed the events or who drew on eyewitness accounts, depicted fighting scenes. The many claims for rewards and spoils of the Kamakura retainers who helped repel the invaders went unheeded and contributed further to disenchantment with the shogunal regents.

The final blow that overthrew the Kamakura came from Kyoto. The junior and senior lines to the imperial succession had become involved in another of many disputes, and the shogunate interfered in the contest. This interference was resented by the reigning emperor, Daigo II, who wanted to keep the succession in his branch, the junior one, of the family. Moreover, as one of the few ambitious monarchs in Japanese history, he wished to regain control of the court from the cloistered emperors. Most audaciously, he desired independence from Kamakura as well, and rallied some of the court and military to his cause.

In 1331, when the shogunate attempted to force his premature retirement, the emperor went into open rebellion. At first he enjoyed considerable success, but Kamakura forces captured him and exiled him to a remote island. Revolts by imperial partisans continued, and in 1333 Daigo II escaped and continued the fighting. The Kamakura general, Ashikaga Takauji, sent to capture him, proved a turncoat. He changed sides, pledged loyalty to the emperor, and seized Kyoto for the monarch. Events moved quickly, and in the ensuing military turmoil Kamakura was captured and burned by anti-shogunal forces. In 1333 the Hojo regency came to an end, and Japan entered a new politically and militarily confusing era, termed the Ashikaga, which constituted the last two and a half centuries of the feudal period.

The Kamakura period had noted the height of indirect rule with the existence of emperors, cloistered emperors, royal regents, shoguns, and shogunal regents. The unwieldly chain of command could only operate effectively when exercised by strong men in top posts. This proved to be the case during Minamoto Yoritomo's strong shogunate and the early Hojo regency, although the system broke down in later decades with lesser men and the passage of time. With the growing decentralization of power in the central organs of government came the growing importance of regional forces, such as the constables, stewards, and warriors. Political and economic power spread, as well as culture. Buddhism experienced its golden age, formed its most popular sects, and brought artistic expressions of its faith. Yet despite the rapid spread of the pacifistic religion, militarism was pronounced. Retainers, warriors, and lords provided the backdrop to the militant life, for with the growing insecurity and often left to fend for themselves and for their estates, they assumed more duties and powers in their respective domains, which were scattered throughout Japan. Japanese history became more complex and many-sided.

CHRONOLOGY

960–1279	Sung dynasty in China
1133–1212	Honen, founder of Jodo sect
1141–1215	Eisei, founder of Rinzai version of Zen
1173–1262	Shinran, founder of Jodo Shinshu sect
1192	Yoritomo appointed as shogun
1200–1253	Dogen, founder of Soto version of Zen

1205   *Shin Kokinshu* compiled
1221   Revolt of Emperor Toba II (Shokyu or Jukyo war)
1222–1282   Nichiren, founder of Lotus sect
1232   Joei code
1239–1289   Monk Ippen
1274, 1281 Mongol invasions
1331, 1333 Rebellions of Emperor Daigo II

VII

ASHIKAGA JAPAN (1333–1603)

Aided by his new Ashikaga ally, the victorious monarch, Daigo II, planned to re-establish imperial control over Japan. In the next three years he busied himself at Kyoto with the restoration of civilian government and appointed court nobles to high offices. But the court had neither the troops nor the resources to govern the country. Ashikaga Takauji, after eliminating his chief military rivals, again proved opportunistic and seized Kyoto in 1336. He supported a member of the senior branch of royalty to the throne, and Daigo II, of the opposite faction, fled with some of his supporters to Yoshino, located in the mountains south of Nara, where he established his capital. Japan had now two rival courts at two capitals, a political phenomenon that lasted for some fifty years.

In 1338 Takauji appointed himself shogun, a position which his family retained in Kyoto until 1573. But his shogunate differed from that of Yoritomo. Where the Minamoto and the early Hojo had maintained effective control over all of Japan's many feudal families and the retainers owed them loyalty at least in the initial half of their regime, the Ashikaga never exercised effective control over the warrior class as a whole but only over their few supporters. They kept the Kamakura government structure, but it soon became inoperative except in the capital area. Provincial figures had emerged as powerful competitors for central political power.

Strife

Chaos and decentralization followed the accession of Takauji as shogun. A half-century of general strife ensued and succession disputes divided the northern and southern courts. Many noble families changed allegiance opportunistically. The whole land was in a state of commotion and strife. It was an age of turncoats, of amassing great fortunes and lands, and of losing them. New lords emerged suddenly, and sudden defeats plunged them once more into oblivion. One family, the Yamana, who in 1390 managed to gain control over eleven provinces, which were equivalent to one-sixth of the land area of Japan, was subsequently defeated by the Ashikaga and reduced to governing two provinces. The Ashikaga ruled those areas which they controlled effectively from Kyoto. They established their headquarters in the Muromachi section from 1392 to 1573 (this period is also known by the designation Muromachi). In the capital they maintained their power and controlled the imperial court more effectively than did the Hojo, but political disintegration continued in the countryside. There was little or no obedience to central authority; loyalty, if it existed, was extended only to the immediate lord.

In 1392 the third Ashikaga shogun, Yoshimitsu, persuaded the southern court to return to Kyoto, and he pledged that the throne would again alternate between the two branches. The court returned, but the shogun did not live up to his promise. Daigo II's line never occupied the throne again and eventually disappeared, though some Japanese historians have claimed it as the legitimate one. The later Ashikaga-sponsored emperors were weak and impoverished for lack of imperial funds. One monarch was reduced to selling specimens of his calligraphy on the streets of the capital. Another remained unburied for six weeks. At one time there was no reigning emperor for twenty-one years.

Factional strife continued, and the first half of the Ashikaga period experienced a variety of domestic disturbances. Some fighting was predicated on political grounds. Shoguns pitted themselves against provincial and feudal lords. Lords, backed by their retainers, took on each other. Since no dominating feudal family emerged until the mid-sixteenth century, autonomous feudal entities ruled their own vassals according to their own laws. Economic unrest, following periods of heavy taxation and famine, also contributed to violence. Beginning dimly to realize their importance, peasants rose in revolt and attacked money lenders, pawnshops, and warehouses. Agrarian protest movements on a large scale resulted, although they lacked leadership and continuing programs. The peasants usually demanded acts of grace and moratoriums or cancellations of debts. They burned legal documents. These outbursts indicated some class antagonism to the military or civilian overlords. There were also Buddhist uprisings. Large temples and monasteries with their own military forces acted in an independent manner and sometimes established autonomous political administrations. Members of the Jodo Shinshu sect ruled a province or two for over a century in northwest Honshu, and they instigated rioting elsewhere. Because of their religious fanaticism, they became known as Ikko or the "single-minded" sect.

A low political point was reached during the Onin War (1467–1477), designated after the reign name of the emperor, when succession disputes between the two factions claiming the throne became especially acute. Fighting became endemic in the streets of the capital itself, and in the course of the decade Kyoto was nearly destroyed. So destructive were these years that some Japanese historians have maintained that Japanese history really began only after this period. The Onin War triggered another century of warfare, known to indigenous historians appropriately as *sengoku jidai*, a hundred years of "warring states." Not until the last half of the sixteenth century was this divisive trend arrested.

The process of reunification was slow and tortuous, for in the post-Onin age of strife the shogunate became even more enfeebled and local lords acquired greater powers. Later termed *daimyo,* these lords were despots or petty kings. Each had his strict house laws to govern relations with retainers. The captains of the growing daimyo armies were still mounted, but their position had changed from one of importance in Kamakura to subordination to great lords in Ashikaga times. On the other hand, in the fourteenth and fifteenth centuries the foot soldiers became very important. They gradually displaced the individual knight as the basic military unit. Lines between warriors and commoners were blurred considerably. The distinction between "good" and "low-born" commoners also disappeared, though the latter were replaced by the *eta* or outcasts. These eta came from diverse origins, but the majority probably became outcasts from the nature of their occupations, as tanning and butchery, which violated vegetarian Buddhist precepts against the taking of animal life.

Land ownership as well as society underwent great change. Estates were reshaped during the Ashikaga period. Former private estates over the centuries were assimilated into the daimiates. Court estates shrank in size, and the nobility became particularly impoverished after the Onin War. New estates replaced the vanishing older ones and grew in importance as regional economic and political units, while villages assumed more importance in local administration as the basic units of rural organization. Enjoying considerable local autonomy, the individual or contiguous villages were generally located near shrines, convenient transportation facilities, or sources of water. Their inhabitants paid their taxes to the ruling lord and they performed labor services for him. The old managerial class on the late Heian and Kamakura estates were amalgamated more into the peasant than into the aristocratic ranks, but they retained importance as village headmen. In these times of political elasticity and growing land scarcity, a form of primogeniture developed to replace the practice of division of property. To maintain land and position in family hands, fathers passed on titles to one successor, not necessarily the eldest son but the strongest and the most able natural or adopted heir.

Commerce

Despite military strife, domestic trade flourished. A money economy complemented barter trade. Although the government as early as the eighth and ninth centuries had promoted a money economy, the effort proved premature and failed. The government mint disappeared, but with the resurgence of trade in feudal times, rather than minting new coins, the Ashikaga imported Chinese copper cash. The growth of a money economy coincided with the development of towns and of urban centers. As in later medieval Europe, commercial centers of varying types emerged in the Ashikaga period. There were port towns, such as Sakai, the port for Osaka, which achieved commercial prominence and independent municipal status. There were castle towns like Osaka and Edo (or early Tokyo) built around important daimyo capitals. There were temple towns developing near important Buddhist or Shinto shrines and monasteries. A merchant class rose, probably from enterprising lower echelons of society. Guilds, known as *za*, dating from the twelfth century, also became important in the Ashikaga era. The trading societies, receiving protection from lords or religious orders, found new commercial solidarity among themselves. The widespread political chaos helped to unite them in a common cause within their growing urban centers. They began to develop along the lines of the medieval

European city states, but they did not become a powerful mercantile community as did the German cities. When Japan was closed to the outside world in the seventeenth century, urban society thereafter became stratified along rigid occupational lines.

Overseas trade, mainly with China, also received impetus. It had begun to assume significant proportions in the late twelfth century. At first Koreans were the intermediaries in this trade, but slowly the Japanese themselves appropriated the trade channels. By the fourteenth and fifteenth centuries they began to dominate the China shipping and commercial lanes. Trade was both legal and illegal, private and official. Japanese pirates, known as *wako,* preyed on Chinese and Japanese vessels and proved a serious menace. In spite of the insecurity of sea routes, the China trade proved lucrative for those who participated in it. In 1404 the shogun Yoshimitsu agreed to revive official missions to China. In this resumption of formal contacts, he agreed to recognize Chinese suzerainty and to be invested as the "King of Japan" by the emperor of the Ming dynasty (1368–1644), which had replaced the Mongol in China. For this submissive act he earned the condemnation of later Japanese historians. According to the terms of the treaty, the Japanese were to send every decade a mission of two ships to China. But instead of one mission Yoshimitsu dispatched six embassies in as many years. In 1411 his son terminated the agreement, but trade was resumed in 1432 and lasted until 1549. In these 117 years, eleven official embassies, consisting of up to nine vessels, went to China.

In this international trade, Japanese imported tropical products, manufactured goods, and luxury items as silks, porcelain, books, works of art, and copper cash. Japanese exported sulphur, lumber, gold, pearls, mercury, mother-of-pearl, swords, screens, and painted folding fans, an invention of theirs. The curved swords of medieval Japan were in great demand throughout east Asia. One trade mission to China in 1483 alone brought along 37,000 swords. Not only did the shogun and the court participate in the trade, but also the feudal families, especially those in Kyushu, and Buddhist monasteries, particularly the Zen orders. Proceeds from this China trade helped Zen monks to build monasteries, including that of the Tenryuji in western Kyoto.

Culture

Partly because of its participation in the China trade, Zen Buddhism grew in importance during the Ashikaga period. Paradoxically, in spite of its antischolastic foundations, its monasteries became centers of learning and art. Zen monks, among the first to learn of creative culture trends in China, reintroduced the use of pure Chinese in texts and literary works. They also led in the development of, though they did not create, Japan's first great dramatic form, the *No* ("Ability") drama. Drawing on secular backgrounds, No was given religious impetus. In part derived from *sarugaku* (mimes or "monkey music"), a tradition originating in India, and *dengaku* (Japanese harvest songs), No consisted of symbolic dances and poetic recitations chanted by actors and by an accompanying chorus. The epics of No have remained one of the great dramatic legacies of the Japanese. The drama unfolded on a bare stage with two chief actors wearing masks, assisted by a few subordinate characters. A play usually ran for six hours and was divided traditionally into five parts. Each successive act related to gods, a warrior, a woman, a mad person, and a concluding festive piece. To provide comic relief, *kyogen* ("crazy words") were interspersed between the No acts; these were realistic satires on society of the time.

With its aesthetic perception, Zen culture, through a blend of native tradition and imported ideas, developed other arts. Imported from China, these arts included landscape gardening, flower arrangements, and the tea ceremony. Based on the theory that universal truths and beauty could be appreciated through the expression of the intimate and the simple, landscapes and rock gardens became miniature replicas of nature as a whole. An early name in garden architecture was that of the Zen priest Muso Soseki (1275–1351), who, among other works, created the beautiful and justly famous moss garden of the Saihoji in Kyoto. Both dry and water garden types existed; in the former sand or white pebbles represented water. Most famous of this type is the rock and sand garden at the Ryoanji in Kyoto, of unknown architect and uncertain date.

Bonsai, or dwarf trees, and plant arrangements became another expression of the "cultivation of the little." Flower arrangements, initially associated with the placing of floral offerings before Buddhist deities, in themselves became a fine art, and no Japanese *tokonoma* or alcove was complete without its floral decoration (*ikebana*). In a beautiful but simple environment, the tea ceremony became also an aesthetic spiritual ritual (*cha-no-yu*).

The shoguns might have been weak in military power, but they provided a focus for cultural leadership, and their courts at Kyoto became cultural centers. Of the fifteen Ashikaga shoguns, Yoshi-mitsu was probably the most active in this regard. Not only did he promote trade with China, but he sponsored the arts in the capital, which under his shogunate experienced an outburst of cultural energy. In 1397, upon his retirement to Buddhist orders, he built as his residence the Kinkakuji or the Golden Pavilion in the northern hills of the Kitayama district (which bestowed its name to his age). The beautiful structure unfortunately was burned down by an arsonist in 1950 and only imperfectly restored. Similarly, the eighth shogun, Yoshimasa, also upon his retirement in 1473, built the Gingakuji or the Silver Pavilion in the eastern hills suburb of Kyoto called Higashiyama, also designated as that cultural epoch. These two buildings constituted the most outstanding examples of archi-tecture in the Ashikaga period. Graceful and pleasing, the structures continued to utilize the light architectural forms of aristocratic Japan.

With Zen in the ascendancy, sculptural representations of its priests and deities were effected. Realistic No masks were carved for male players, particularly for those playing women's roles or supernatural beings. The shogun Yoshimitsu patronized No drama and encouraged its development through the actors Kanami (1333–1384) and his son Zeami (1363–1443). His successor Yoshimasa also surrounded himself with talented cultured men, whose ranks included the "three amis" of No: Noami (1397–1471), his son Geami (1431–1485), and his grandson Soami (d. 1525).

Harking back to Sung art concepts, Ashikaga painters sought to convey the essence of nature in a few bold ink brush strokes, termed the *sumi-e* style. In these paintings they eliminated minor details, and they placed man and his works in small, insignificant stature so that they blended with or were subordinate to the natural setting. Josetsu, active around 1400, of whose work only one extant copy exists, painted in this style. Among the greater artists in this man-ner were his disciple Shobun (fl. 1414–1465) and the latter's dis-ciple Sesshu (1420–1506). The last-named was probably the greatest of Japanese painters in this tradition.

Other schools and styles flourished. The Kano school, commencing with a father Masanobu (1434–1530) and son Motonobu (1476–1559), transformed landscape painting into an art monopolized by a hereditary school of painters, who as professionals worked on commissions from their patrons, the shoguns. Its adherents worked on a grandiose scale, covering screen panels of silk or paper with bright decorative compositions in the Chinese style. It endured as the paramount school of painters until the nineteenth century. The Tosa school, another hereditary line of scroll painters, was founded by Yukihiro and lifted to greater heights by Mitsonobu (1438–1525). These took for subjects sacred and secular historical topics in the Yamato-e tradition. The imperial court patronized this school.

In prose, military epics and court miscellanies continued to be composed. Describing wars and campaigns from 1318 to 1368 is a work with the incongruously worded title of *Taiheiki* (*Chronicle of Great Peace*). A court poet, Yoshida Kenko (1283–1350), who later became a Buddhist monk, in the mid-fourteenth century composed *Essays in Idleness* (*Tsurezuregusa*), a miscellany of stories and personal observations. In poetry, the *renga* or chain poem appeared, in which the traditional thirty-one syllable tanka was split, alternating three- and two-line units of 5-7-5 and 7-7 syllables respectively. The chain poem, a verbal scroll to match the picture scroll, proved popular, and it became a game of literary art.

Reunification

Against the backdrop of political disunity and cultural growth, the reunification of Japan proceeded in the latter half of the sixteenth century. In this process of reconsolidation three contemporaneous names stand out—Oda Nobunaga (1534–1582), Toyotomi Hideyoshi (1536–1598), and Tokugawa Ieyasu (1542–1616). So prominent were they that the Japanese have usually designated them only by their given names. The latter two started their careers as lieutenants of Nobunaga, but each in succession as subsequent top military leader came to bring more of Japan under his sway. Yet their tactics were disparate. Their differing personalities were reflected in popular epigrams. Of Nobunaga it was said, "If the cuckoo doesn't sing, I'll kill him"; of Hideyoshi, "If the cuckoo doesn't sing, I'll make him"; and of Ieyasu, "If the cuckoo doesn't sing, I'll wait until he does."

Nobunaga, the first of the trio, was the son of a relatively obscure lord in a province bordering Nagoya. A courageous and able general, he built his fortunes on his father's estates and branched out to conquer neighboring lords. Attracting the attention of the reigning emperor, who was seeking the support of a military man, he was invited by imperial commission to restore order in Kyoto. He accomplished that task, but he did not become shogun himself. Rather, he dominated the figurehead Ashikaga who was titular possessor of that office until 1573, after which the shogunate remained vacant for some thirty years. Controlling the capital or heartland of Japan, Nobunaga from this strategic location enhanced his power. From his position as only one of many feudal lords, he rose to prominence through his abilities and the maximum use of opportunities that presented themselves.

Nobunaga located his headquarters near Kyoto at Azuchi, a castle town on Lake Biwa. After disposing of his immediate enemies, he directed his efforts against the Buddhists, who posed serious political and military threats. On these grounds, rather than on religious antipathy, he used military force and divide-and-rule tactics to eliminate their strongholds. In 1571 he subdued the Enryakuji temple of the tendentious Tendai sect on Mt. Hiei, where he laid waste to the three thousand buildings and slaughtered most of the twenty thousand inmates. In a ten-year campaign, he conquered the rebellious Ikko sect in northwest Honshu, and he leveled their stronghold in Osaka. Buddhism never again regained a strong temporal position in Japan. Toward his secular and religious foes Nobunaga could be cruel. He massacred thousands, burned captives alive, and killed noncombatants. Through forceful measures he was master of half of Japan by the time he was assassinated in 1582 by one of his lieutenants.

Four of Nobunaga's leading vassals appointed themselves regents for Nobunaga's successor, his infant grandson. The regency was a failure, and Hideyoshi, who had been pacifying west Honshu, seized power. Hideyoshi's own story had a "rags to riches" theme. Born of humble origins, he was a foot soldier, who through sheer ability and the breakdown of class lines of the time rose in ranks. Lacking even a surname, he adopted three of them in succession until he finally settled on Toyotomi ("Abundant Provider"). He came to terms with Tokugawa Ieyasu, who ruled the Kanto area. He conquered northern Honshu, Shikoku, and Kyushu in huge campaigns that involved up to 250,000 troops. Like his predecessor, Hideyoshi declined to become shogun, but he assumed the old title of kampaku, hitherto held only by the Fujiwara. Faced with realities, this family simply adopted him in order to maintain tradition. Hideyoshi located his capital at Osaka, where he rose to power, but near Kyoto he built a palace called Momoyama, which bestowed its name to a period of Japanese cultural history (1573–1615).

Quite ostentatious, his palaces and castles were huge, ornamental, and flowery. He restored prestige to the imperial office and rebuilt the royal palaces. At Kyoto he erected a Daibutsu or Great Buddha statue, larger than those at Nara and at Kamakura, but it was destroyed in an earthquake of 1596. Artists turned out flowery gold screens, beautiful textiles, elaborate No costumes, lacquer ware, and half a dozen types of decorative or utilitarian ceramics, such as Karatsu, Raku, Shino, Oribe, Bizen, Iga, and Shigaraki. Main pottery centers were in Kyushu, which received fresh artistic impulses from neighboring Korea and continental China. The Tosa school continued as did the Kano in painting. The latter particularly flourished under Motonobu's grandson, Eitoku (1534–1590). Hasegawa Tohaku (1539–1610) founded another school.

Hideyoshi's domestic policies reflected his background. He ruled through the feudal structure of vassalage. Akin to Yoritomo's system, it centralized authority in practice, but the general permitted the daimyo in theory to enjoy local autonomy. Possibly because he retained the daimyo system and imposed his will through the lords, he was able to reunify Japan more quickly than otherwise would have been the case. Reminiscent of the Taika reform, he conducted an exhaustive land survey of all Japan and had the population registers kept up to date. In 1588, through a "sword hunt" edict, he disarmed all non-samurai, and he tried to prevent those of common birth, as he had been, from rising in society. Through other decrees he endeavored to fix class distinctions, freeze occupations, and forbid changes in residence. He minted gold, silver, and copper coins, and he augmented military settlements with financial rewards to his ex-enemies. Although he stripped the nobility of power, he was generous to the court. In his latter years a strain of megalomania became pronounced, and he turned to extreme measures. After the birth of his son, Hideyori, he killed his nephew, children, and wives. As Yoritomo had done, he practically eliminated his family. Not stopping there, he proposed grandiose yet desperate schemes in foreign policy.

Desiring to subjugate China, Hideyoshi hoped to achieve this goal by an invasion of Korea. His foreign policy was probably motivated partially by a desire to divert attention from internal problems and to keep his numerous military followers occupied. China was an attractive magnet, and Hideyoshi in his grand, deluded dreams wanted it. He equated the subjugation of the Ming empire of some 65 million souls with a domestic campaign. In 1590 he informed the Korean ambassadors of his plans of conquest. Two years later he established advanced headquarters at Kyushu, and he gathered some 150,000 troops for the invasion. Though Hideyoshi himself never landed in Korea, his force of nine armies landed in south Korea. They proceeded north to capture Seoul and Pyongyang in the west and to reach the Tumen River in the extreme northeast frontier. His troops slaughtered thousands of Chinese and Koreans and sent their ears and noses back to Japan, where they were buried in the famous ear mound at Kyoto.

The campaigns, however, bogged down. The winters were severe, and the Korean navy played havoc with supporting Japanese sea lanes. Included in the Korean maritime arsenal were the bizarre tortoise boats that confounded the enemy. These strange-looking vessels had strong roofs, resembling turtle shells, covered with iron plates and spikes, which covered the whole ship. Long and narrow, the iron ships were heavily timbered to withstand the shock of collisions. They had rams at either end and a battery of oars that could be manipulated in either forward or reverse directions with equal speed. Faced by a stalemate on land and sagging sea support, the Japanese negotiated with the envoys of the Ming, who had dispatched troops to Korea to help stop the Japanese. The long talks proved fruitless. The Ming rejected Japanese demands, and instead, they sent an embassy to Japan to claim investiture, which Chinese emperors traditionally considered their sovereign prerogative to confirm rulers of neighboring lands. The infuriated Hideyoshi redeclared war, and new invasions proceeded. But in 1598, after a brief illness, Hideyoshi died, and the Korean adventure collapsed. The men returned home, bringing with them Korean printers and potters who were to enrich Japanese cultural life.

Hideyoshi's ambitions knew no bounds. He wanted to incorporate into a Japanese empire the Philippines, Indochina, and Siam. He desired a base near the mouth of the Yangtze River in central coastal China from which to direct his overseas conquests. He had two maps of the world, which in his times meant east Asia. One was on a folding screen in his palace, and another was on a fan, which, while cooling him, literally fanned his ambitions. Despite his foreign failures, Hideyoshi secured for himself a high place in Japanese history, ranking as possibly the greatest premodern popular figure. Many books and plays were written about him, and the corpus of popular literature on his exploits remained voluminous. His personality was domineering, but his domestic and foreign policies were based on his personal power, and some policies did not long survive his lifetime.

The five regents appointed to administer affairs of state for Hideyoshi's young son cooperated no better than the four for Nobunaga's heir. Tokugawa Ieyasu, a stay-at-home who bided his time in the Kanto plain, arose to the top in the ensuing free-for-all after Hideyoshi's death. In the struggle for power, Ieyasu won out in 1600 in the battle of Sekigahara, a town controlling a vital pass near Lake Biwa. Three years later he assumed the title of shogun, and the country embarked upon the Tokugawa period, the last of the traditional Japanese political eras.

Western Intrusion

Concurrent with domestic controls came the outlawing of foreign trade, foreign contacts, foreign ideas, and the foreign religion of Christianity. By the time the doors slammed shut to outsiders in the early Tokugawa period, the Japanese had been exposed not only to the rich Chinese markets but to the first European traders and missionaries. The Portuguese were the first Westerners to land in Japan. The traditional story relates that in 1542 or 1543 Portuguese sailors voyaging along the south China coast were blown off course to the shores of Tanegashima, a small island off the southern coast of Kyushu. They brought with them firearms, in the use of which they instructed the local inhabitants and which came to be called *tanegashima* after the island. More Portuguese ships appeared, and the southern feudal lords took readily to the idea of trade with foreigners as well as to the utility of firearms.

Commercial contacts with southern Japan were soon followed by missionary endeavors. The Jesuit Francis Xavier, who had been preaching in Asian Portuguese colonies, was persuaded in Goa by one Anjiro, a Japanese youth carried there on a Portuguese ship, to go to Japan to convert the people. In company with a brother missionary, Xavier landed at Kagoshima in southern Kyushu in mid-summer of 1549. He remained in the country two years, preaching in western Japan and in Kyoto. Other Jesuits arrived to carry on the cause. In spite of linguistic problems, the Japanese at first received the clerics well, and Nobunaga himself bestowed favors on them. Converts were made from the ranks of both commoners and daimyo. The leaders were not only impressed with the fire arms brought by the Westerners but with cultural aspects of Christianity. Some, for political reasons, saw in the new faith a counterpoise to Buddhism. Others professed to see resemblances to Buddhism in doctrine and in country of origin, for Catholicism had come to Japan from India. There were probably many sincere converts, as well as those who joined the church from political or economic motives.

In defiance of imperial and papal rulings, the Spanish followed the Portuguese into Japan. In 1581, when Portugal and Spain were united under Philip II, the monarch confirmed to his Portuguese subjects the exclusive right to trade in Japan. Four years later the Pope conferred upon the Jesuits the sole right to enter Japan as missionaries. Although Hideyoshi at this time was involved in campaigns of domestic conquest, he sent an embassy to Manila to demand recognition of Japan as suzerain power. In reply, the Spanish governor sent two missions to Japan that included four Franciscan friars disguised as ambassadors. More Jesuits and missionaries of other orders arrived, and they were permitted to land on the understanding that they would not preach Christianity. They accepted this prohibition but violated it by preaching not only in the countryside but in the cities of Nagasaki, Kyoto, and Osaka.

After Hideyoshi had completed the subjugation of western Japan, he issued a decree in 1587 ordering all Christian missionaries to leave Japan. However, engrossed in other matters, for a decade he made little effort to enforce the decree. But he became increasingly suspicious of the political implications of Christianity. The idle boasting of a Spanish pilot to the effect that missionaries were preparing the way for a political conquest quickened his fears. He was irritated by sectarian feuds among the various Catholic orders, and his authority had been defied by open preaching. In 1597 he ordered the first major wave of executions of Christians. Six Franciscans, three Japanese Jesuits, and seventeen Japanese laymen were crucified at Nagasaki.

Other Westerners arrived. The Dutch followed the Portuguese and the Spanish, but they limited themselves to trade alone. In 1600, the first Dutch ship reached Japan. It was one of a fleet of five vessels that sailed by way of the Straits of Magellan, and when blown from its course in the central Pacific it sought refuge in Kyushu. The pilot of the vessel was an English sailor, Will Adams, who, because of his wit and maritime ability, was employed by Ieyasu as adviser in matters of commerce and navigation. Other Dutch ships arrived, and a Dutch factory, or warehouse-residence-office complex, was constructed at Hirado, an island near Nagasaki. By the time Ieyasu had assumed the shogunate, Westerners had a toe-hold in Japan. Their activities and peculiarities gave rise to pictorial representation known as *namban* or art portraying Western themes. But they were not to keep their precarious position in Japan for long, for in the process of Tokugawa control and the self-imposed policy of isolation for the country, their progress was nipped in the bud.

In a new era, the Tokugawa restored order to the country. They reversed the trend toward political and economic disintegration that had accelerated during the Ashikaga period, which had caused the loss of effective central control and the persistence of widespread and chronic strife in many forms. In these previously chaotic times, social and economic lines had been rearranged. Estates changed hands, land holdings grew or shrank, lords won and lost power, villages assumed importance as semiautonomous administrative units, cities sprang up, and guilds formed. Commerce and trade registered gains at home and abroad. Cultural vitality was maintained. The Japanese practiced popular arts, appreciated impressionistic type paintings, developed early dramatic forms, wrote poetry, and erected architectural gems. But Buddhism had seen its heyday, and it was checked as a potent political force. Oda Nobunaga dealt the blow, and his two military successors continued the policies of eliminating the divisive forces in the land. Because of their campaigns, Japan once again achieved political reunification by the turn of the seventeenth century.

CHRONOLOGY

1275–1351	Landscape architect Muso Soseki
1283–1350	Poet Yoshida Kenko
1333–1384	No actor Kanami
1336–1392	Northern and southern courts
1338–1573	Ashikaga shogunate
1363–1443	No actor Zeami
1368–1644	Ming dynasty in China
1392–1573	Muromachi subperiod of Ashikaga
1397	Shogun Yoshimitsu builds Golden Pavilion
1397–1471	No actor Noami
ca. 1400	Painter Josetsu flourished
1404–1549	Intermittent missions to China
1414–1465	Painter Shobun flourished
1420–1506	Painter Sesshu
1431–1485	No actor Geami
1434–1530	Painter Kano Masanobu, founder of Kano school
1438–1525	Painter Tosa Mitsonobu
1467–1477	Onin War; initiates *Sengoku Jidai* (century of fighting)
1476–1559	Kano Motonobu
1473	Eighth shogun Yoshimasa builds Silver Pavilion
1525	No actor Soami dies
1534–1582	Oda Nobunaga
1536–1598	Toyotomi Hideyoshi
1539–1590	Painter Hasegawa Tohaku

1542–1616	Tokukawa Ieyasu
1542?	Portuguese arrive
1543–1590	Tosa Eitoku
1549–1551	Francis Xavier in Japan
1571	Nobunaga destroys Enryakuji temple on Mt. Hiei
1573	Shogun's title vacated
1573–1615	Momoyama cultural subperiod
1587	Hideyoshi decree expelling missionaries
1588	Hideyoshi's "sword hunt" decree
1592–1598	Hideyoshi's Korean campaigns
1597	Hideyoshi authorizes first wave of Christian executions
1600	First Dutch ship arrives with English captain, Will Adams
	Pivotal battle of Sekigahara

VIII

TOKUGAWA JAPAN (1603–1868): (1) STABILITY

Tokugawa Ieyasu and his immediate successors were faced with the fundamental choice of resisting or accepting change. Recalling the previous periods of political disunity and of the terrible civil wars, they chose as their foremost policies political stability and national isolation. They resisted change, tried to control and freeze society in a number of ways, and suppressed many of the creative tendencies in the land. In these goals they were successful, for Japan was to enjoy some two and a half centuries of political stability and seclusion. But these ends were achieved only at great costs, for the shoguns retained outmoded forms of feudalism at a time when Western countries in these same centuries were breaking their traditional shackles and were forging ahead in domestic and foreign affairs. Some of the later shogunal advisers endeavored to introduce policies of limited modernization, but their short-term attempts to come to grips with changing times proved abortive.

Society

As Nobunaga and Hideyoshi had ruled from bases near their own sources of power, so did Ieyasu as shogun rule from his new military stronghold at Edo, or present-day Tokyo, on the fertile Kanto plain. Just as the Minamoto and the Hojo had also previously ruled at Kamakura some distance from Kyoto, so the Tokugawa established themselves in familiar territory away from the imperial capital. From their great fortress complex, the fifteen Tokugawa shoguns ruled Japan. Protected by wide moats, great embankments, and stone walls, the shogunal fortress was arranged in a series of concentric structures with an overall diameter of over two miles. The inner circles of the great fort now constitute the imperial palace in the center of Tokyo where the emperor and court, having remained in Kyoto for almost eleven centuries, moved in 1868. Augmenting this impressive physical symbol of shogunal rule was the centralized administration at Edo, composed of a variety of positions and organs to service the shogun. At the top of the political structure was a prime minister, a post sometimes left vacant by the shoguns. A council of state of half a dozen elders advised the Tokugawa on weighty political matters, while a similar number of junior elders managed the affairs of the petty vassals. A large bureaucracy implemented the civil administration, and a corps of *metsuke* or secret police spread out from Edo throughout the countryside to ferret out subversives and malcontents.

Located three hundred miles from Kyoto, the Tokugawa nonetheless kept rigid controls over the emperor and the court, which, as sources of potential trouble, were isolated from the daimyo. All previous shoguns had accepted the concept of the divinity of the emperor who was the sole source of political authority, and the Tokugawa continued this tradition. In theory shogunal powers derived from the emperor, and Edo rulers effected measures through the Kyoto imperial channels. But they stationed representatives at the capital to keep a watchful eye on royal affairs. All visitors, prior to making appointments at the court and with the emperor had to clear with these deputies. Although the source of theoretical political power, the emperors in reality continued to be weak. The practice of abdication continued, and of the fifteen emperors during the Tokugawa shogunate, ten left office before death.

The Tokugawa also imposed controls over the daimyo or feudal lords, who were grouped into three categories. First were the major and minor cadet or branch families of the shogunal line itself. Outside of Edo, the major branches were centered in three strategic areas in central Honshu: at Mito, east of Edo; at Nagoya, near the geographical center of the Tokugawa lands; and at Wakayama, south of Osaka in the west. Then there were the so-called *fudai* or "inside" lords, who had been allies of, or were friendly to, Ieyasu prior to the fateful battle of Sekigahara. They were given some liberties and a degree of autonomy in local affairs. Finally, there were the *tozama* or the "outside" lords, who had been enemies of the Tokugawa prior to Sekigahara, and who always remained a potential source of trouble. Located mainly in western areas, they resented their subordinate position and much later in the 1860's some of them proved instrumental in the downfall of the shogun.

Through the principle of *sankin kotai*, or "alternate attendance," all daimyo were required to spend some time at Edo. Most spent every other year there, and they left their families behind as hostages in Edo when they returned to their fiefs or *han*. Others spent only part of a year in residence. Reminiscent of a similar policy of Louis XIV in France, this double residence proved costly to the lords, usually claiming about a quarter of their annual income. Rank and status improved obligations, and, as a more extreme example, one rich lord maintained, besides his home quarters in northwest Honshu, four costly residences at Edo staffed by ten thousand retainers. The trains of these lords and their followers to and from the shogunal capital proved an economic boon to the country. Roads were extended and improved. Towns sprang up with merchants, hostelries, and service professions benefitting directly from these endless processions. Edo itself reached a population of over a million before the end of the era.

All daimyo were also ranked according to the assessed value of their rice land production, the major economic factor in Japanese life. To attain rank as daimyo, the landlord had to record an annual minimal assessed yield of 10,000 *koku* (about 50,000 bushels) of rice. In the early seventeenth century, Japan raised an estimated annual production of some 24.5 million koku from daimyo fiefs of ten thousand koku or more. Of this total, the Tokugawa possessed over a third, or 8.5 million koku. They controlled as fiefs most of the fertile rice lands of central Honshu (as well as that island's most important cities of Nagoya, Kyoto, and Osaka, in addition to Edo). Some 150 fudai lords possessed about 6 million koku. The remaining 120 tozama lords, plus those with holdings in miscellaneous categories, reaped 10 million koku. The most extensive daimyo holdings, which were tozama, exceeded one million koku, although the average lord had 100,000 koku. The size of the lands and the number of daimiates varied in the course of the Tokugawa period as families became extinct or as fiefs were amalgamated or divided by the shoguns. Because of this economic factor that was based on assessed rice land yields, stringent social and military hierarchical arrangements, rights, and privileges arose.

Not only were the lords ranked, but all society was divided into occupational groups, who were intended to remain hereditary. Following both Hideyoshi from whom the Tokugawa borrowed so much and from hierarchical Confucian doctrines that once again became important during this period, the Tokugawa froze Japan's population into four classes. The highest class numbering some 10 per cent of the population were military administrators drawn from the daimyo and their samurai, the latter now a generic term loosely applied to the military class as a whole. As members of the hereditary aristocracy, the samurai were permitted two swords, a long one for warfare and a short one for harakiri. Second in rank were the peasants, the primary producers, probably constituting about 85 per cent of the populace. Rated high in theory but in reality treated with disdain, the peasant in the Tokugawa structure, as in earlier Japanese times and in traditional Chinese society, lived poorly. Attention was paid to agriculture but not to the agriculturist, who bore the brunt of taxes and agrarian rents. The third and fourth social ranks constituted the artisans and the merchants respectively, who, as secondary or tertiary producers, according to Confucian thought, bordered on economic parasitism. Despite their real intellectual and cultural status, merchants were placed last because theoretically they were an unproductive class. There was to be no change in class for any individual, and distinctive dress, habits, and symbols were prescribed for each class.

A multitude of codes governed Tokugawa life. In Japanese history each political era or shogunal dynasty has had its own codes, and in this respect the Tokugawa were no exception. Ieyasu started the codification process, and his successors continued it. There were several basic types of decrees. One group of laws governed royal affairs. Consisting mainly of moral maxims, they enjoined the court to study diligently, to observe proper protocol, to follow regulations on dress and etiquette, and to behave discreetly. Other laws were directed at the feudal nobility. Also embracing moral and educational tenets, these stipulated that the daimyo and their military followers, in the absence of any campaigns to fight, were to redirect their efforts to intellectual pursuits, to the study of literature, and to the practice of frugality. Public laws, posted on notice boards to be read to the illiterate populace, were also predicated on ethical bases, which were important foundations for Japanese legal and administrative life. Finally, overall and comprehensive codes, such as the Hundred Regulations of 1742, applied to all. These covered both criminal and civil subjects, procedures to follow in filing suit, and sentences to be imposed. Decapitation was decreed for adultery, banishment to peripheral areas such as Hokkaido was imposed, and confession by torture through four progressively more horrible stages was permitted. The continued rain of edicts sought to stabilize the populace. Augmenting social measures were others that closed Japan to foreign influences.

Isolation

Westerners, initially welcomed by Hideyoshi and Ieyasu, were subjected to increasingly restrictive measures in the early decades of the seventeenth century. By the inception of the Tokugawa shogunate a Dutch factory, as noted above, had been constructed at Hirado. In 1641, the Dutch were forced to move to Deshima, a small artificial island in Nagasaki harbor. The English came last to Japan and left the earliest. They maintained an unsuccessful factory at Hirado from 1612 until 1623, but abandoned it to concentrate their commercial efforts in India and southeast Asia. The French had no trading interests in Japan.

Ieyasu initially reversed the stern policy of his predecessor *vis-à-vis* Christianity, and he befriended even the Spanish missionaries in order to maintain trade ties. But the nonproselytizing Protestant Dutch and English traders persuaded the shogun that it was not necessary to tolerate Christianity in order to keep commercial contacts. About 1613, pursuing his policy of political stability, Ieyasu reverted to Hideyoshi's policy of persecuting Christians. In 1617 his successor executed European and native Christians. In the next few years the persecutions mounted in earnest, and all missionaries were killed or were forced to flee Japan. Thousands of Japanese Christians were faced with martyrdom unless they renounced their faith. A common practice of the time to ferret out Christians was to order those suspected of the faith to tread upon a cross or some other sacred symbol or icon, and to execute those who refused.

The persecution of Christians came to a dramatic climax in 1637–1638, when the peasantry of Shimabara near Nagasaki, in a daimiate early associated with Christianity, in desperation rebelled against economic, agrarian, and religious oppression. With leadership provided by some dissatisfied *ronin* (masterless samurai), 30,000 peasants in an old fortress held out for almost three months against the assault of 100,000 shogunal troops supported by Dutch naval power. The Christian rebels eventually were exterminated. After this catastrophe Christianity, which had embraced an estimated half a million converts, ceased to exist as an organized, formal religion in Japan. The intertwined political, economic, and religious character of the uprising alarmed the bakufu, and it gave impetus to the exclusion policy.

Tied to the proscription of Christianity was the cessation of most foreign trade contacts. In the Tokugawa zeal for maintaining the status quo, the doors were closed to most commercial contacts, and, at this time foreigners were in no position to retaliate. Although the English left Japan voluntarily, the Spanish were expelled in 1624, and the Portuguese were ejected in 1638 because of suspected complicity in the Shimabara rebellion. When a Portuguese mission returned a few years later in an effort to reopen trade links, its envoys were summarily executed. Only the Dutch trading post at Deshima, established in 1641, was permitted to operate, but the merchants of the Dutch East India Company were kept in virtual year-round imprisonment. Under close supervision Chinese merchants were also permitted to visit and to trade at the port. Some foreign contacts were additionally maintained with China by individual daimyo controlling Tsushima Islands in the Korean straits and the Ryukyus to the south. The Tokugawa shoguns did not cut off all contact with foreign countries, but this policy of limited, controlled trade contributed to the later downfall of the Tokugawa, since modern foreign ideas continued to seep into Japan through Deshima.

As aliens were not allowed to enter the country, so in 1637 the Japanese were forbidden to leave the country. Those abroad were not permitted to return since the Tokugawa feared that they might return with subversive ideas. Another decree prohibited the construction of large ships that might be used in overseas trade. As a result, the indigenous merchant marine was restricted to small vessels engaged in limited coastal commerce among the home islands. The overseas expansion of Japanese trade and commerce came to an abrupt end. Many Japanese abroad were permanently cast adrift from their homeland, to be absorbed by the native populations of the cities of southeast Asia. The dynamic quality of Japanese international relations noticeable in Ashikaga times was thwarted, and the country closed at a time when Europeans were beginning to expand. Had the process of Japanese overseas expansion been permitted to continue, in the absence of similar drives in contemporaneous Chinese, southeast Asian, or Indian empires, it is intriguing to speculate just where and how the Japanese would have encountered and reacted to Western forces of expansion in Asia.

The Occident left little immediate and appreciable impact during Japan's "Christian century." Christian theological ideas were difficult to understand, and the social doctrine of individuality conflicted with vassal-lord relationships. There were political reasons for leaders to fear the faith, for the shogunate could reasonably envision a possible alliance among the daimyo converted to Christianity, who then would also enjoy special relations with Western powers. Some religious opposition to Christianity existed in the central government, but it was based mainly on political grounds and was not basically different than Nobunaga's bloody suppression of Buddhist orders. Not viewing their policies for the eradication of Christianity as peculiar or unique, the leaders of a reunified Japan treated the alien faith as a domestic issue. But in spite of the suppression of their religion, Westerners bequeathed some secular legacies to Japan. Firearms began to play an important part in Japanese military campaigns. Castle construction on a grand scale with massive stone walls and moats received impetus. The Portuguese contributed a few words to the Japanese vocabulary. Some new plants, as tobacco and potatoes, were introduced. The more fundamental Western secular effects were not immediately discernible, for modern political and economic ideas were to enter Japan in later years through the Dutch base at Deshima.

Effects of Isolation

In its aim of securing national political stability, the isolationist policy of the Tokugawa proved successful. For two centuries or more, no major revolution, strife, serious disturbances, or grave incidents threatened their rule. Japan slumbered fitfully on in its ocean-protected, semi-isolated cocoon. The peace of the land was broken only by occasional, small-scale, and sporadic eruptions of man and of nature, as fires in Edo, earthquakes, rice riots by impoverished country or city dwellers, and in 1707 the last eruption of Fuji. Nothing occurred on a national scale to threaten the existing Tokugawa structure.

A good example of the carefully imposed political stability of the time is reflected in the true story of the forty-seven ronin which illustrated the potential stresses that could arise between samurai obligations to the ruling shogun and the former lord. In 1700 a lesser feudal lord, insulted by a higher lord within the shogun's palace, drew his sword and wounded his antagonist. Since the act of drawing a sword within the palace was an offense that carried a death sentence, the Edo authorities ordered the lesser lord to commit harakiri and appropriated his domains. His feudal retainers lost their samurai status and became dispossessed men. Forty-seven of these ronin vowed to avenge themselves upon the daimyo who had caused their master's disgrace. To quiet the suspicions of the police, who were anticipating such an act of revenge, they bided their time. Their leader took up a life of debauchery to cast off suspicion. Finally, one winter's night, two years later, they reassembled at Edo and took vengeance by beheading their lord's old enemy and several of his samurai. By taking justice into their own hands, they had defied shogunal authority, but they became heroes through their self-sacrificial act of loyalty to their lord. Caught in cross currents, the bakufu debated the case for over a year, when finally it permitted the ronin to commit harakiri. Today the simple graves of the forty-seven ronin lie side by side in a Tokyo temple compound that has become a national shrine.

The centuries of stability, seclusion, and conformity left their mark on the Japanese. The adventurous, spirited people of earlier centuries were transformed into a regimented nation by the nineteenth. On all issues they looked to their leaders for guidance, and without dissent they obeyed authority. Patterns of social intercourse were firmly set. Society became structured and rigid, but the crowded Japanese managed to live together on their small islands in peace and with few outward signs of friction. Yet the feudal outlook and structure were preserved long after they had become outdated. On the other hand, in part because of the attitudes formed in the Tokugawa period, Japan accepted Western norms more easily than any country in Asia. After being opened by the Western powers, it forged ahead of its Asian neighbors. Paradoxically, the Tokugawa legacy proved to be both a boon and a bane.

CHRONOLOGY

1609–1641	Dutch at Hirado
1612–1623	English at Hirado
1613	Ieyasu commences persecutions of Christians
1617	Ieyasu's successor continues persecutions of Christians
1624	Spanish expelled
1637–1638	Shimabara Christian rebellion
1637	Japanese forbidden to leave the country
1638	Portuguese expelled
1641	Dutch move to Deshima
1700–1702	Incident of the forty-seven ronin
1707	Mt. Fuji's last eruption
1742	Hundred Regulations

IX

TOKUGAWA JAPAN: (2) CHANGE

Try as they did, the Tokugawa shoguns could not completely freeze social and economic patterns over a period of two and a half centuries. Signs of change and of growth were too pronounced to be ignored. Yet Japan, unlike European countries which sloughed off medieval concepts, grafted new elements onto the old traditions. She advanced to another and unique stage in her form of feudalism, that of modernization based on feudal elements. Surface stability was maintained, but economic, social, and intellectual currents were stirring underneath. By the time the West arrived to help open Japan's doors in the mid-nineteenth century, the Japanese themselves were more than ready for change.

Social and Economic Trends

One aspect of change was the growth of cities and towns. This trend towards urbanization continued during the Tokugawa regime which itself contributed to the phenomenon. Warriors followed their lords to castles, samurai concentrated in or near the chief cities in each of the *han,* and the processions to and from Edo of the daimyo trains favored trade. By the mid-eighteenth century, Kyoto and Osaka each had half a million inhabitants, and Edo itself a million. About twenty other cities had populations ranging from 50,000 to 100,000.

In the first half of the period, Japan's population doubled from 15 million to 30 million, when, paradoxically, it levelled out despite the continuance of peace and prosperity.

The growth of urban life was accompanied by an increase in numbers and in influence of the merchant class. The merchants might have been relegated to a low rank in society, but they possessed the money and thereby great economic power. Their capital opened up new areas to cultivation; their loans to the military, who needed money rather than grain to pay for their many expenses in both town and country, made them creditors of daimyo and samurai. While in theory the military-administrative group was the highest social class, distinctions were breaking down because of contact and marriages with other classes. Sons of merchants were adopted by military families, and sometimes the reverse was true. The cities were hubs of mercantile activity. In them banking facilities flourished, and grain markets, particularly those in Osaka and in Edo, dealt in volume transactions and speculated in futures. Within the more efficient and larger daimyo and shogunal holdings, trade barriers were eliminated, and commerce flowed more freely along domestic routes than in earlier eras. The shogun's territory was the most suitable for commercial activity, since it contained the largest cities with the greatest wealth, offered the most protection, and had proportionately fewer military men and contingents to support than had the daimyo on their less extensive holdings.

In towns, guilds broke down into smaller and more individually run units, though merchant associations continued to fix credit rates, stabilize prices, and control distribution patterns of particular products. Family wholesale and retail commercial firms grew in importance. One of the largest private enterprises in the world today, the Mitsui, began in the early Tokugawa years. In 1620 the family was operating a sake, or rice wine, brewery in the strategic area near the national Ise shrine. By judicious investment and expansion, it soon branched out to deal in rice transactions, pawnshop operations, and haberdashery outlets. In 1691 the family became the banker for both court and shogun and through succeeding years continued to flourish and grow.

While merchants luxuriated, the military became impoverished. Participation in the good but expensive life of the cities caused the daimyo and the samurai to fall into debt. The daimyo received their chief income from land taxes, which constituted a certain percentage of the produce of the peasant, though in the latter years of the Tokugawa up to 20 per cent of the tax was paid in money. From these proceeds of rice or its equivalent, the daimyo in turn supported through fixed stipends the samurai, whose living costs were rising. Sometimes the lords defaulted or retrenched on their payments to their retainers, who in turn tried to squeeze more out of the farmers. Peasants were forced to occasional rebellion or flight, and strains developed in the economic arrangements of the military pyramid.

The agrarian economy was also in a state of flux. As long as the villages paid their taxes, they maintained their semi-autonomy. But villagers remained overtaxed, for the feudal mentality of the Tokugawa continued to overemphasize agrarian taxation and neglected taxation of urban sectors. Yet through reclamation and irrigation projects, the acreage of arable land increased. New plant types augmented diets, and commercial fertilizers added to yields. In addition to subsistence farming of the necessary grain produce, commercial or cash crops were cultivated such as cotton, sesame, sugar cane, and tobacco. Village industries expanded with such enterprises as silk production, textile weaving, cotton spinning, and sake brewing. Entrepreneurial skills developed in the country, and by the end of the Tokugawa era in every village there was at least one wealthy farming family that had more land than the others as well as profitable auxiliary handicraft industries. But other villagers became poorer, went into debt, or became dispossessed. They drifted to the cities, where they formed the base for an unskilled or semi-skilled urban labor force. Through shifting patterns, encouraged by the growth of tenancy, the rise of a wage-laboring class, and a variety of crops that required special, intensified skills, large extended families and large land holdings tended to break down over the centuries into smaller agrarian groupings.

The seventeenth century registered the greatest argicultural, population, and urban growth in any period of Japanese history to that time. This growth and expansion reached its peak in the Genroku period (1688–1704), named after the year period of the reigning emperor. In the latter decades of the era, however, commercial growth slackened somewhat. This was due in part to governmental retrenchment policies that insisted on the primacy of an agrarian base for revenues rather than on more comprehensive national financing. Monopolistic practices by merchant associations restricted fuller trade, and the purchasing power of the shoguns and the daimyo, who constituted the major buyers and consumers of the time, did not develop appreciably. Yet in the eighteenth century there was increased agricultural production and commercialization. Overall continued economic growth was possible despite restrictions, in part, because the lower classes, excluded from political activity, could pursue economic ends fairly single-mindedly.

In the process of readjustment to realities, by the end of the Tokugawa all major classes had become dissatisfied with their status. The peasants remained overtaxed, and while they produced most of the national wealth, they shared only minimally in its increase. Despite their economic importance, the city merchants and artisans lacked commensurate political and social standing. The military-administrators had prestige but also increasing debts. These changes in Japanese society had repercussions in the development of Japanese life.

Culture

Whereas the court in aristocratic Japan and the Zen monks in Ashikaga times had dominated the cultural life of their respective periods, the *chonin* or townsmen in the great cities of Edo, Osaka, and Kyoto dominated the new Tokugawa culture. The cities became centers of art and culture. Despite the sumptuary laws of the shoguns regulating the spending of money, city folk enjoyed a degree of social freedom and of flamboyant fashions. Amusement quarters flourished, and the *geisha* or professional female entertainer provided a new kind of social relationship for Japanese men. Since polite mixed society did not exist, the Japanese male turned to these avenues of entertainment and to the houses of prostitution for romance and for social intercourse, which were almost nonexistent in prearranged marriages and formalized family life. The rise in these forms of popular entertainment indicated the decline in the status of woman in Japan from its relative eminence in the classical and early medieval periods.

Reflecting more prosperous and ostentatious times, Tokugawa architecture also became more complex and more gaudy than it had been in earlier periods. Gone was Zen simplicity and the deep religious spirit in art. The magnificent palaces and public buildings, such as the Nikko shrines, which were the mausoleums for Ieyasu and his grandson, were elaborately constructed. More simple and traditional construction, resembling the earlier Fujiwara style, is the Katsura Detached Palace, an imperial villa near Kyoto. On the campus of the International Christian University at Mitaka, a suburb of Tokyo, is the Kusa-no-ya (Grass House), a prototype of a Tokugawa tea house.

Sculpture was second rate and lacked the spiritual impulse of Buddhism. Only minor results were recorded in the plastic arts that produced such miniature products as the *netsuke*, or the small ivory carvings used in the fastenings of tobacco pouches and pillboxes.

Ceramic art reached a new height at Arita, an area in Kyushu with its port of Imari. Other prominent ceramic names included those of Kakeimon, Nabeshima, and Kutani. Lacquer production continued as well as textile. Folk art (*mingei*) took its place alongside the aristocratic.

In the graphic and pictorial arts, gorgeous decorative screens and panels depicted brightly colored scenes. The Kano school persisted with Eitoku's grandson Kano Tanyu (1602–1674) and his brother Naonobu (1607–1650). Other contemporary artists included Honami Koetsu (1558–1637), Tawaraya Sotatsu (1576–1643), Ogata Korin (1658–1716), and Maruyama Okyo (1733–1795). The adherents of the Nanga (Southern) school, which wanted to return to the techniques of the Chinese style, flourished in the Kyoto area. Their ranks included amateur painters who pursued the art for pleasure rather than for money.

Ukiyo-e, pictures recording fleeting impressions of the contemporary secular life—the "floating world," became prominent. Ukiyo-e became particularly associated with woodblock prints, perhaps the type of Japanese art best known to the West. At first the woodblock prints had been illustrations in printed works, but soon they evolved into independent works of art. The prints were considered quite vulgar in Tokugawa times, and they did not achieve distinction until later decades. Quite complex in process, the production of a woodblock print involved not only the artist, but a publisher to sponsor the print, an anonymous but expert woodcutter to cut the scenes (each color or shading required a separate cutting), and finally a printer who produced the final result by careful superimposition of the various cuts onto the same print.

One of the earliest artists (they are usually known by their given names) in the medium is Hishikawa Moronobu (1618–1694). He was followed by Suzuki Harunobu (1725–1770), Torii Kiyonaga (1752–1815), and Kitagawa Utamaro (1753–1806), who portrayed sophisticated, sensuous ladies. Toshusai Sharaku (active for only a brief span of some ten months in 1794 and 1795), who may have been a No actor, sketched fierce representations, bordering almost on caricature, of Kabuki types. The most familiar of the artists to the Westerner, however, were Katsushika Hokusai (1760–1849), who produced a series of thirty-six views of Fuji, and Ando Hiroshige (1797–1858), whose work includes two sets of the fifty-three stations on the Tokaido road.

In literature, there were new developments in the Japanese drama. Puppet drama emerged. It was variously called *joruri* after its texts, *bunraku* after the puppets, and *gidayu* after the personal name of one of the earliest playwrights to compose in this medium. These puppet tales were recited to the accompaniment of the three-stringed *samisen*, a plucked instrument like the banjo. Puppet drama developed at Osaka, where today the Bunrakuza is the outstanding theater. The chief name in the development of puppetry was Chikamatsu Monzaemon (1653–1724). His librettos drew their inspiration basically from two sources, historical drama and contemporaneous domestic themes. One of his most popular plays was *The Battles of Koxinga*, which dealt with the daring exploits of a pirate of Japanese-Chinese descent who ravaged the Chinese coast during the Ming era. The play's initial Osaka run lasted seventeen consecutive months. At first the puppets were small in dimension, but in time they were enlarged to two-thirds the actual size of human beings and three men on stage were required to manipulate each figure.

A second dramatic form to emerge at this time was Kabuki. Its development dated from the early seventeenth century in Kyoto, where a renegade Shinto priestess led a troupe of dancers and actors in salacious dances. Because of the low moral tone of Kabuki, the authorities soon banned women from the stage, and the drama was limited to performances by men actors, as early Shakespearean drama had been. The Kabuki texts borrowed from a variety of sources such as puppet themes and librettos, the No drama, and secular tales. Like No, the Kabuki often used an onstage chorus to chant the narrative portions to instrumental accompaniment. Stage settings were quite realistic and elaborate; often visually striking tableaux were struck. A revolving stage added to the sense of drama, and a runway from the stage into the pit gave the audience a sense of participation in the play. Through hereditary lines of great actors, the Kabuki tradition was kept alive, and the Kabukiza theater in Tokyo is the greatest contemporary exponent of the art.

Poetry experienced the further refinement of the earlier five-line, thirty-one syllable tanka through the renga or chain poem to the *haiku*, which reduced the poems even further to three lines of seventeen syllables arrayed in a 5-7-5 syllabic pattern. This concise poetic form pleased bourgeois society, who amused itself by composing in the medium. Haiku appeal lay in its stress on sharp wit through brevity and on mental dexterity. Probably the greatest composer of haiku, who also composed chain poems, was Batsuo Basho (1644–1694), a former samurai and haiku master at Edo.

Finally, the growth of printing stimulated the development of literature. Literacy was necessary for city life and commerce, and new stimuli for printing came from the Korean printers brought back by Hideyoshi's armies and from the Jesuits who had operated a press to print Christian tracts. Movable type was known to the Japanese, but it was not used. Instead, printers employed the wood-block medium, which permitted the inclusion of illustrative material. Many very popular booklets were printed in kana. Among these booklets were collections of moral maxims, short tracts on miscellaneous topics, historical writings, guidebooks, and sundry anecdotes.

The novel as a literary form was influenced by the new urban society. One of the more prominent novelists of early Tokugawa times was Ihara Saikaku (1642–1693), an Osaka townsman, who presented amusing and colorful portrayals of city types. His first important work was *An Amorous Man*, which sold so well that he followed it with sequels such as *An Amorous Woman* and *Five Amorous Women*. Many novels were pornographic but were popular in spite of Tokugawa censorship. Other stories reflected Japanese traditions. One dominant theme in Tokugawa novels was the clash in an individual between *giri*, or duty, and *ninjo*, or passion. A typical theme might be the futile love of a rich young man for a geisha, an attachment that ran contrary to his family duty and social obligations. Neither love nor duty won out, and the solution in the impasse was for the two parties to commit double suicide, which was viewed as a romantic, reasonable, and respectable escape from an unresolvable situation in Japan at that time.

Intellectual Trends

Cultural changes in Tokugawa Japan were accompanied by intellectual changes. The latter were derived from two contributing streams. Foreign intellectual influences advocating modernization seeped into Japan chiefly through the Dutch at Deshima, while internal intellectual trends promoted the restoration of power to the emperor. In the early years of the exclusion policy, the European powers were in no position to protest its disadvantages to them. But changes that were occurring in Europe during the Tokugawa regime placed Europe and the United States in a position to challenge Japan. Fundamental changes in the West included increases in wealth and in population in disproportionate relation to Japan; improved military and naval technology which through the clipper ships and steamships made easier Western contact with the Far

East; and, particularly, the rise of Russia and America on the world scene. In the late eighteenth and early nineteenth centuries, Japan received warning signals of the expansion of Western interests in Asia and their own home islands. The Japanese noted more foreign shipping along their coasts, and they came into contact with more missions trying to enter the country. They were also cognizant of British territorial encroachments in India and of the Western exaction of special rights from a weak China.

The Dutch were the main source of foreign ideas. Yearly the manager of the company went to Edo to make his report, while the shoguns kept continual check on the Dutch through local daimyo on Kyushu. Certain lords assigned samurai to learn Dutch, and these men in time became valuable interpreters, although sometimes they fell under suspicion by their countrymen because of association with Westerners. In 1720 Edo, safe in its isolation, removed the long-standing bans on the study of Western subjects and on the importation of European books, with the exception of those relating to Christianity. A small but intellectually vigorous group of students of the European sciences arose. Some social sciences, technology, and medicine were studied, but pursuit of philosophy or the humanities was frowned upon. A text on anatomy was translated into Japanese, and a Dutch-Japanese dictionary was compiled.

By the middle of the nineteenth century, Japanese scholars were well-versed in some Western sciences such as gunnery, smelting, shipbuilding, cartography, and medicine. They built model steam engines, and they erected brick furnaces. Although few in number, they became a valuable nucleus of scholars who would seize the initiative in conducting scientific work on a much grander scale later when opportunity was available. Cognizant of the superiority of Western technology, some Japanese concluded that modernization was necessary. They helped to lay the groundwork for change before the Westerners in strength arrived in Japan.

Among the few thoughtful Japanese who pondered on the desirability of importing Western ideas to strengthen the country were some samurai. In their ranks was Honda Toshiaki (1744–1821), a gifted man, who was a samurai from a tozama fief in a west Honshu province somewhat removed from Edo influence. He learned the Dutch language, studied mathematics and astronomy, and opened a school. He wrote on a variety of subjects, including shipping, foreign affairs, and the conservation of natural resources. In 1798 he composed a volume entitled *A Secret Plan of Government* in which he proposed state control of industry, commerce, shipping, and colonization. He was among the first Japanese to see that the closed economy of Japan, with its modest resources, was incapable of supporting an expanding higher standard of living in a capitalist society without the benefit of growing trade. In defiance of official Tokugawa edicts, he argued for a merchant marine capable of overseas traffic, and he advocated establishment of commercial relations with Russia. To enhance national power, he argued that Japan needed gunpowder, metals, ships, and colonies. He was even disposed to accept the validity of Christianity.

Another representative of the military class who thought along similar lines was Sato Nobuhiro (1769–1850), a native of northern Japan. He had definite views on the necessary relation of colonies to a strong homeland. He declared that the country's leaders could not sit idly by but that they should seize lands around the Japanese perimeter, including Korea, Manchuria, and eastern Siberia. Such conquests, he argued, would entail reorganization of the country. To this end he advocated a unified national army command, a unified national government, the end of feudalism, and a strong economic base. In his *Maritime History of Nations,* he argued that the greatness of nations lay in commerce and the navy. An imaginative man, ahead of his time, he foretold Japan's future remarkably, but his works were suppressed by the Tokugawa authorities, who still hewed to the isolationist policy.

Complementing this small but rising group of Japanese who wished to transform Japan into a strong, modern power in world affairs were Japanese intellectuals who were dissatisfied with the bases of existing governmental structures. They criticized the Tokugawa shoguns guardedly, for the secret police were omnipresent. They aimed their barbs indirectly through a comparison of Japan with strong European powers. These thinkers did not coalesce into any political movement because of government repression and censorship. Criticism remained in a theorizing vein. Nevertheless, one result of this intellectual activity was the denial of the legitimacy of Tokugawa rule and support for the emperor to play the central role in national life. Two areas of speculation contributed to this end: Confucianism and Japanese historical studies.

As Buddhism went into a precipitous decline during the era, the Tokugawa advocated Confucianism as the official doctrine in the hope that it would contribute to stability by its emphasis on proper relationships between rulers and subjects, its sense of loyalty to the duly constituted political authorities, and its stress on harmony. The shoguns sponsored a school of Confucianism at Edo, and samurai were enjoined to participate in its studies. Fujiwara Seika (1561–1619) left the Buddhist fold and initiated the school. His disciple, Hayashi Razan (1583–1657) was adviser to Ieyasu. His descendants founded at Edo the official Confucian university and in 1670 finalized a history based on Chinese forms, *The Comprehensive Mirror of Our Country*. Other histories were compiled by schools and individuals, such as Arai Hakuseki (1657–1725), a shogunal official.

The official philosophy, borrowed from China, was known as neo-Confucianism because of metaphysical accretions from Buddhist and Taoist thought. As crystallized in the Sung dynasty by the Chinese philosopher Chu Hsi (1130–1200), the school recognized a moral law or order in the universe, to which man was to adapt himself. Known in Japan as Shushi, the school pleased the Tokugawa since the core of the thought emphasized loyalty. It set great store on the importance of learning, but it insisted on orthodoxy. Other variants of neo-Confucianism arose both in Japan and China, including that known in Japan as O-Yomei, derived from the Chinese philosopher, Wang Yang-ming (1472–1529), of the Ming dynasty. Wang's teaching was opposed to that of Chu Hsi because it held that self-knowledge was the highest type of learning and it emphasized intuition and introspection as means to acquiring knowledge. Since this approach could encourage independence of thought and of action, the Tokugawa shoguns discouraged it.

The Tokugawa, like earlier Japanese advocates of Confucianism, also omitted or ignored other fundamental aspects of the Chinese ethical system, such as the concepts of the mandate of heaven and of the right to revolt. According to both Confucian and neo-Confucian theory as it developed in traditional Chinese thought, the emperor of China ruled by virtue. When the emperor was virtuous good times followed; if his evil acts brought misfortune, as in an accumulation of disasters, he could be overthrown. Since there were no shoguns in China, blame fell directly on the monarch and not on any usurping authority. But within the existent structure of Japanese politics, critics leveled their charges against the actual rulers of Japan, who were the shoguns, not the emperors. Arguing abstractly rather than pointedly, Japanese students of Confucianism inferred that within the Japanese system the shoguns had been military usurpers who ruled not by virtue but by arms and conquest. The implication was that the emperor was the legitimate ruler and should rule in fact.

The necessity of restoring power to the emperor was a theme simultanaeously advanced by those Japanese who were reinterpreting their national history. Again, samurai and ronin, lacking formal military functions, took the lead in domestic historical studies. Their ranks were swelled by certain Shinto scholars, including Motoori Norinaga (1730–1801), who resurrected the early *Kojiki* and *Nihon Shoki* as bases for imperial power. In their own national history, they sought the origins of dissatisfaction with the contemporaneous regime. They recreated the Sun Goddess myth that emphasized the divinity and the central role of the imperial family. They idealized the semi-historical and historical periods through the tenth century. They glorified the preshogunal Heian period, which they interpreted as the high point in Japanese art, culture, and politics. During those centuries they saw a peaceful, prosperous country ruled by just monarchs. Subsequent eras, they continued, were degenerate, since imperial power had been usurped by the military, who had neither the virtue nor the legitimacy to rule.

Again, to avoid direct criticism, the historians did not include the Tokugawa period in their studies but rather provided the inference that their works were tracts for the times. Because of strong government controls, no revolutionary movement, no party organization, and no national leadership emerged to correlate and coordinate the ideology that was subversive to the bakufu. Nevertheless, these concepts culminated in the downfall of the shogunate and the restoration in 1868 of the emperor to a central position in Japanese politics and life.

CHRONOLOGY

1558–1637	Artist Honami Koetsu
1561–1619	Scholar Fujiwara Seika
1576–1643	Artist Tawaraya Sotatsu
1583–1657	Scholar Hayashi Razan
1602–1674	Artist Kano Tanyu
1607–1650	Artist Kano Naonobu
1618–1694	Woodblock artist Hishikawa Moronobu
1642–1693	Novelist Ihara Saikaku
1644–1694	Poet Batsuo Basho
1653–1724	Playwright Chikamatsu Monzaemon
1675–1725	Scholar Arai Hakuseki
1658–1716	Artist Ogata Korin
1688–1704	Genroku period
1720	Ban on most Western studies removed

1725–1770   Woodblock artist Suzuki Harunobu
1730–1801   Scholar Mootori Norinaga
1733–1795   Artist Maruyama Okyo
1744–1821   Honda Toshiaki, advocate of Westernization
1752–1815   Woodblock artist Torii Kiyonaga
1753–1806   Woodblock artist Kitagawa Utamaro
1760–1849   Woodblock artist Katsushika Hokusai
1769–1850   Sato Nohuhiro, advocate of Westernization
1794–1795   Woodblock artist Toshusai Sharaku flourishes
1797–1858   Woodblock artist Ando Hiroshige
1830–1844   Tempo era

X

TOKUGAWA JAPAN:
(3) WESTERN INTRUSION

By the mid-nineteenth century, Japan faced two crises. In Japan itself there was discontent among all major classes in Japanese society and a growing ideology that saw a need for Japan's modernization and for strong imperial power. The second crisis resulted from the gradual but forceful expansion of the West backed by great economic and military strength. The interacting crises were brought to a head by the United States in the guise of Commodore Matthew C. Perry. Yet he only represented the culmination of Western efforts to open Japan. The Russians, expanding eastward into Siberia through the centuries, had early probed Sakhalin Island and the Kuriles. One Russian expedition landed in a Japanese jail. They halted further activity between 1813 and 1852, when the czar dispatched an admiral on a mission to Japan to seek its friendship against the British and the Americans. This Russian mission had arrived in Nagasaki as Perry steamed into Tokyo Bay in mid-1853. During the first half of the nineteenth century, the British embarked on fitful trips to or near Japan, but they made no effort to open the country.

End of Isolation

A decade after the British had taken the initiative in opening China with the first Western treaty, the United States concluded the first treaty between Japan and a Western power. There were several reasons for strong American interest in Japan. By the early 1850's the United States had expanded its borders to the Pacific. California had been admitted to the Union, and the northwest coast was being opened. Now a Pacific power, the United States had the west coast as a base for further expansion into the great ocean, and the great circle route via the Alaska coast was the shortest way to Asia. Moreover, Japan could be reached before China, and even those Americans who dreamt of a great China trade and of vast Chinese markets saw the necessity of Japan as a way station.

By this time, the American whaling trade in the North Pacific had become highly important, and up to two hundred whaling ships plied those seas each year. Some of the ships were wrecked on Japanese coasts, where sailors were summarily executed or imprisoned in accordance with the prevailing laws and policy of seclusion. Japan was thought to be rich in coal deposits, and Americans emphasized the need for coaling stations there to meet the requirement of the new steamships. In addition there was great naval interest in the Pacific, an interest reflected in the naval rank of some of the official American personnel and missions to Japan and to other Pacific countries. Finally, a policy of *realpolitik* dictated the necessity of freezing European powers out of Japan by getting there first, and this power position interested not only the navy but some civilian officials in Washington as well.

At least two dozen times before Perry, American ships had come to Japan. In 1791 efforts by two merchant vessels to initiate fur trade failed. Six years later, an American ship under Dutch charter entered Nagasaki. In 1815 Captain David Porter, a hero of the War of 1812, sought to convince President James Madison of the necessity of introducing the Japanese to the modern world. The first American diplomat to Eastern countries, Edmund Roberts, conveyed a letter from President Andrew Jackson to the Japanese emperor, but the envoy died in Macao prior to arrival in Japan. In 1837 an American businessman in Canton organized an embassy to repatriate seven Japanese sailors, who had been stranded abroad, but none were permitted to land. Caleb Cushing, who in 1844 had concluded the first United States treaty with China on the heels of the British, was authorized to deal with Japan, but he had left China prior to the arrival of his instructions. In 1846 two United States navy vessels sailed into Tokyo Bay, but they were repulsed by Japanese authorities when the American Commander refused a showdown. Three years later, another naval official at Nagasaki using opposite tactics, forced the Japanese to surrender fifteen

American sailors who had been in chains for months in Japan. In 1851 the commander of the American squadron in Asian waters was ordered to visit Japan, but he was recalled from his command and Perry took his place.

Perry at the age of sixty was a distinguished naval officer. He was among the most articulate of the navy's policy makers in advocating a strong expansionist stand. Applying the concept of manifest destiny to overseas areas, he was interested in securing naval bases in the Pacific and in establishing a large number of American settlements there. Before departing, Perry read all available books about Japan, which numbered about forty. In them estimates of Japan's area ranged from 9,000 square miles to 266,000 square miles (it was some 140,000 square miles). Population density was said to be from 184 to 4000 per square mile (it was about 210), and the total population was reported at between 15 million and 50 million (it was approximately 30 million). Edo alone was thought to have a population of 10 million.

With four ships, including the first two steamships ever seen in Japan, Perry, bypassing Nagasaki, sailed directly into Tokyo Bay on July 8, 1853. His arrival did not take the Japanese by surprise, for the Dutch had warned the shogun that the Americans were coming. But the appearance of the squadron precipitated more immediate crises in Japan, although Perry was unaware of the domestic problems then prevailing in Japan. He insisted on dealing only with top-ranking officials of the shogunate, and to them he presented President Millard Fillmore's letter requesting peace and friendship, free trade, good treatment of shipwrecked whalers, and provisioning of coal for vessels. Displaying great firmness, Perry promised to return within a year with a larger force to implement the requests and sailed away after a stay of nine days.

The shogunate was thrown into confusion. It was in a particularly vulnerable position, since the shogun was ill (he died before Perry returned), and the shogunal advisers were divided in council. They recognized that if they acceded to the requests, other nations would certainly make demands, as they had in China. On the other hand, if they did not grant the requests, the Americans might resort to the use of force to gain compliance. Force was implied in Perry's tactics and was overtly used by Westerners in obtaining their first Chinese treaties between 1842 and 1844.

After Perry had departed, to help resolve the dilemma the shogunate embarked on several unusual steps. It lifted all restrictions on shipbuilding in order to permit the Tokugawa themselves and the daimyo to construct naval vessels and steamships. It also took the unprecedented step of requesting the opinions of the lords on the appropriate course of action to take with respect to the foreign stipulations. Going further, it consulted with the emperor on the issue. For the first time in six and a half centuries of shogunal rule, the bakufu had requested imperial advice on an important problem of state. Though the shogunate probably had political motives in sharing responsibility for any decision that might be taken, the precedent for consulting other parties had been set. And while the bakufu had expected a uniform reaction, it received mixed replies, although the majority of the lords opted for continued isolation.

The dilemma remained unresolved when Perry returned in February, 1854, earlier than planned, to forestall British and Russian advances. Under the threat of the seven-ship fleet, the Tokugawa had no choice but to conclude a treaty with the Americans. After several weeks of negotiations that involved exchanges of gifts and official receptions, the treaty was signed on March 31, 1854. Sometimes termed the Treaty of Kanagawa, after the small port town south of Tokyo now part of that megalopolis, it contained few provisions. It called for peace between the two countries, for the opening for supplies of the relatively inaccessible ports of Shimoda in central Honshu and Hakodate in Hokkaido, for good treatment of shipwrecked sailors, for limited trade, for consular residence at Shimoda, and for the most-favored-nation clause (which meant that a privilege extended by Japan to one country, or the most-favored one, would be extended to all).

Perry did not worry about details. He wanted to sign a treaty, any treaty, before European ships took advantage of the foothold gained by American ships to secure concessions for themselves. The treaty was rushed to the United States, where the Senate promptly and unanimously ratified it. The Japanese emperor also approved it, and the necessary exchange of ratifications subsequently took place in Japan. What both Perry and the Japanese feared did happen, for the fleets of seventeen nations followed the Americans into Tokyo Bay. Within two years of the Kanagawa treaty, additional treaties had been concluded between the Japanese and the major European powers.

Perry's success was due in part to its timing, to the domestic crises in the country, to Japanese awareness of Chinese diplomatic defeats, and to the commodore's own tactics of firmness, determination, and show of strength. Perry's mission made a great impact on Japan, but was paid little attention at home. The American press and President Franklin Pierce almost ignored it. Congress took issue with the "outrageously extravagant" cost of printing the official report on the mission. New York City presented Perry with a set of silver plate, and Boston merchants honored him with a medal. Perry at the time was better known in Japan than in his homeland, for his significance then was lost to his countrymen, not to be realized until a later day. As "Mr. Dooley" (the humorist Finley Peter Dunne) expressed it, "Whin we rapped on the dure, we didn't go in, they come out."

Western Rights and Japanese Reactions

In accordance with provisions of the Kanagawa treaty, Townsend Harris was sent as first consul general in August, 1856, to reside at Shimoda. Harris, a New York City merchant with some previous experience in Asia, possessed an excellent mind and a fine character, and was an abstemious bachelor. He had fallen on harder days and welcomed the assignment. He arrived in Japan alone, unknown, and unwelcomed. Shimoda was a remote town with a poor harbor. The Japanese, who only grudgingly accepted American treaty terms, hoped to quarantine and isolate the American representative. They almost succeeded in their aims. Harris wrote in his diary that he had not received a letter from home in over ten months. At one time he received no instructions from the Department of State for one and half years. He was forced to live in a cockroach-infested temple, and vendors at the markets sold him their worst food.

But Harris was a patient man. As the Japanese witnessed encroaching European interests in China in the late 1850's, he advanced the timely argument that were the shogun to deal first with the United States, he would receive a more favorable treaty as a model for ensuing arrangements. In 1857 he concluded a convention with the shogunate that permitted the right of residence at the two open ports of Shimoda and Hakodate, the provisioning of supplies at Nagasaki, and extraterritoriality, or extrality for short, in criminal cases (this was the juridical right in foreign countries for aliens to be tried according to their own laws by their own authorities).

Harris then traveled to Edo to conclude a full-scale commercial treaty. He proceeded there with a retinue of 350, performed no obeisance, and was the first Westerner received in audience by the shogun. No gunboats accompanied him. Despite the lack of show of force, a new treaty was signed on July 29, 1858, on an American ship in Tokyo Bay. The terms of the treaty were wide-ranging. They provided for diplomatic representation in the capitals of both powers. They opened to trade four new ports—Nagasaki, Kanagawa, Niigata, and Hyogo (Kobe), they permitted the right of residence at Osaka and at Edo, and they broadened extrality to include civil cases. No opium was permitted into Japan (its importation into China had been the immediate and ostensible cause of the Anglo-Chinese War of 1839–1842, dubbed the Opium War). Religious freedom was granted to foreigners, customs duties were regulated on exports and imports, and the usual most-favored-nation clause was included. On one year's notice, revision was possible after July, 1872. The treaty also provided for American mediation, if requested, between Japan and other powers, for purchase of weapons and ships in the United States, and for hiring American technical assistants. Within three months, the British, French, Russians, and Dutch also concluded treaties.

The bakufu seemed satisfied with the terms, but the emperor did not consent to their ratification at the time. Accepted by European powers as the model, the 1858 Harris treaty, in spite of imperial disfavor, remained the fundamental document in Japanese foreign relations until the turn of the century. It was a great personal and official victory for Harris, for suasion had succeeded as much as the earlier policy of implied force. This time, ratifications were exchanged in 1860 in Washington. A Japanese diplomatic mission of seventy, representing those factions that accepted the treaty, proceeded to the United States where it became the object of great curiosity and the recipient of lavish entertainment. Elevated to ministerial rank, Harris remained in Japan until 1862 despite failing health, to preserve American gains.

The bakufu continued to be squeezed between conflicting pressures, and the differing reactions to the shogunal request for information as to how to handle Perry revealed varying attitudes to this issue among the Japanese. Many remained unreconciled to the presence of the increasing number of foreigners in the land, and they continued to press for an exclusion policy. Despite the consolidation of initial treaties with the West, rejection of the West was advanced by some thinkers. An adherent to this school of thought was Aizawa Seishisai, a Mito samurai, who in 1825 had advanced his creed in the *New Proposals*. His work had been occasioned by the appearance of foreign shipping in Japanese waters and the detention of crewmen from a British whaler in the Mito feudal domains. The opening portion of Aizawa's tract presented the concept of *kokutai*, the essence of Japanese nationalism. Welding together imported and native concepts of Shintoism, Confucianism, and *bushido* (the code of the warrior), the author identified the Sun Goddess with heaven, ascribed to her the moral law and political order among men, and related the Confucian virtues of loyalty and of filial piety to Shinto worship. Kokutai had simultaneous religious, ethical, and political overtones. Emphasizing the uniqueness of Japan, it had little place for the accommodation of foreign ideas. Aizawa argued that alien contacts were useless for Japanese development.

Another school of thought in regard to Westernization advocated instead the opening of Japan gradually and from within through a process of self-strengthening and blending of Western science and Eastern ethics. Akin to ideas earlier advanced by Honda Toshiaki and Sato Nobuhiro, Sakuma Shozan (1811–1864), a samurai from a central Honshu province, submitted an eight-point program to his daimyo as the basis for shogunal policy: fortify strategic coastal points, construct armaments, expand the merchant marine, develop efficient maritime trade, build Western-type warships, introduce a modern school system, establish an open but firm system of rewards and punishments, and inaugurate a merit system in selecting government officials.

Following this tradition was Sakuma's disciple, Yoshida Shoin (1830–1859) from Choshu, who had been adopted into the samurai class. In disobedience to the exclusion edicts, he tried to stow away on one of Perry's ships but was apprehended. He advocated selective borrowing from the West, the abolition of feudalism, the emancipation of the peasants, and the building of a modern army. He had no concrete program of action to promote his aims, but he conceived instead a spectacular act of bravery to dramatize his ideas. He attempted to assassinate one of the shogun's representatives in Kyoto, and for this act, which failed, he was executed at Edo. Nonetheless, his self-discipline and bravery transformed him into a heroic figure for later generations.

A few Japanese advocated complete Westernization. In this group was Fukuzawa Yukichi (1834–1901), a pioneer of modernization. Born in Kyushu in a lower samurai rank, he early learned Dutch and English. He traveled to the United States in the 1860 diplomatic mission. Seven years later he returned on a second trip, and also traveled in Europe. As Japan eventually opened its doors to Western ideas in the latter half of the nineteenth century, Fukuzawa was in the vanguard. He promoted the ideas of utilitarianism and of liberalism, founded a newspaper, and established Keio University. His accommodating approach won out in the early decades of modernization, but the advocates of self-strengthening and of kokutai were also to have their day.

The Final Decade of Tokugawa Rule

In the decade following the 1858 treaty settlement, the economic effects, some of them adverse, of Westernization were immediately registered in Japan. The volume of exports and of imports through foreign channels grew appreciably because of the low tariff rates imposed on Japan by the unequal treaties, and it had an unsettling effect on the domestic economy. Fuel products, such as kerosene, were imported in large quantities. Cotton yarn could be imported more cheaply than silk or cotton that could be raised in Japan. Since Japanese domestic industry was still in the handicraft stage, its products could not compete with cheap imports in mass proportions. A resultant depression of handicraft industries occurred both in the cities and in the countryside. The process of economic dislocation in the late Tokugawa period resulted in many revolts by peasants. With their fixed incomes, the military, already in economic straits, suffered further reverses with the influx of goods and with rising prices.

The political situation was also getting more complex. The years after 1858 witnessed a struggle between factions supporting the emperor and those backing the hard-pressed shogun. Subsequent to the conclusion of Western treaties, the influence of the shogunate lessened. That of the emperor, court, and certain tozama grew, particularly the four clans of Tosa in Shikoku, Hizen and Satsuma in Kyushu, and Choshu in western Honshu. Supporting the imperial institution, these daimyo attacked the joint enemies, bakufu and foreigners. The action of the shogun in signing the Harris treaties without the consent of the monarch provided ammunition against the Tokugawa. The court informed the shogun, who had already promised the foreigners to implement terms of the treaties, that the treaties would not be accepted until the aliens were expelled. Japan teetered on the brink of civil war, and the lives of foreigners were endangered. Samurai and other ultra-patriots attacked foreigners and tried to discredit the shogunate with the slogan "revere the emperor and expel the barbarians." With so much bitter opposition, it was surprising that only a few Westerners were killed in this decade. Three Russian naval officers were murdered, the Dutch interpreter for the United States legation was cut down, and a British diplomat, C. L. Richardson, was killed near Yokohama when he did not dismount as the high-ranking, anti-Western lord of Satsuma passed by him.

Harris believed that the shogun was doing his best to preserve order, but the English reacted strongly to the Richardson incident. They demanded an apology and an indemnity. Getting no satisfaction, in August, 1863, their fleet bombarded Kagoshima, the capital of the Satsuma fief. This proved to be a turning point in the anti-foreign campaign, for the Satsuma, after a face-saving formula of claiming to have driven away the foreign fleet, had been so impressed with British power that they became friends of the English. The clan became the leading advocate of a modern navy, patterned on the British model, in Japan over the next half-century, and its members filled top-ranking naval positions.

Meanwhile, the court and the Choshu clan had been acting independently. On his own authority, in 1862 the emperor cancelled the institution of alternate attendance, and he fixed June 25, 1863, as the date for closing the country. When that day arrived, despite the shogun's objections to the royal ultimatum, Choshu began shelling foreign ships from their capital of Shimonoseki, which guarded the narrow but strategic strait between Honshu and Kyushu, a major shipping lane to China. Foreign ships, including an American merchant vessel, were damaged.

The United States retaliated by dispatching a warship to punish the recalcitrant lord. In the resultant fray, five Americans were killed and six were wounded. The Congress applauded the brave act and directed the Treasury to compensate the crew for meritorious service. The French also sent two ships to punish the Choshu, who continued obstreperous, and, in contravention of treaty terms, closed the strait for a year. Finally, in September, 1864, a joint expedition of seventeen ships (nine British, four Dutch, three French, and one American vessel), defeated the daimyo, from whom a $3 million indemnity was demanded. Eventually the United States realized about $800,000 of this sum, but an act of the Congress in 1883 returned the proceeds to the Japanese, who used some of the money to construct the Yokohama breakwater.

Like Satsuma, Choshu learned its lesson by force. It dropped its opposition to the foreigners and instead concentrated its efforts against the shogun. Choshu leaders became paramount in the development of Japan's modern army, as Satsuma had been with the navy. The emperor also capitulated to Western force. His consent to the 1857 and 1858 treaties was obtained in late 1865, after a show of naval strength off Osaka by an allied undertaking of nine ships (five British, three French and one Dutch). At that engagement the American charge d'affaires, lacking a ship of his own nationality, hitched a ride with the British.

With foreign issues settled and the Western powers placated, the tozama daimyo concentrated on the shogun's downfall. The times were conducive to change. In September, 1866, the shogun died, and in the following February the emperor was also gathered to his ancestors. Another shogun and a young emperor ascended to their respective positions. In the new atmosphere, the tozama in 1867 sent an ultimatum to the Tokugawa demanding that he surrender his shogunal powers. Already predisposed to do this, the shogun renounced his political rights, and he declared his intention to retire. On January 3, 1868, the court issued a rescript announcing the restoration of power to the emperor. The monarch, through the advisers, then asked the ex-shogun to surrender his lands. This request was refused, and not until May, after some months of fighting, did the Tokugawa relinquish their territories. Treated well in defeat, the former shogun was given princely rank, and the family turned their fortunes to business enterprises.

As the central figure in the restoration period, the fifteen-year-old emperor Mutsuhito assumed the reign name of Meiji (Enlightened One). Through his tozama advisers he chose to follow a policy of Westernization which was enunciated in general terms through two proclamations. In April, 1868, the Charter Oath, drawn up by a few young advisers in the emperor's name, in five short articles pledged the establishment of deliberative assemblies and the decision of all matters by public discussion; declared that all classes, high and low, were to unite in vigorously effecting affairs of state; permitted the common people, no less than the civil and military officials, to pursue their individual callings; sought to break off "evil customs" of the past; and stated the desire to seek knowledge throughout the world to strengthen the foundations of imperial rule. The so-called constitution of June, 1868, supported similar ends. To symbolize the new era, the capital moved from Kyoto to Edo, renamed Tokyo (Eastern Capital), where the Meiji emperor ruled until his death in 1912.

Another political period began in Japan. Many new ideas and forces were in evidence, but old ways persisted. As she had done before, Japan was to borrow and utilize foreign ideas to an appreciable extent, this time on her road toward modernization and international status. But this borrowing was only part of the story of the rise to power, for native institutions were not wholly discarded in the process. The Japanese were once again to strike their own balance between contemporary and traditional elements.

CHRONOLOGY

1811–1864	Sakuma Shozan
1830–1859	Yoshida Shoin
1834–1901	Fukuzawa Yukichi
1853	Perry first in Japan
1854	Perry or Kanagawa treaty
1856–1862	Townsend Harris in Japan
1857/1858	Harris treaties, concluded with shogun, without imperial consent
1860	Exchange of ratifications in Washington of 1858 treaty
1863	Satsuma subdued
1864	Choshu subdued
1868	Meiji restoration; capital to Tokyo; Charter Oath (April); and June constitution

PART THREE

MODERN JAPAN

With the Meiji restoration Japan started on its way to modernization and world status. In the almost half-century of Mutsuhitu's rule, the country laid the bases for domestic strength and foreign expansion. Then, over the next several decades, through World War I and the 1920's, Japan in imperial guise rose to even greater heights of international standing and home productivity by a combination of factors unique to the land and times. But, after Japan had built up one of the greatest empires in the world, momentarily and through force, the success story culminated in the tragic resolution of World War II. Once again the country reverted to its pre-Perry status, its energies confined realistically and territorially to its home islands. Within only a century the historical process had gone full cycle.

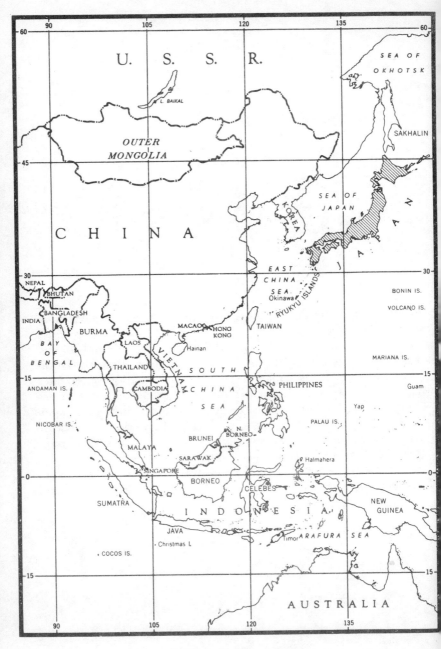

Japan in the Asian setting

XI

MEIJI JAPAN (1868–1912):
(1) POLITICS

In the four and a half decades that constituted the Meiji period, Japan modernized her political, economic, and social institutions and achieved the status of a world power. National wealth increased during this period, for both the agricultural and industrial segments of the economy kept pace with the burgeoning population. Economic modernization, political stability, and the stimulus of foreign trade contributed to steady development. Policy was directed by oligarchic ruling groups, and Japanese society responded quickly to their direction. The lack of any appreciable difference or conflict in outlook between rulers and ruled in regard to national goals helped to smooth the process of modernization.

Background

Meiji Japan may be conveniently divided into two periods. During the first two decades, until about 1890, the leaders were primarily concerned with internal changes and laid the foundations for modernization. In political affairs, they dealt with immediate and pressing matters of state, such as the achievement of stability, the consolidation of unified domestic rule, and the establishment of effective government organs. In this initial period the formulation of long-range goals was of secondary import. In economics, because of the great scope of programs involved, financing remained precarious in the years immediately following the restoration, though pragmatic steps were taken to solve adverse budgetary conditions.

Modern industries were instituted. The textile industry was one of the first to show appreciable gains. Appearing on the industrial scene at the time were the *zaibatsu* or cartels that became a dominant characteristic of Japanese economic life. In cultural matters in the early Meiji years, many Japanese seemed to go overboard in adopting Western customs and ideas, and Western philosophies of education temporarily won prestige.

In the latter half of the Meiji period, after 1890, Japan became a world economic and political power. Internal growth matched foreign expansion, for each element sustained the other. Once immediate political considerations had been met, the government turned to the side-tracked issue of constitutionalism, which it resolved at a leisurely pace and in a conservative manner. In economics, more lasting fiscal solvency resulted from retrenchment policies of the 1880's. Similar to the nineteenth-century economic pattern in England, Japan, after registering growth in the textile field, emphasized heavy industry. The zaibatsu grew in economic and in political importance, and they began overseas operations. In cultural affairs, the pendulum swung back to revival of the traditional ways, and the national system of education, after early experiments involving heavy doses of Western philosophies, was put on a more securely Japanese footing. Japan now became an empire.

In a Cinderella-type story, Japan within the Meiji period became a modern state. The young reformers, who in the early years of the restoration began to modernize Japan, saw their goals achieved within their lifetimes. Their aim was reflected in the slogan to "enrich the nation and strengthen its arms." They desired to build up both military and industrial power in order to achieve equality with the West and were successful in effecting progress in economic, social, political, and cultural spheres. They displayed a readiness to experiment with new methods and to push boldly ahead, but they concurrently adhered to traditional ideals and virtues. By 1912 Japan had acquired all the requisites for a modern state, the first in Asia to do so. She possessed a strong national government, a constitution, a military based on universal conscription, a wide-ranging educational program, money economy, a growing industrial, commercial, and urbanized society, adequate labor supply in city and country, and sufficient food production. Agricultural yields helped to increase national wealth, and industry and modernization were sustained by growth in the rest of the economy. In their own way, the Japanese met the challenge of the times.

Yet it is debatable whether the success of Meiji Japan, which is held up as a model of early modernization, has contemporary relevance for economically underdeveloped countries desiring to pursue a similar end. Meiji Japan faced no ideological conflicts, as some modern states experience. She had fewer sources of foreign aid and hesitated to use those available for fear of strings attached. Change was evolutionary, and Japan did not rush toward modernization. Conditioned by historical background, particularly the centuries of regimented Tokugawa rule, the Japanese were prepared to accept leadership and direction from above. Features unique to Japan prevailed in the latter decades of the nineteenth century and the early years of the twentieth. Some of the factors contributing to Japan's modernization were not easily exportable nor are they applicable now.

Both the leaders of modernization and the Japanese people accepted common values, such as loyalty to the emperor and devotion to the nation. While there was naturally some dissent and extremism during the Meiji years, the leaders and the populace focused on the imperial office as their sanction for modernization. The Emperor Meiji was the great symbol of Japan's modernization. Yet because of the sanctity of his person, little was known of him. Even in Tokyo, he remained apart from the world. The throne continued divine and mystical in concept. Augmenting imperial seclusion and aloofness was the emperor's personality. Not wishing to dominate the government, he relied heavily on his advisers. He won their admiration with his accommodation, and because of agreement between emperor and advisers it was easy to maintain the exalted position of the throne. Modern Japanese nationalism, already possessing features dating to Tokugawa times, required little stimulus from the West. National consciousness and emperor worship combined into a national creed in the form of state Shinto. Moreover, the presence of a historic strain of Confucian ethic, with its reliance on vital moral forces and on moral guidance devolving from sage-kings, enhanced the imperial role in the modernization process.

Realignments

In the decade following the restoration, all major classes of Japanese society were affected by change. The daimyo were liqui-

dated as a class. Their samurai, particularly those of the han of
Satsuma, Choshu, and others of western Japan, in an effort to avoid
further civil war, persuaded their own lords to surrender their
domains to the emperor. These leading daimyo complied and the
rest of the lords, taking the cue, followed in similar action. Typical
of the "grass-roots" samurai who persuaded their lords to relinquish
their lands was Kido Koin (1833–1877) of Choshu, a disciple of
Yoshida Shoin. He had early realized the futility of his fellow
clansmen's violent antiforeign demonstrations when Choshu was
so weak. He reorganized his clan's forces and led them against the
shogunate in the unrest of 1867 and 1868. He engineered the coalition of forces that eventually overthrew the Tokugawa and abolished
feudalism. Rather than precipitate domestic strife over the issue,
Kido used his persuasive talents to convince the daimyo to surrender
their fiefs as a patriotic gesture and moral obligation.

By 1869, within a year of the restoration, no feudal domains remained in Japan. All land had reverted in name to the emperor.
Because of the tremendous nature of the change, for the two years
between 1869 and 1871 the daimyo were appointed as governors
of their former estates, and they were permitted to retain one-tenth
of former revenues as salaries. In 1871 the fiefs were entirely
abolished, and the land was divided into new political divisions
called prefectures, political and administrative structures that have
lasted into contemporary times. This act terminated the status of
daimyo as feudal lords, although the government eventually pen-
sioned them off with lump-sum payments in the nature of government bonds (a form of payment which helped to insure support of
the new regime).

The old daimyo left the political scene, but many were incorporated into the new peerage that was created. The government
bestowed upon them titles of nobility, divided into five ranks, in
accordance with the size of their previous domains. The last Tokugawa shogun received the rank of prince, and the former holders
of the smallest estates became barons. Some of the former daimyo,
using their capital and bonds judiciously to build up commercial
ventures, became part of the growing capitalist class in Japan. In
some ways, they were better off in the new society. The government
cancelled or assumed most of their debts, the ex-lords had no more
samurai to support, and their income was generally higher in their
newer ventures.

The merchants welcomed the restoration. They helped to finance
it, for they desired political changes to assure them status com-

mensurate with their economic growth and importance. Since the government had shouldered the previous debts which the military owed to the commercial class, the confidence of the zaibatsu and merchants in the new regime was generally assured. However, the farmers, who were the largest group in the population, became worse off. The majority of them had not been tenants, since under the laws of the Tokugawa the land could not be alienated. Within a few years after the restoration, about a third of the farmers became tenants through the legalization of processes by which landlords could acquire more land. The peasantry by and large became a dispossessed class.

The samurai, probably the most important group in the restoration, were phased out of existence. Constituting with their families some two million or 5 per cent of Japan's population, they lost traditional rights and privileges over a period of years. With the introduction of universal military training in 1872 and 1873, they lost their time-honored position as warrior-aristocrats. With the disappearance of a class of feudal lords with their fiefs, the samurai also lost their traditional revenues. As in the case of the daimyo, the government paid the samurai pensions over an eight-year period (1868–1876) in lieu of the former hereditary stipends. In 1876 the government commuted these pensions into relatively small lump-sum final payments. Now ordinary subjects, the ex-samurai were left to fend for themselves. Some managed well, for they used their payments to start successful business enterprises. Others were attracted to the officer corps of the new army or to the police forces. The final blow to samurai privilege came in 1876, when the government prohibited them from wearing the traditional two swords that had marked them as a separate class with special feudal rights.

For some samurai conservatives, these developments had been too drastic. They went into opposition against those of their own class or clansmen who were directing the changes. The most serious samurai revolt broke out in Satsuma itself. There conservatives rallied around Saigo Takamori (1827–1877), one of the ex-samurai himself but one who felt that the new government was going too far in its reforms. Saigo opposed the universal conscription law, capitalist interests in government, the official policy of not using ex-samurai in foreign wars, and what he termed an appeasement policy toward Koreans who had mistreated Japanese envoys in summary fashion. Disgusted with the trend of events, he returned from Tokyo to Satsuma, where he built up his forces and rebelled in 1877. The new imperial conscript army with modern weapons roundly defeated his samurai forces. Saigo's rebellion was significant as the last protest of a dying feudal system, for the great majority of the Japanese, including samurai, tacitly or openly concurred with the policies of realigning social classes. Although he died for a lost cause, Saigo became a hero revered by future generations of Japanese patriots.

With little effective dissent to hamper them, the leaders borrowed administrative techniques, centralized government control, adopted the Western calendar, provided for religious toleration, and modernized the law enforcement, financial, postal, and juridical systems. One early restoration leader who favored change directed by a ruling group was Okubo Toshimichi (1830–1878). Also of Satsuma and a boyhood friend of Saigo, he differed with his clansman on the nature and the extent of internal reforms and of foreign policy goals. Okubo stressed the necessity of achieving internal stability, of systematizing progress, and of concentrating on domestic rather than on foreign affairs. Transcending clan loyalties, he enlisted in his cause capable supporters from other fiefs. A chief engineer of Japan's modernization, Okubo served as minister of finance and minister of home affairs. He was a moderate who stood for the evolution of constitutional government. In 1878 he was assassinated by an assailant who explained that he was motivated by a desire to revenge Saigo's death for which Okubo, as home minister, had been responsible. Within one year three early heroes of the restoration—Kido, Saigo, and Okubo—had died in the prime of life. Yet others came forth to plan and to consolidate the policies begun in early Meiji times.

New Leadership

One such emerging figure in Japan's second and newer line of political leadership was Ito Hirobumi (1841–1909). Of lowly Choshu samurai background, Ito rose through a hierarchical society to pinnacles of power. As a youth he had vigorous induction into bushido, the code of the warrior. From his teachers, among whom was Yoshida Shoin, he inherited strong traits of self-discipline and loyalty. He was also early impressed with the necessity of acquiring Western knowledge. In 1863 he went to Europe on an English ship, and on his return he became, as Kido had become, a leading Choshu advocate of coming to terms with the West. After the restoration, he rose to become an important member of the inner government oligarchy. His first appointment was in the new Bureau of Foreign

Affairs, and he later moved to Finance, Industry, and finally to the prime ministership. A second mission to the West in 1870 included a stay in the United States. Ito made a third trip to the West in 1882–1884 as the head of an imperial commission to study constitutions and was impressed by the new Germany of Bismarck, which resembled Japan in some ways, and by the centralized concepts of Prussian statism.

Although he thought of himself as a moderate supporting neither despotism nor democracy, Ito was at times openly hostile toward parliamentary forms of government. In his quest for a constitution appropriate for Japan, he came into conflict with leaders of newly emerging political parties and movements that also demanded a voice in constitution making. His chief opponents arose in Tosa on Shikoku and Hizen in Kyushu, which, as former tozama clans, had helped overthrow the shogunate but which, subsequent to the restoration, found themselves outpaced by the Satsuma-Choshu clique in gaining government office and political influence. They founded political parties and complicated the Meiji political scene.

Political parties were a novelty in nineteenth-century Japan, and the word had to be coined in the Japanese language. A Western concept, parties had no place in traditional Japanese political thought, where open criticism of duly constituted authorities was not tolerated. Itagaki Taisuke (1837–1919) of Tosa was an early proponent of political parties. After the restoration he served as a councillor or cabinet member in Tokyo, but in 1874 he returned home to establish the first Japanese political party, which was called the Public Society of Patriots. The next year at a conference at Osaka, the party petitioned the government to establish a legislative asssembly and a judiciary and to call a conference of prefectural governors to consider a future form of national government. Not entirely democratic in nature, the party drew its strength mainly from Tosa samurai. It desired that parliamentary participation be limited to ex-samurai and to a small class of wealthy peasants. Despite its self-imposed restrictions, within a few years the party outgrew its local origins to become established on a national basis. It showed some strength in forcing political concessions from the central government, for in 1878 the government called for elected prefectural assemblies.

Put into effect the following year, the franchise was extended to males who paid at least five yen or more in land taxes. Acting solely in an advisory capacity, the prefectural assemblies were nonetheless the first elected legislatures in the non-Western world. In

1880 similar assemblies were constituted in towns and in smaller units of local government. Giving with one hand and taking with the other, the government passed that year gag ordinances that required the stamp of official approval three days prior to holding any political meetings and the reporting of all names and addresses of groups and parties at such meetings.

Allying himself with Itagaki in the opposition to the government was Okuma Shigenobu (1838–1922) of Hizen. After the restoration was announced, he joined the foreign office in Tokyo and became a cabinet member. In March, 1881, he presented the emperor with a memorial outlining steps towards achieving a parliamentary form of government. He suggested a definite date for the opening of a parliament, thinking in terms of a year or two. The impact of Okuma's sudden political demands on his colleagues was dramatic, and Ito, a gradualist and a conservative, particularly took issue. Four months later, in July, Okuma went on to challenge the government's economic policy, charging that insiders were profiting from the proposed sale of the assets of the Hokkaido Colonization Office, which in the previous decade had been given responsibility for the development of that island. Crying scandal, he forced a showdown in the cabinet not only on the issue of the disposition of government-owned industries and lands, but on the personalities dictating policies. Ito and his faction won, for the liquidation of assets of the Office to private interests proceeded as planned. Okuma was forced out of office, but the throne promised a constitution by 1890. To advance their views in the matter, the opposition founded new and broader political parties. In 1881 Itagaki formed the Liberal Party, and the next year Okuma organized the Progressive Party. The government responded by creating in 1882 the Imperial Party that followed the official line.

The Meiji Constitution

Ito was commissioned to draw up a constitution and began work after his return in the early 1880's from the trip abroad to study constitutional governments. To eliminate the danger of pressure from the various political camps, all work was done in official privacy within the imperial household. A privy council worked with Ito and ratified the document. Finally, on February 11, 1889, the traditional anniversary of the founding of Yamato state, the emperor bestowed the constitution upon the people as a royal gift. The realization of representative government, which was the first east of the Suez, had been drafted by an oligarchy, was bestowed through imperial grace upon the people, and was accepted obediently by them. The constitution, which took twenty-one years to prepare, became official in a ten-minute speech by the emperor. The document lasted fifty-eight years without amendments until a new version replaced it during the post-World War II occupation.

The Meiji constitution consisted of a preamble and seven chapters with seventy-six articles. At the apex of political power was the emperor, whose traditional position of divinity was affirmed. As fountainhead of sovereignty, sacred and inviolable, the direct descendant of the gods, the emperor enjoyed special powers. He could issue imperial ordinances, executive acts in the general interest, and emergency laws when parliament was not in session. Also conferred on him were parliamentary powers. He was supreme commander of the military forces, convoked and prorogued parliament, declared war and made peace, sanctioned all laws, and controlled foreign affairs conducted by the cabinet. Government in his name was the source and wellspring of power. Attached to the emperor was the Imperial Household Ministry with its two important positions of Lord Keeper of the Privy Seal and Minister of the Imperial Household. Imperial House Law, taking precedence over parliamentary law, governed such matters as succession and other royal affairs.

The parliament or Diet, as it was termed by Japanese, was bicameral. The upper chamber, or the House of Peers, resembling the English House of Lords, embraced members of aristocratic standing. Its membership was divided into six categories: princes of the imperial blood; princes and marquises; representatives of counts, viscounts, and barons, who served seven-year terms; imperial appointees for life selected because of special service to the state; delegates from the Imperial Academy with seven-year terms; and representatives of the highest taxpayers. The lower body, or House of Representatives, initially consisted of 300 members (this was raised to 381 in 1900 and to 466 in 1925), who were elected by males over the age of twenty-five who paid an annual tax of fifteen yen or more. All statutes required majority vote of both houses, but they were subject to imperial veto. The Diet was convoked annually by the emperor. It had the right, although it was not usually exercised, to initiate legislation, for most bills were presented instead by the government. Parliamentary power over finances was constricted. It did not apply to fixed expenditures in the budget, and it was not permitted to regulate expenditures of the imperial household or bureaucratic salaries.

Another constitutional organ was the privy council. Initially created to review and accept the constitution, it remained as the highest formally constituted advisory body in the land. Its membership of twenty-six was selected by the emperor on the advice of the prime minister. In turn, the prime minister was appointed by the emperor, on the advice principally of elder statesmen. On matters of state he had direct access to the throne. A limited bill of rights for all subjects was incorporated into the constitution, but its provisions could be changed by law. Despite its modern form, the Meiji constitution embraced some time-honored Japanese political concepts, all of which were at variance with Western jurisprudence. These included the ideas that the ideal state was the patriarchial family headed by the emperor as father of the nation, that government by men prevailed above government by law, that group obligations took precedence over individual rights, and that man by nature was created unequal. Here was another example of the persistence of traditional Japanese ideas.

Extraconstitutional Groups

Omissions in the constitution proved to be as important as its provisions, if not more so. Although not stipulated in the document, several extraconstitutional groups developed and gained in power and influence over the years. The bureaucracy, one such collective group, assumed importance. It had started on an experimental basis, and the emperor appointed to it military and civilian personnel. Cliques, particularly from Satsuma and from Choshu, filled the ranks of earlier bureaucratic offices. In 1899 an imperial proclamation laid the basis for an examination system. Placed on a merit basis, the bureaucracy, which came to embrace some half a million civil servants, became impervious to the popular or parliamentary will. It enjoyed its own *esprit de corps,* and cabinets usually included members from its top ranks.

Bureaucrats affiliated with special interests, such as military or industrial groups, could exert influence for good or ill in their autonomous role. In the top rank of the bureaucracy was the cabinet, which predated the constitution. In its early years it embraced the heads of ten departments. Yet the most influential political group was another extraconstitutional and advisory body, the *genro* or elder statesmen, as Ito, who derived essentially from Satsuma-Choshu ranks. These few men acting as a closely knit oligarchy ruled Meiji Japan in the name of the emperor.

Military leaders, some of them also from genro ranks, assumed prominence in Meiji Japan. Endeavoring initially to separate military and civilian affairs, the constitution stipulated that the military were not to vote. In 1882 an imperial rescript prohibited military involvement in political affairs. Yet the military conceived itself as protecters of kokutai, the national spirit. The professional soldier, far from eschewing politics, entered into it. Paradoxically, despite the restrictions placed on them, the military in time became more and more important. In 1878, in addition to the already existing cabinet post of Minister of War, the emperor under genro advice created an army general staff headed by a chief responsible to him. In 1893 the same procedure was extended to the navy, and the chief of the naval general staff was also to report directly to the throne. Such organs as the Board of Field Marshals and Fleet Admirals and the Supreme War Council were composed of top-ranking military planners. A dominant position for the military in Japanese politics was assured when in 1900 an ordinance provided that only generals and lieutenant-generals on the active list could be appointed to the traditionally civilian cabinet post of Minister of War, reporting directly to the emperor. Similarly, only admirals and vice-admirals on active duty could be appointed as Minister of the Navy. Unlike most parliamentary governments, where the prime minister had a relatively free hand in selecting ministers for various portfolios, no cabinet in Japan could be formed after 1900 without military consent. A modern-day bakufu had re-emerged in cabinet ranks.

The new military man was best exemplified by Yamagata Aritomo (1838–1922). Like Kido and Ito, he was a Choshu clansman. He also benefitted from tutelage under Yoshida Shoin. Yamagata was orphaned at the age of five and was raised by a strong-willed grandmother, who was said to have later committed suicide lest he be torn between family and patriotic duties. In the prerestoration Western attacks on Choshu, Yamagata helped to organize clan defenses. He discovered that while the peasant conscripts fought as bravely as the samurai, sheer fighting spirit was no match for modern arms. At the earliest opportunity, Yamagata embarked on a world tour to study the military organization of the advanced Western powers. On his return he took a leading part in the establishment of the new conscript army, which defeated Saigo's rebels. Yamagata enjoyed a long and honorable government career. His military positions included those of Minister of War, Chief of General Staff, and Field Marshal. He also participated in politics, serving twice as Home Minister and as Prime Minister and three times as President of the Privy Council. He finally became a prince in the new Meiji aristocracy. After Ito's assassination in Manchuria in 1909 by a Korean he assumed until his death the position of senior elder statesman and principal adviser to the throne. Under leadership such as his, Japan commenced its experience with constitutional government.

Government and Party Relations

With leadership consolidated in Satsuma and Choshu civilian and military ranks, constitutional government began with the promulgation of the document in 1889. However, parliamentary machinery did not change the basic nature of Japanese politics, which remained oligarchic. The "in" group, who controlled the government, held at bay the political parties spearheaded by the "out" clans of Tosa and Hizen. The struggle between clan leaders was reflected in the Diet from the first elections of 1890 until World War I, when party government (defined as a system in which the prime ministers are generally chosen from the parties controlling majorities in parliament) was instituted. It remained difficult to reconcile government absolutism with party participation. Government leaders endeavored to maintain the status quo, and they narrowly interpreted the already constricted constitution. They meant to preserve the prestige of the throne, and they shied away from passing liberalizing measures. And while their opponents in parliament pleaded for the extension or provision of more political rights, the degree of this opposition's liberalism was also questionable. Often more concerned with individual prestige and party positions than with the extension of popular rights, Itagaki and Okuma followed courses of expediency and of opportunism. Because Japanese politics were dominated by strong personalities, factions which formed around these personalities rather than around political programs became a dominant strain in party alignments and realignments.

In the first parliamentary elections of July 1, 1890, all but 27,000 of 450,000 eligible voters (in a country of some 35 million) went to the polls. In part, voters turned out in large numbers to gain the respect of the Western countries and because of simple faith in the magic of constitutionalism that brought them the right of franchise for the first time. Of those voting, 91 per cent were commoners and 9 per cent were ex-samurai; the latter were represented in the Diet in proportion to their numbers. Some prefectures elected only commoners. In its report on the election, the government noted that electioneering, considered notorious, was not widespread, and instead candidates depended on family name or position to win votes. Not many speeches were given and few issues were discussed. Itagaki's Liberal Party and Okuma's Progressive Party won a combined total of 171 out of 300 seats in the lower house of the first Diet. With this mandate, the parties set about to rid Japan of the unequal treaties, and they proposed drastic cuts in the government budget. They envisioned parliament as a means to exercise some control over the government, while government leaders held a contrary view, resulting in rapid estrangement between the parties and the oligarchs.

In the first seven years of the constitution (1889–1896), the government oligarchs worked at cross purposes with the parties. Yamagata headed the first cabinet (1889–1891) under the constitution. He called on the House of Representatives to act in unison with the government. The parties responded instead by proposing budgetary cuts, including salaries of bureaucrats. The government replied by invoking the legal provisions prohibiting any reduction of fixed expenditures. It went further and resorted to intimidation of party members by hired gangsters, and it bribed weak-kneed members to modify their views. Yamagata also made a private deal with Itagaki, whose Liberal Party suddenly announced support of the government by requesting only a 6 per cent, rather than an original 10 per cent, cut in the budget. Disliking the give and take of politics, Yamagata resigned office shortly afterwards, and Matsukata Masayoshi of Satsuma, a former minister of finance and protegé of Yamagata, became prime minister (1891–1892). No fresh point of view emerged in the government, because the majority of members in the old cabinet were carried over into the new. The same parliamentary controversy arose over the budget, which now had been expanded to include expenditures for naval and shipbuilding programs.

Meeting with continued opposition, the government dissolved the Diet, and in the special elections of February, 1892, perhaps the most brutal in Japanese history, at least twenty-five persons were killed and nearly four hundred wounded. Yet the government did not succeed in cowing the House into submission, for in the new Diet the parties won 163 out of 300 seats. This time Ito accepted the premiership (1892–1896) in a cabinet that included several genro. The fight over the budget was again immediately repeated. This time Ito, through a unique strategem, secured an imperial announcement stating that the emperor was contributing 350,000 yen a year for six years toward military programs and was requesting all civil servants to contribute 10 per cent of their salaries to the military budget. Losing face, the Diet voted the budget, and then turned its attacks on foreign policy issues. In 1894 the war with China provided the government with welcome relief from domestic considerations.

From 1896 to 1900, the government oligarchs, represented by the three prime ministers from their ranks, cooperated to a degree with the parties. They realized that party support was preferable to party antagonism, and they extended limited political promises as concessions. With backing from the Progressive Party, Matsukata formed his second cabinet (1896–1898), to be followed by Ito's second premiership (1898). By this time an open break in the genro had emerged between the civilian Ito and his military clansman Yamagata. Itagaki and Okuma, on the other hand, in the summer of 1898 had temporarily settled their differences and had merged their followers into a coalition Constitutional Party. In an election that year, the new party won 260 of 300 seats, and this overwhelming party majority precipitated a serious government crisis. Yamagata advised the emperor to suspend the constitution, while Ito, who had worked most closely with its formulation, rather than terminating or vitiating it, recommended that the party take over the cabinet. Ito won his point and Okuma became prime minister.

The first real Japanese party cabinet was short-lived. The genro and the bureaucracy were not favorably disposed toward it, and the two coalition factions themselves could not cooperate. A dispute arose over a vacated cabinet position, and Itagaki resigned when Okuma filled the post with a man from his own faction. Yamagata again stepped back into office (1898–1900). In this period the government enacted important measures. The land tax was increased, voting qualifications were reduced, the civil service was put on a merit basis, and, as noted, the military took over the cabinet posts of Ministers of War and of Navy. These measures were passed in parliament because of their support by Itagaki, who though in political opposition was not democratic and enjoyed a working relationship with Yamagata.

In a third phase (1900–1913), the oligarchs took over, or directed the political parties. As head of the new Seiyukai Party (Association of Friends of Constitutional Government), Ito for the third time formed a cabinet (1900–1901). He gave prestige to it, and he attracted adherents from the ranks of the disintegrating Constitutional Party. But it was his last term in office, and two new genro, Prince Saionji Kimmochi, a court noble, and Katsura Taro, a Choshu general, protegés of Ito and of Yamagata respectively, as heads of parties alternated as premier between 1901 and 1913. Saionji held the post twice, and Katsura was premier three times. The country finally tired of the seesawing, and with the Emperor Meiji's death at sixty in 1912, the accession of a new emperor and of new men as premiers augured changes in the Japanese political scene.

CHRONOLOGY

1827–1877	Saigo Takamori
1830–1878	Okubo Toshimichi
1833–1877	Kido Koin
1837–1919	Itagaki Taisuke
1838–1922	Okuma Shigenobu
1838–1922	Yamagata Aritomo
1841–1909	Ito Hirobumi
1874	Itagaki founds Public Society of Patriots
1878	Army general chief of staff created, responsible to emperor
1879	Elected prefectural assemblies
1880	Elected town and local assemblies
1881	Okuma's memorial on parliamentary government; throne promises constitution by 1890; Itagaki forms Liberal Party
1882	Okuma forms Progressive Party; Imperial Party of government
1889	Constitution promulgated
1890	First parliamentary elections
1893	Navy chief of staff created, responsible to emperor
1898	Itagaki-Okuma form Constitutional Party
1900	Active military men as Ministers of War and Navy; Ito heads Seiyukai Party

XII

MEIJI JAPAN: (2) ECONOMICS AND SOCIETY

As Japan modernized the political structure, concurrent changes were proceeding in economic and social life. Light and heavy industries both were developed and helped to lay the groundwork for the country's rapid rise to world power. Supported in part by government policies and financing, private industries grew in number and size, to dominate the economic scene by late Meiji. Rural life continued along traditional lines, but cities expanded, and it was in urban areas that social change was most noticeable.

Economics

Japan's leaders had achieved a new political structure and also turned toward directing an industrial revolution. In typical Japanese fashion, economic changes were initiated by the state. The programs were so large and so basic that only the government possessed the funds and the ability to execute plans. There was relatively and proportionately little capital in private hands of merchants, daimyo, and samurai. Even if private parties had the funds, they often did not desire to gamble on large-scale undertakings, at least not without official support. In addition to direct official control and operation of key industries, the government did extend considerable aid and subsidies to encourage the development of certain specified private industries. The government did not adhere to any preconceived concepts of state socialism or of dedication to private enterprise but rather used pragmatic means to solve economic problems. Noting the situation in China in which foreign loans brought foreign interference, they eschewed loans from abroad, and they held to a minimum foreign economic advisers, fearing that foreign assistance might come with political strings attached.

Despite the desire to industrialize, there were several fundamental obstacles to Japan's industrialization. Capital was relatively scarce even for government investments, and the government in the early Meiji decades resorted to deficit financing. Also lacking were the supporting structures for industry, such as adequate systems of distribution, transportation, communication, and advertising. Foreign competition was keen, and the low import duty of 5 per cent imposed by the unequal treaties proved a handicap. Political power was potentially weighted against change, and industrial advancement implied dislocations and rearrangements in social and economic patterns. Yet by 1890 Japan was ready for an economic "breakthrough," at least in certain key industrial areas. Cotton spinning mills started the trend, and other fields followed. With Matsukata as Minister of Finance in the mid-1880's the transfer of many government enterprises to private hands resulted in the first industrial boom, and cartels expanded their operations. In the mid-1890's another surge in industry occurred. In part as a result of the war with China, light industry became more diversified, and heavy industry became extensive. Chemical fertilizer plants, cotton weaving mills, electrical industries, coal and steel factories, sugar refining, and the manufacture of machine tools were among the more important industries. Wartime commitment in the campaigns against Russia accelerated industrial growth. In the second half of the Meiji period, industry had come of age and Japan registered sustained economic growth.

In line with the general policy to "enrich the nation and strengthen its arms" the government directly developed and controlled certain services and public utilities. In 1872 the first railway, only eighteen miles long, was completed between Tokyo and the port of Yokohama, but it took time to develop a national system of railroads because of the rugged Japanese terrain. The government constructed paper mills, cotton spinning plants, and other light industrial complexes, which were sold in the 1880's to private interests. Besides the liquidation of some interests, government aid to private industry included extending low rates of interest, setting up model factories, giving technical advice, advancing long-term loans, and guaranteeing profits. The phenomenal growth of certain industrial interests resulted, and small fortunes skyrocketed into great economic empires, which branched out in all directions through interlocking companies.

The largest of these new zaibatsu, the Mitsui, traced its origins to merchant interests of the early seventeenth century. After the restoration the family moved its headquarters from Kyoto to Tokyo, and there embarked on a program of modernization. It diversified its interests, and its members studied commercial techniques abroad. Mitsubishi, the next largest, was founded by a samurai from Tosa, who had supervised subsidiary operations of that fief in Nagasaki. Subsequently, he transferred interests to his own firm and, while particularly active in shipping, the firm also diversified its activities. The third largest zaibatsu, the Sumitomo, grew out of an old merchant firm of the early seventeenth century which, after the restoration, concentrated on copper mining activities and allied enterprises. Yasuda, the fourth largest, was started by a peasant entrepreneur who, prior to the restoration, ran away from home in western Honshu to Edo, where he became a moneychanger. After the restoration, he went into banking, railroads, and other businesses. Cartels such as these four were larger than their contemporary counterparts in the West. They were essentially family corporations, their interests were not necessarily confined to any one branch of industry, and they had their own banks and credit facilities to finance operations.

The financing of Meiji economic enterprises had begun precariously. In 1868 official receipts were only a third of expenditures. Government financial burdens were heavy. Military campaigns were expensive as was the assumption of shogunal and feudal debts and the pension payments to former daimyo and samurai. It took two-thirds of the national budget itself to support the ex-samurai in the early years of the restoration. Deficit financing was practiced, but with expansion in the economy came rising confidence in the new government. Bond issues were floated at home. In 1871 Ito and Okuma standardized the currency, adopted the decimal system, and promulgated the yen as the standard coin. A mint was set up at Osaka. Matsukata's retrenchment policies in the next decade further helped to stabilize finances. Government industrial enterprises, except for war industries, communications, and public utilities, were sold, usually to insiders, at 11 to 90 per cent of original investments. New taxes, a centralized bank system, reduction in volume of paper currency, and lower interest rates helped to solidify the government's economic foundations.

Nevertheless, agriculture remained the chief source of wealth, and in the first fifteen years of the Meiji 80 per cent of government revenues came from land. In 1873 the land tax was fixed at 3 per cent in money on the assessed value of land rather than on harvest yields, so that the farmer was responsible for the same tax in times of good or bad crops. In Meiji Japan, as in earlier eras, the peasant bore the brunt of taxation. Whether as landowner paying taxes or as tenant farmer paying rent, which usually amounted to between 45 and 60 per cent of the crop, his lot was financially difficult.

Rural life continued with little change. The size of the average farm remained small, averaging about two acres. Leading a marginal existence, the family of some five to eight members tilled the fields in traditional manner. Agriculture was mostly unmechanized and involved the use of simple tools and series of hand operations. The main agricultural activity continued to be rice cultivation, which required the use of much water, development of extensive irrigation systems, and cooperative family and village endeavors in planting and in harvesting the crop. Conservative rural society emphasized old, traditional, and authoritarian values. Generally the family and village remained self-sufficient, consuming about one-third of the produce and selling the rest. Isolated from modernization processes, much of agrarian society remained embedded in unchanging ways. Low standards of living persisted, although as rural as well as urban population grew, some farm hands moved to cities to provide a source of cheap labor in industry.

The cities grew in population and in importance in pace with their commercial and industrial complexes. The capitalist group remained small, and with a concentration of private wealth in few hands, the zaibatsu exerted economic influence far beyond their numbers. The urban middle class was small but growing. Bureaucrats, professionals, intellectuals, and students swelled its ranks. But most numerous were the unskilled industrial laborers, who made the goods but who could hardly afford them, since they lacked adequate purchasing power. These economic groupings in cities affected the political scene. The industrialists, with important commercial and trading interests, expressed their political outlook through parliamentary parties. The growing middle class also reflected its desires through the Diet, but its interests did not always coincide with those of the government. And as the urban middle class grew, the government had greater difficulty in keeping it in

line, for this class displayed the more liberal trends in Japanese
political life.

Society

The modernization and industrialization of Japan was reflected in
its social life. An extensive but orthodox educational pattern was developed by the government. The early Meiji leaders showed wisdom
in discerning the importance of education in a modern state. One
base for power included a literate, and possibly indoctrinated, population, soldiers who could read and write, and trained technicians.
Study abroad was encouraged, and among the two dozen political
leaders only two (Saigo and Okuma) had never been to Europe or
to the United States. At first, foreign experts were hired to develop
educational systems and were highly respected. They proved valuable but expensive, and by the turn of the century only a few of
them remained as language teachers. In 1871 the Ministry of Education was formed and embarked on a great program of universal
education. It built thousands of schoolhouses and trained tens of
thousands of teachers.

By the early twentieth century, six years of primary coeducational
schooling had become compulsory for all. Girls could go on in
government schools to middle schools for four or five years, but
there their education ended, unless they entered private institutions.
In the educational structure, after the primary grades, boys could
advance through lower technical to higher technical schools, or
they could proceed up through five-year academic middle schools
to three-year higher schools, and finally to three years at government
universities (or four years in medicine). Tokyo Imperial University,
with antecedents dating to shogunal schools that combined into one
faculty in the year following the restoration, was formed in 1877.
It reorganized eight years later into a multifaculty organ, and it
enjoyed particular prestige. Other government universities were
founded in the main cities. Private mission and secular schools
augmented publicly supported ones. In 1868 Fukuzawa Yukichi
established a school that eventually grew into Keio, and in 1882,
Okuma formed an institution that became Waseda. In 1875, a
Japanese Christian, trained in the United States, founded Doshisha
in Kyoto.

The overall educational system was geared to Japanese requirements. The general populace was taught to read, larger groups of
literate people found semi-skilled jobs, and a small core of highly

educated men entered the professions and the bureaucracy. The Ministry of Education asserted authority over all schools, including private Japanese and Western mission schools. Curricula combined Occidental and Japanese subjects; students both pursued Western sciences and used Chinese characters. Foreign languages, notably English, were taught. Books were translated from Western languages, and newspapers appeared and multiplied. Universal education transformed Japan into the first Asian country with a literate populace, a fact which helped to explain its concurrent rise to industrial power and military strength. But the Japanese rejected the ideas of democracy and of equality in education. To the Japanese leaders, the purpose of education was not to permit youth to enjoy a richer life but was rather to provide competent citizens as a base for a strong state. These official goals prevailed, and as stated in the Imperial Rescript of 1890, the core of Japanese education emphasized morality, social harmony, and loyalty. Education became an instrument of government that existed for the sake of the country and not for that of the students. Japan pioneered in authoritarian techniques of using education as a means of political tutelage.

The formulation of patriotic state Shinto buttressed political indoctrination. State Shinto was administered by a separate department of religion, which also took charge of the varying particularist Shinto sects that continued to worship individual kami. State Shinto stressed the importance of the imperial shrine at Ise, the imperial house, the national heroes, and ancestors. It inculcated devotion to the emperor and encouraged patriotism by reiterating the time-honored concepts of divinity of the emperor, Japan as the land of the gods, and a benevolent but expansive manifest destiny.

As Shinto returned to favor, so Buddhism and Christianity suffered. Even before the long-standing ban on Christianity was removed in 1873, Protestant missionaries arrived from England and the United States. At first welcomed, they founded schools and won some converts, but Christianity was not adopted wholesale by the Japanese. Whereas in the early seventeenth century perhaps 2 per cent of the population had embraced Christianity, in its Catholic form, in 1889, less than a quarter of 1 per cent were converts (40,000 Catholics, 29,000 Protestants, and 18,000 Orthodox). Christian theology made only a limited imprint in Meiji Japan, although Christian principles of social responsibility and of humanitarianism probably had greater, although more indeterminate, effect.

More secular ideas had varying degrees of impact. Marxism was introduced to Japan later than other Western ideas. Initially not interested in, and later not permitted to indulge in, protest movements or unorthodox ideologies, the Japanese concentrated on more abstract systems of philosophy. But in the 1880's students and intellectuals became concerned with social issues resulting from urbanization and modernization. In 1883 a rickshawmen's union protested technological unemployment. It was disbanded, but the union attracted wide interest. Articles exposed working conditions in coal mines and factories. With the slow growth of the social conscience, books with Marxist flavor were translated into Japanese. After 1892 Socialist magazines were founded. In 1898 a small group, including some Christians, established the Society for the Study of Socialism. Early Socialist endeavors bore fruit by the turn of the century, and more labor unions were organized in the railroads and in the iron works. In 1901 the Social Democratic Party was formed, but the government ordered it dissolved within three hours of its founding. A journal, *Heimin Shimbun (Common People's Newspaper)*, was founded in 1904. It managed to eke out a precarious six-year existence, although it was suppressed from time to time. Protest action by the lower classes was something new in Japan, and the government remained alert to any flare-ups. By 1911 twenty-three leading Socialists had been tried and twelve executed. Leaders temporarily disappeared, to emerge in the more liberal decade of the 1920's with greater influence in intellectual and academic circles, especially among faculties in economics and in history.

Other secular aspects of modernization made more visible impact. Foreigners started the first modern press in Japan in English, but in 1870, in Yokohama the first regular Japanese daily, the *Mainichi*, was issued. Nine years later the *Asahi* chain was established, and into contemporary times the two proved to be the zaibatsu of the newspaper industry. To help rid the country of unequal treaties, the government embarked on legal reforms. Individual, rather than joint family, ownership of property was provided for, but census statistics continued to recognize the validity of the old extended family as the appropriate demographic base of society. Laws were publicized, torture was abolished, and law court procedures were modeled after Western practices. Legal reforms proceeded on a piecemeal basis, but those which did not rest on popular acceptance or on understanding proved ineffectual and were dropped. By the turn of the century the three basic law codes of a modern state—

criminal, civil, and commercial—had been adopted. In 1873 the Gregorian calendar with its seven-day week and Sunday holiday was adopted.

In the earlier decades of the Meiji a mania for Westernized customs developed in urban society. The Charter Oath stipulation of 1868 that "evil customs" had to go was taken literally. Buddhists took wives, raised families, and ate beef (*sukiyaki* was supposedly invented because of the Western taste for meat dishes). Instead of wearing the traditional long hair done up in a top knot, men cut their hair. Married women stopped blackening their teeth and shaving their eyebrows. Sensitivity to Western opinion and desire to follow the latest fads stimulated extremes, but by 1885 the irrational imbalance for things Western was countered by a conservative reaction. Superficial Westernized customs, such as ballroom dancing and costume parties, were discarded, while the more lasting and significant imported technological and scientific innovations lost their onus of association with trivial Occidental peculiarities. Perspective was regained, and although Western influence continued to be strong, it was opposed in some quarters and more rationally evaluated in others.

Meiji literature reflected the impact of Western thought. Translations of European and American classics were popular, although many translators were students rather than professional writers. A creative native style developed in the novel. During the early restoration years, novelists treated political themes, but with the advent of the constitution they redirected their talents to other themes. One familiar literary strain portrayed the tensions of modernization. With pressures on individuals and families, cultural schizophrenia resulted in the main characters, for modern and traditional values were in conflict. In the late nineteenth century, prominent themes of novels were pessimism and inaction. A typical Meiji novel might portray a hero, a sensitive soul, perhaps an artist with aspirations and individual goals, trying to meet and to resolve conflicting social and family demands made upon him. Self-doubt and self-denial complicate the resolution of his problems, and the hero, brooding on the bitterness and complexity of life, Hamlet-like lapses into paralysis and indecision.

CHRONOLOGY

1868   Fukuzawa Yukichi founds Keio University
1870   *Mainichi,* first Japanese newspaper, issued
1871   Ministry of Education established; currency reforms
1872   First railroad, Tokyo to Yokohama
1873   Land tax framed; ban on Christianity removed; Gregorian calendar adopted
1875   Doshisha University established in Kyoto
1877   Tokyo Imperial University founded
1879   *Asahi* newspaper chain founded
1882   Okuma establishes Waseda University
1888   Society for the Study of Socialism created
1890   Imperial Rescript on official goals of education
1901   Social Democratic Party founded
1904   *Heimin Shimbun* founded

XIII

MEIJI JAPAN: (3) FOREIGN RELATIONS

The energy devoted to strengthening the nation was also reflected in the creation of the foundations of empire. Taking the cue from the imperialist tenor of the times at the turn of the century, Japan embarked on two major wars, one with China (1894–1895)ʾ and one with Russia (1904–1905). As a result, it gained territorial acquisitions on mainland Asia and offshore islands. In 1910, after long careful periods of watchful waiting and careful diplomatic maneuvering, it annexed Korea. It came to diplomatic accommodation with the major European powers as well as with the United States. By 1911, all the unequal treaties had been terminated and replaced by others based on equality.

Background

Prior to the restoration, in the latter years of seclusion, there were individuals in Japan who had urged a vigorous continental policy.

Russia's march eastward across Siberia awakened fears, and some Japanese had early advocated the acquisition of Kamchatka peninsula and Sakhalin Island. Others, including Yoshida Shoin, advocated the seizure of Formosa, Korea, Manchuria, and the Philippines as well. After the restoration, although the primary concern was with charting domestic affairs, a concurrent military build-up laid the basis for the initial acquisition of territories of the islands surrounding Japan and on the Asian mainland.

Essential in a world of force was reliance on force, some Japanese argued, which could be used either for self-defense purposes or for supporting foreign conquests. The conscript laws of the early 1870's made youths liable for seven years of service—three on active duty, two years in the first reserve, followed by another two in the second reserve. European uniforms were adopted, foreign advisers were hired, and, because of German military successes in Europe, the Japanese army modeled itself after Prussian organization and discipline. The country was divided into six military districts, and an efficient standing army of 400,000 was attained around the turn of the century. In 1869 a naval training station was created in Tokyo with English advisers and instruction in English, since England was the leading naval power of the day. In another six years, Japan had her own naval academy, arsenal, and naval medical facilities. She had constructed her first war vessel at Yokosuka near Yokohama but still depended upon the use of foreign ships and torpedo boats against the Chinese and the Russians in later campaigns.

As Japan built up her army, she sought to terminate the unequal treaties with the West. As early as 1872, Iwakura Tomomi, a court noble, was sent abroad to negotiate treaty revision. His mission was not successful since Japan had not taken enough strides toward modernization to please the Western powers. A decade later, the foreign minister called a conference of interested parties to give up their rights regarding extraterritoriality and tariff controls. This move also was not successful. The foreign office then proceeded to negotiate individually with the respective powers on revisions, and it made some progress. In 1888 Mexico, although a minor power, gave up extraterritoriality and recognized Japan's tariff autonomy. In 1894 treaties with Great Britain and the United States, to be effective in five years if other powers took similar steps, were signed abolishing extraterritoriality and the most-favored-nation clauses and providing for reciprocal rights of travel, residence, navigation, and religion. By 1899 Japan was the first Asian country to free itself of extraterritoriality; in 1911 Japan had resumed complete control of its own tariff schedules. By this time, Europeans and Americans had been favorably impressed with the rapid strides made by the Japanese in modernizing, and they were willing to give up their rights when the legal and administrative systems in Japan approximated their own. The Meiji leaders had won their point. In following Western models, they had eliminated special Western privileges.

Japan also turned to overseas expansion. Within a decade of the restoration, Japan's borders had widened. More complete control was imposed on the island of Yezo or Hokkaido. Under the Tokugawa, Yezo had been a daimyo fief and few Japanese lived there. Now the economic development of the island was encouraged, and American experts were employed to assist in the development of that frontier area. Further north, Japanese landed on the Kuriles and Sakhalin, where they encountered Russian rivalry. In 1858 temporary accommodation had been reached between the two powers in a treaty that declared joint possession of Sakhalin. Later, the Tokugawa shogun proposed a division of the island at the fiftieth parallel, but no agreement was reached on the issue. In the post-restoration period, another compromise was sought. In an 1875 treaty, Japan surrendered its claims to Sakhalin, and Russia in turn surrendered its claims to the Kuriles, and so Japan acquired legal title to that island chain. In 1878 the Bonins, a desolate island group in the Pacific but with potential strategic importance, were also annexed. Two years later they were incorporated into the Tokyo metropolitan prefecture.

Japan, Korea, and China

Japan then came into collision with China, first in the Ryukyus and Formosa and then in Korea. To the south, the Ryukyus, claimed by China, were absorbed into the growing empire. In an anomalous situation, the inhabitants of that archipelago were related to the Japanese by blood, and for two centuries they had been considered part of the Satsuma fief. But they had also paid tribute to China through their ruler, who, moreover, had entered on his own into treaty relations with Western representatives including Perry. The Japanese forced the complicated issue of sovereignty over the islands. In 1871 some shipwrecked Ryukyuans were massacred by aborigines on the east coast of Taiwan (Formosa), which was claimed also by China. The next year, Japan took action against the Chinese by formally annexing the Ryukyus. Only after some delay, in 1874, did she dispatch a punitive force to Taiwan itself. Encountering superior military might, the Chinese settled the dispute by paying Japan an indemnity for the costs of the expedition as well as for the murdered Ryukyuans. The Japanese then left Taiwan. China eventually gave up its claims to the Ryukyus, but the Japanese were to return within two decades in force to reoccupy Taiwan.

To the west, Japan like China had long historic interests in Korea. The ancient Yamato sovereigns had planted colonies on the southern Korean coast. For centuries there was close contact and transmission of ideas between China and Japan through Korea. Hideyoshi had tried to conquer Korea and incorporate her into Japan. During the early seventeenth century and into the nineteenth, Korea enjoyed commercial relations with both Japan and China. Korea had always been important geographically. The peninsula commanded the sea approach to Manchuria, eastern Siberia, and north China. In the hands of a strong power, it could be a "dagger pointed at the heart of Japan."

In early Meiji times, a new wave of interest was directed toward the mainland. Western powers were encroaching in Korea; France, Great Britain, and the United States were interested in trade; Russia, through treaties with the Manchu rulers of China, had extended her borders to the Pacific. Ever-present China was also involved in Korean politics, and in the first half of the nineteenth century Korea was more an appendage of China than of Japan, despite the weakness of the former country. China, who had been in and out of Korea since the second century B.C., did not easily surrender her rights and claims of suzerainty. To complicate matters, against the background of international competition for Korea, the country was weak internally. The Yi dynasty was in its final stages. Its officials were backward, conservative, sterile, and quite unable to discern winds of change. Korea truly lived up to her name, the "Hermit Kingdom."

The early policy (1868–1876) of the Meiji leaders was to establish the fact of Korean independence and sovereignty and so eliminate Chinese influence. They sent commissioners to investigate conditions there, and the mission reported that were China to take decisive action, Korea might become subject to a foreign power. While China disclaimed any responsibility for acts by the Koreans, the Chinese declared, anomalously, that although Korea was nominally a vassal of China, she had the power to make peace and to declare war. In 1874 Korea, in the nebulous status of a semisovereign state, agreed to receive an envoy from Japan and to send one in return.

When the Japanese envoy arrived at Seoul, he was refused an imperial audience. Incidents ensued, and in the following years a Japanese gunboat that was surveying the entrance to the Han River, on which Seoul, the capital, was located, was fired upon. After demonstrations of Japanese naval force in 1874 and 1875, the Koreans were frightened into signing the Treaty of Kanghwa in February, 1876. This first Korean treaty of modern times, signed with a country itself still chafing under unequal treaties, asserted the independence of Korea (which denied Chinese suzerainty); opened two ports to Japanese trade in addition to Pusan where the Japanese already resided; and provided extraterritorial privileges for Japan. Other powers, including the United States in 1882, followed in concluding similar treaties with Korea.

China refused to recognize the growing Japanese role in Korean affairs. For the next decade (1876–1885) a cold war in Korea ensued between China and Japan. Although the Korean king oriented his policies toward the Japanese, China endeavored to reassert her influence through factions in the Korean court favorable to her. A struggle ensued in Seoul between those who wanted to learn from the West, as Japan had, and those conservatives who desired to resist change, as China was doing. Rivalries beset the court; mob demonstrations got out of hand. In 1882 the palace was attacked and the Japanese legation was damaged. Japan exacted an indemnity, demanded a mission of apology, extracted new privileges, and stationed an army in the capital. In turn, China began to deal more positively in order to keep Korea in her orbit. Chinese troops were likewise augmented, and after clashes with Japanese troops, more turbulence ensued. Ito was dispatched to China to conduct negotiations to resolve peacefully the conflicting Asian interests in Korea. In 1885 a Sino-Japanese convention was signed. Both countries pledged to withdraw troops, and if either side found it necessary to return troops to quell disorders, it had to notify the other concerned power.

The following decade (1885–1895) was marked by uneasy coexistence between China and Japan in Korea. During this interim, more Western powers became involved in Korean affairs, but the chief struggle remained between the two Asian protagonists. Japan was committed to maintain her position in Korea. After the events of the 1880's no Japanese cabinet could have withdrawn from Korea and survived. Yet the truce with China could not last indefinitely. In 1894 one of the many sporadic internal uprisings broke out in Korea. Both China and Japan sent in troops to suppress it. Although the rebellion had terminated before the arrival of either army, more friction resulted between Japan and China. Open hostilities finally broke out in July, 1894, when Japanese ships fired on Chinese warships and on a British merchant ship transporting Chinese troops to Korea. Formal declarations of war followed. The war was brief, and the Chinese were decisively defeated within nine months. Their small fleet was routed, and their armies were quickly expelled from Korea. Japanese troops moved into Manchuria, where they captured the naval base of Port Arthur on Liaotung peninsula in south Manchuria. They occupied as well the naval base of Weihaiwei on Shantung peninsula opposite Manchuria. Now commanding the sea approaches to north China, the Japanese were in a strategic position to move on to the Chinese capital at Peking.

Defeated but haughty, the Chinese sued for peace with a people whom they regarded with contempt. But they sent a top diplomatic envoy, Li Hung-chang, to arrange treaty terms with Japan, which was represented by Ito at the bargaining table. Each delegation had an American adviser. In the course of the negotiations, a Japanese attempted to assassinate Li. Losing face, the Japanese softened somewhat their severe treaty provisions. In the chief terms of the Treaty of Shimonoseki of April, 1895, China recognized Korean independence. She ceded to Japan the Liaotung peninsula, Formosa, and the Pescadores, a small group of islands lying some twenty-five miles off western Formosa. China also paid an indemnity, opened four new treaty ports, extended the most-favored-nation clause, and promised a new treaty of commerce. Japanese troops occupied Formosa, and in October, 1895, a Japanese general set about pacifying the island. The next year a civilian administration was commissioned, and Formosa became an integral part of the Japanese empire.

The Japanese were less successful in retaining the Liaotung peninsula. Within six days of the treaty, Germany, Russia, and France counseled Japan to surrender her claims there, allegedly because Japan's presence would be a menace to Peking and to the independence of Korea. Japan interpreted the act, known in history as the Triple Intervention, as a thinly veiled threat, but she was not strong enough to defy the three European powers. After extracting an additional indemnity from China, Japan acquiesced and withdrew from the Asian mainland. The experience was a bitter one, for it constituted the most humiliating diplomatic defeat for Japan prior to World War II.

Japan, Korea, and Russia

After her defeat in 1895, China was replaced by Russia as the most serious challenger to Japanese interests on the northeastern Asian mainland. Between 1895 and 1904 Russian interests and influence increased in both Manchuria and Korea. Although China had been recently defeated, by the end of 1895 Japan felt less secure in her economic and political interests in China because of Russian presence. The Russians were completing the Trans-Siberian Railroad, which ended in Vladivostok, and in the course of Czar Nicholas II's coronation festivities in St. Petersburg in 1896, they concluded a fifteen-year treaty of alliance with China that pledged Russian protection of China. In return, China granted Russia the right to construct the Chinese Eastern Railroad through northern Manchuria as a short cut to Vladivostok. As Manchuria appeared to be moving into the Russian orbit, so did Korea, because her monarchs now looked to Russian support in order to counterbalance Japanese interests there.

Not desiring war at the time, the Japanese explored alternatives to contain Russia. On this matter, Japanese foreign policy, far from being monolithic or united in character, was flexible and a matter for experimentation and debate. Three points of view emerged from policy discussions on how to contain Russia. One school, which included Fukuzawa Yukichi, advocated an alliance with the British, for England, like Japan, seemed threatened in Asia by Russian expansion. Others, including Okuma, advanced the idea of an alliance with China and Korea. Although it was an unrealistic alternative at the time, Okuma argued that Japan's safety lay not in any alliance with a Western power, which would exploit Japan, but rather with the two mainland powers. The trouble was that both China and Korea were backward and weak, although both had great resources and potential strength. Implicit in Japanese thinking was the idea that China and Korea could be developed under Japanese leadership and direction in a type of Pan-Asian movement. The third view, advanced in 1895 by both Yamagata and Ito before their split, was to seek accommodation with Russia itself and to delineate respective spheres of influence.

The last viewpoint prevailed initially. Japan endeavored to reach a modus vivendi with Russia in Korea, which constituted the more immediate consideration. While in Russia in 1896 for the czar's coronation, Yamagata proposed to the Russians a division of Korea at the 38th parallel. The Russians declined the offer. But that same year Yamagata concluded with the Russian foreign minister an agreement to establish a condominium over Korea. The joint venture did not work out, and in 1898 the Japanese foreign minister concluded with the Russian ambassador in Tokyo an agreement declaring the abstention by both powers from Korean affairs.

Meanwhile, the Russians pushed on in north China and Manchuria. In 1898, as part of a general scramble for concessions, Russia received from China leaseholds on the Kwantung peninsula at the tip of the Liaotung peninsula in south Manchuria, where Port Arthur and Dairen were located. It also received the right to construct a railroad branching from the Chinese Eastern Railroad and cutting across south Manchuria to Port Arthur. Now entrenched in an area from which they had helped to force the Japanese only three years previously, the Russians established a naval base at Port Arthur, and they moved ominously closer to Peking. There, at the turn of the century as a result of the Boxer uprising against the West, the Russians participated in an international expeditionary force that marched on the Chinese capital to quell the rebellion. Their troops remained in the area and in Manchuria until 1902, long after the suppression of the outbreak. Convinced that no accommodation was possible with Russia, the Japanese, who had once advocated a Russian alliance, now began to favor the notion of one with England. Ito held out to the last for an arrangement with Russia.

Desiring to end their isolation, advance their interests in Korea, and contain Russia, the Japanese negotiated with the British, who in turn envisioned Japan as a counterpoise to Russia in Asia. Fearful that Japan might ally herself with Russia against their own interests, the British in 1902 concluded with the newly rising Asian power the ten-year Anglo-Japanese alliance, thereby ending centuries of "splendid isolation." Its terms confirmed the integrity of China and of Korea, although Britain recognized special Japanese interests in Korea. The two signatories affirmed neutrality in the event that one of them was engaged in war with a third party, but each would aid the other if either were attacked by two or more other powers. Three years later, in a revision of the alliance, Britain recognized the paramount rights of Japan in Korea, and each now pledged to aid the other should either be attacked by only one other power. Renewed in 1911 for another decade, the Anglo-Japanese alliance survived until the Washington Conference of 1921–1922, when it was replaced by the Four Power Treaty, with France and the United States as additional subscribers.

Despite the alliance with the British, in 1903 and 1904 the Japanese continued efforts toward rapprochement with Russia. They suggested a Russia-in-Manchuria swap for Japan-in-Korea, an arrangement recognizing Russian supremacy in Manchuria and Japanese predominance in Korea, but the Russians stalled. The conflicting positions relative to political paramountcy in Manchuria and Korea finally erupted in war. On February 6, 1904, the Japanese severed relations with Russia. Two days later they torpedoed the Russian fleet at Port Arthur, and on the fifth day they declared war. Segments of the United States press termed the sequence of events as "bold initiative." The Russians sent troops into Manchuria and Korea and dispatched their Baltic fleet halfway around the world to Korea, only to be destroyed by Admiral Togo Nakagoro in a great battle in the Tsushima straits off Kyushu. In the eighteen months' war, major battles were fought in Manchuria on Chinese soil. The military engagements ended in stalemate, and the Japanese asked President Theodore Roosevelt to mediate. The Russians accepted the proffered mediation, and both belligerent parties met at Portsmouth, New Hampshire, to conduct peace negotiations.

The Treaty of Portsmouth of September, 1905, reflected the stalemated military situation. Japanese demands were not fully met. Japan received not all but only the southern half of Sakhalin. She did not get an indemnity and did not acquire the coveted Maritime Provinces along the Siberian Pacific coast. But, subject to China's consent, Japan succeeded to the twenty-five year Russian territorial, railroad, and commercial leases in the Kwantung peninsula and in south Manchuria. The Russians also acknowledged Korean independence. Despite the restraints of the treaty, Japan was strengthened in Asia and achieved the status of a world power. Commencing as the underdog in the war, she emerged with prestige. Japan fired the imagination of Asia, for here at last was an Asian power fighting a white power on an equal basis. Asian nationalists took heart, while the Western powers, including the United States, began to reevaluate their positions in a changing Asia.

The 1905 Peking treaty with China confirmed the Portsmouth concessions in south Manchuria, and the agreement laid the legal foundations for Japanese economic and political growth there and in north China. In 1906 Japan created the South Manchurian Railroad, which became the chief agent of Japanese penetration in that area. Japan not only operated the railway, but also managed mines, hotels, schools, hospitals, ships, and research institutes. She stationed troops to maintain security, and over the years, these troops increased vastly in number until they were designated in time the Kwantung army. A governor-general ruled the Kwantung leased areas. Port Arthur became a strong naval base, and in the adjacent free port of Dairen a Chinese official collected the customs tariff under Japanese aegis. Pushed out of Manchuria in 1895 by the Triple Intervention, the Japanese in 1905 returned for a longer stay.

Japan, Korea, and World Powers

The Treaty of Portsmouth recognized Japan's paramount interests in Korea as well. In late 1905 Ito went to Seoul to negotiate a treaty which transformed Korea into a Japanese protectorate. Korean foreign relations came under Japanese management, and a Japanese resident-general, of whom Ito was the first, was stationed in the capital. Ito launched reforms, but complaining of the slow pace of modernization, he forced the abdication of the Korean king. In 1907 a new Japanese-Korean agreement was signed that placed in Japanese hands the administration of all important affairs of state, official appointments and dismissals, and all laws. The Korean army was disbanded. Finally, on August 22, 1910, a treaty of annexation terminated Korean sovereignty. The country, now a colony of Japan, was renamed Chosen. Japanese divisions were stationed there, and subsequently, the government of the country was placed under a Japanese general. Chosen became the Japanese headquarters on the Asian mainland.

Korea played a key role in the Japanese movement into China, as had Formosa in southward expansion. To Korea, the Japanese brought law, order, and prosperity, but all efforts were made for Japanese benefit. In the regimented colony, rice production increased, the fish catch in Korean waters quadrupled, and reforestation proceeded. Economic gains were noticeable, but the Koreans did not participate in them. In a double standard of wages and opportunities, the Japanese got the better jobs and offices. Study of the Japanese language was made compulsory for Koreans. Hatred of Japan became widespread, but rebellion was impossible because of military controls. Some anti-Japanese leaders, such as Syngman Rhee, left the country. They took up residence abroad, to continue the fight against Japanese rule over their homeland.

Having confirmed its paramount position in south Manchuria and Korea, Japan came to terms with the leading European powers. With Britain there were no problems, for the alliance sealed diplomatic friendship. With France, there were no disputes, although Japan had resented the Triple Intervention. After England had signed the Entente Cordiale with France, Japan also came to an agreement with the French. In 1907 an agreement signed in Paris pledged mutual respect for Chinese independence and territory, and Japanese in Indo-China and Indo-Chinese in Japan were to be accorded most-favored-nation status.

The Russians did not remain enemies. With czarist Russia, Japan concluded four agreements to delineate respective spheres of influence in east Asia. In 1907 two conventions, one public and one secret, were signed. The former constituted a routine reaffirmation of the Open Door policy in China, while the latter divided Manchuria into two spheres of special jurisdiction, Japan in the south and Russia in the north. Japan also recognized the primary interests of Russia in Outer Mongolia, while Russia accepted Japan's position in Korea. In 1910 the two parties agreed to consult each other on effective measures in case the status quo in east Asia were threatened. In addition to north Manchuria, in 1912 Russia was allotted the area of western Inner Mongolia as its place of influence and eastern Inner Mongolia was added to Japan's. In 1916, with Russia bogged down in World War I, Japan pledged munitions and supplies to Russia, and the signatories promised not to be a party to any arrangement or treaty directed against the other. A secret convention also established a five-year defensive alliance, and the two nations pledged mutual assistance should war result from the defense of their interests in China and border areas. By World War I Japan had swung Russia, as well as England and France, into support of its policy of expansion on the Asian continent.

The story was otherwise with regard to the United States, for a change took place in Japanese-American relations. Prior to 1905, they had been cordial. The United States did not intervene in the Sino-Japanese War. Its sympathies were with the Japanese in the war with Russia, and in 1905 it closed its embassy in Seoul and dealt with the Koreans through the Japanese. In return, Japan looked on the United States as the one great Western power from which it had nothing to fear. Japanese students came to the United States. American markets sopped up Japanese tea and raw silk, and the Japanese in turn bought American cotton, machine goods, and raw materials.

The tide turned after 1905. Although some Japanese blamed the United States for the compromised terms of the Treaty of Portsmouth, more serious and long-range problems were emerging. The issue of Japanese immigration into the United States was becoming a diplomatic question. Unskilled Japanese coming to the west coast, where they received low wages, alarmed labor leaders, who claimed that American workers could not compete on similar terms. (Census statistics for 1900 revealed 80,000 Japanese in Hawaii and 24,000 in the United States compared with 90,000 Chinese in the territorial United States). In 1900 Tokyo imposed restrictions on emigration to the United States, and in 1907 the government concluded with Washington a gentleman's agreement to prevent more laborers from emigrating.

Americans formulated more extreme measures. In 1905 in San Francisco a league to exclude Japanese and Koreans was organized. The next year San Francisco school officials attempted to segregate Japanese students, who numbered only eighty, from American pupils. President Theodore Roosevelt interfered, and the idea was dropped but on the condition that the federal government stop immigration of Japanese into the continental United States from Hawaii, Mexico, and Canada. These discriminatory moves occurred at the same time as the San Francisco earthquake and fire, disasters in which the Japanese Red Cross contributed very heavily in relief measures. In 1907 the Congress passed an act authorizing the president to prevent further immigration, and the president by proclamation then prohibited Japanese movement from Hawaii, Mexico, and Canada.

Power politics complicated immigration matters. Now committed in the Philippines, wrested from Spain in 1898, the United States was concerned with possible Japanese thrusts toward the archipelago, which Roosevelt termed an "Achilles heel." Washington was also pledged to maintain the open door of equal commercial opportunity and treaty rights in China. In attempting to preserve Philippine territory and Chinese treaty rights, United States policies toward Japan became contradictory. Endeavoring to contain Japan's commercial and financial expansion, Secretary of State Frank Knox in 1909 proposed the purchase by China of Japanese and Russian railroads in Manchuria with funds provided by those powers that had pledged to uphold the open door. The neutralization proposal called for the operation of the railroads by an international board until China could repay the international loan. The Japanese and the Russians found this unacceptable, and the suggestion tended instead to throw the Japanese and the Russians closer together (the 1910 treaty reflected their concern about encroachment on Manchurian interests).

On the other hand, American policy seemed to accept Japanese territorial expansion. Agreements in 1905 between Secretary of War

William H. Taft and Prime Minister Katsura in Tokyo and in 1908 between Secretary of State Elihu Root and the Japanese ambassador Baron Takahira in Washington confirmed Japan's paramount position in Korea, while Japan affirmed that she had no designs on the Philippines. Despite these temporizing arrangements, Japan was coming more and more into conflict with the United States over mutual Asian territorial and commercial concerns. The disparate positions of Americans, who advocated equal treaty rights (implied in the Open Door policy), and of Japanese, who advanced special rights, in time escalated and finally culminated in war. Ironically, the country that had introduced Japan to Western ways was to receive the brunt of Japanese modernization in its military manifestation.

CHRONOLOGY

1858	Russian-Japanese joint occupation of Sakhalin
1872	Iwakura mission abroad to end unequal treaties; Ryukyus annexed
1874	Taiwan incident; Ryukyu indemnity paid by China
1875	Japan gives up Sakhalin; Russia gives up Kuriles
1876	Treaty of Kanghwa with Korea
1878	Japan acquires the Bonins
1885	Sino-Japanese convention on Korea
1894–1895	Sino-Japanese war
1895	Treaty of Shimonoseki; Triple Intervention
1896	Japanese-Russian condominium over Korea
1898	Japanese-Russian abstention in Korean affairs
1899	Japan frees self of extraterritoriality
1902	Anglo-Japanese Alliance
1904–1905	Russo-Japanese war
1905	Treaty of Portsmouth; Anglo-Japanese Alliance amended; Peking treaty with China confirming Portsmouth; Korea a Japanese protectorate; Taft-Katsura notes
1906	South Manchurian Railway created
1907	French-Japanese treaty on reciprocal rights of citizens; Russo-Japanese treaty on Manchurian spheres; gentleman's agreement with United States
1908	Root-Takahira understanding
1909	Knox proposal of railroad neutralization in Manchuria
1910	Korea becomes a Japanese colony; Russo-Japanese treaty to keep status quo
1911	Japan resumes tariff control; Anglo-Japanese alliance renewed
1912	Russo-Japanese agreement on Inner Mongolia spheres
1916	Russo-Japanese treaty of aid and moral support

~~~ XIV

IMPERIAL JAPAN (1912–1922):
WORLD POWER

The story of imperial Japan in the three and a half decades between the death of the Meiji emperor and the end of World War II is one of political success distorted into military failure. The only non-Western country to meet the modernizing challenge of the Occident, Japan continued its spectacular progress, which was initiated in the Meiji period, well into the 1930's.

After the death of Emperor Meiji in 1912, his son ascended the throne and inaugurated the Taisho ("Great Righteousness") period. His reign, which lasted to 1926, has been called Taisho democracy by Japanese historians because of the relative liberalism of the times. Concurrent with the accession to the throne of a new emperor was the termination of the alternating premierships of Saionji and Katsura. The cycles came to an end the following year, accompanied by outbursts and rioting by mobs, which surrounded the Diet building and demanded the end of genro rule. An admiral was next designated as prime minister, but when the navy was implicated in financial scandals relating to battleship construction, the Diet refused to pass the budget, and the prime minister resigned. In 1914, Okuma, now eighty years of age, in command of a new coalition party, the Kenseikai, assumed the post. The aging aristocrat, earlier a champion of representative government, led an administration marked by unprecedented chauvinistic nationalism.

This included the presentation of the Twenty-One Demands to China, an action which resulted in the strengthening of the military.

After two years in office, Okuma was replaced by Marshal Terauchi Seiki, a general and former governor-general of Korea. His term was marked by domestic wartime problems, profiteering, inflated prices, and widespread rioting over the high price of rice. In 1918, his cabinet fell, and Hara Kei (or Takashi), head of the Seiyukai, the majority party, in parliament, became prime minister. Except for the brief interlude of the Okuma-Itagaki party coalition in 1898, Hara Kei was the first party man, and the first commoner, to be prime minister. His appointment was epochal, for it heralded the end of rule by the genro and the beginning of rule by party politicians, the men of new Japan in commerce, industry, and finance. Party government, with interruption between 1922 and 1924, lasted until 1932.

Background

Further changes brought with them new and urgent problems, fresh leadership, but divided counsels. For in the first half of the twentieth century, the sons and grandsons of the Meiji reformers lived in a world different from that of their forebears. The second and third generations had to face and to resolve such pressing issues as providing employment and benefits for a burgeoning population, increasing food imports, regulating economic cycles, achieving military security in an ever-growing empire, and adjusting to the social and intellectual ramifications of modernization. National wealth increased but all groups, particularly the tenant farmers and factory workers, did not share proportionately in the increase.

As new groups emerged and the political structure was rearranged, a larger and more diverse leadership replaced the smaller, unified Meiji oligarchy. The new elites included the military, the bureaucracy, the political parties, the zaibatsu, the middle classes, and the various legal and nonlegal bodies close to the emperors. The emperors themselves became more symbolic and more removed from decision-making procedures. With no strong and effective mechanisms for settling disagreements among the various factions, except for each to claim that it spoke in the name of the emperor, these forces operated in countervailing fashion through the 1920's, although by the end of the next decade predominance was gained by the military.

Plural political elites were accompanied by plural political philosophies. A growing liberal strain of opinion, spearheaded by Minobe Tatsukichi, professor of administrative law at Tokyo Imperial University between 1900 and 1932, implied that the emperor was only the highest organ of the state rather than an absolute independent entity. His theory had some acceptance among intellectuals of the 1920's, but traditional views continued to be strong. Kokutai, or national policy, continued to emphasize the uniqueness of Japan, its strong moral base, its familial character, and its Shinto statism. This more extreme position eventually won out in the 1930's, because advantages were passing to rightist civilian and military groups at a time when Japan was becoming more responsive both to forces from the outside world and to internal reactions to these external forces. For too long, Japan existed in a compromised world of restrictions and of partial freedoms, in a delicate balance of authoritarianism and liberalism.

Japan's economy, despite fluctuations, continued to expand. By the turn of the century, a firm basis had been laid for modern industrial development. A few indices revealed continued expansion. Between 1914 and 1930, production of raw materials went up 46 per cent, and in the last half of the 1920's the overall increase in economic productivity reached 59 per cent. Gains provided an impetus for further growth. From an exporter of raw and semi-processed materials during the Meiji period, Japan was transformed into a producer of finished goods. Newly acquired colonies and expanding foreign markets, particularly in south Manchuria and in north China after 1905, helped to sustain the growing economy, but they contributed only a small percentage of total Japanese raw materials and of the ratio of foreign trade. Yet the psychological awareness of economic dependence on overseas areas became more intense as the decades progressed. As Japan industrialized, she became more tied to world trade, and she experienced the modern capitalistic phenomenon of booms and recessions. In part because of an overambitious rate of industrial investment and of official expenditures that helped to create a lopsided and top-heavy government sector in the mixed economy, by 1913 the Japanese economy was floundering.

The advent of World War I helped to bail the country out of its economic doldrums. The war diverted the industry of European competitors to production of armaments and industries, while Japan's arms production was considerably smaller. Her military participation was limited and allowed her to continue the industrialization process. Japan was virtually free to produce for

Asian markets and to make inroads into European and African markets. She displaced Great Britain as the chief foreign economic power in China and by filling Allied war orders changed from a debtor to a creditor nation. But a year or so after the end of the war, deflation set in, prices collapsed, and government expenses declined.

As Japan broadened its domestic base, so it expanded abroad. Imperial Japan capitalized on its pre-eminence in Asia to consolidate either forcibly or peacefully territorial and diplomatic gains achieved during World War I. She displayed tractability in foreign affairs of the 1920's in several major instances. She pulled out of Siberia after the Russian Revolution and the subsequent intervention there. She agreed to the arrangements of the Washington Conference of 1921–1922, which reduced her naval strength considerably.

The foreign policy of imperial Japan was concerned essentially with China. Japan's paramount interests were centered on the Asian mainland, where they were facing crises by the end of the Meiji period. In China, the two-and-a-half-century rule of the Manchus, the last of some two dozen traditional dynasties in Chinese history, was coming to an end. China's political order, weakened in the nineteenth century by internal decay and external forces, was collapsing, and the empire, which dated to the third century B.C., came abruptly to an end in 1912. The Manchus were replaced by a nominal republic, headed by a warlord, established in Peking that same year. Recognized by Japan and the Western powers, it did not command universal Chinese loyalty. In south China, a rival government was established, and other warlords operated independently throughout the country. Instability in Chinese politics implied difficulties in the preservation of Japanese economic privileges in the chaotic country. And the Japanese had great interest in China and in Manchuria, considered a part of China but under the rule of a warlord. One-fifth of Japanese capital was invested in Manchurian industries, and the same proportion of Japanese imports, including necessary iron and coal, came from China. Extensive investment was augmented by psychological commitment as well, for the Japanese envisioned limitless resources and endless markets in China.

In order to preserve Japanese economic rights in a politically confused China, several possibilities were open to Japan. She could practice, on the one hand, a policy of nonintervention in internal Chinese affairs and wait "until the dust settled." The advantage of such a policy was to avoid identification with any of the several Chinese factions contending for eventual mastery over all of the country. The disadvantage was that Japanese interests might suffer in a chaotic interim of indefinite tenure. On the other hand, Japan could pursue a policy of intervention. She could encourage revolution in China and by backing some Chinese faction she could shift the balance of power in its favor. As a third tactical move, a combination of the two policies could be achieved by treating China and Manchuria separately with interference condoned only in the more economically important Manchuria. The last policy eventually won out in the 1920's, but prior to that time, in the course of World War I and in the postwar settlements, Japan fished most extensively in the muddied Chinese waters.

Japan and World War I

Japan entered World War I essentially for two reasons: specifically to honor commitments under the Anglo-Japanese alliance and broadly to extend her Asian interests. According to the terms of the alliance, as amended in 1911, each signatory was to support the other if it were attacked by a third party. When Great Britain entered the war, the Japanese, recalling their obligation, as well as Germany's role in the Triple Intervention of 1895, pressed for war. But Britain, realizing that Japan could expand its Asian operations (which did occur, since Japan took over the German islands in the central Pacific), was cautious in invoking the alliance. Japan went ahead on her own and served an ultimatum to Germany demanding the surrender of German interests in Shantung, which was a peninsula and province in north China opposite south Manchuria. Britain could not restrain Japan, the protesting but weak Chinese tried to but were powerless to act, and the Americans remained neutral. Japan declared war, hostilities erupted in a one-sided war, and the Japanese unilaterally took over German rights in China. Granted to Germany through unequal treaties by a powerless China, Germany's rights in Shantung were extensive. The more important provisions included a ninety-nine year lease on Kiaochow Bay, with its fine modernized port city of Tsingtao; an approximately thirty-mile wide belt around the bay where foreign troops could be deployed; the operation of a railroad between Tsingtao and Tsinan, the inland capital of the province; the right to mine coal within ten miles of the railroad; and the previous consultation of China with Germany, and now Japan, on any decisions affecting Shantung.

Firmly ensconced in Shantung, a province particularly important to the Chinese because it was the home of Confucius, their greatest sage, Japan made further demands on China. The most extreme of these were presented in January, 1915, to the Peking government by Okuma's cabinet. Known collectively as the Twenty-One Demands, they indicated the extent of Japanese interest in China and had they all been granted, China would have become a Japanese protectorate. The demands were grouped into five categories. Group One confirmed Japan's newly won rights in Shantung, and Japan was to consent to any future disposition of them. This precluded a German return to Shantung after the war. The Japanese were adamant on this point because the previous humiliation of the Triple Intervention and the compromises of the Treaty of Portsmouth still rankled Japanese foreign policy makers. Group Two related to Japan's position in south Manchuria and in eastern Mongolia. Japan demanded that the leaseholds, shortly to expire, of Port Arthur, Dairen, and the South Manchurian Railroad, be extended from twenty-five to ninety-nine years. She also sought more extensive economic and residence rights for her citizens in eastern Mongolia and in south Manchuria (Russian interests in the Chinese Eastern Railroad continued in north Manchuria).

Group Three of the Demands dealt with a program to promote Japanese industrial activity in the central Yangtze valley by giving the Han Yeh-p'ing Company, a Sino-Japanese concern, the mining monopoly of iron and coal property in central China. Group Four concerned the nonalienation of Chinese coastal territory. Group Five included a variety of demands, designated by the Japanese as "requests": the hiring of Japanese as advisers, the granting of interior lands to Japanese individuals and groups, the placing of Chinese police under joint administration in designated areas, Chinese purchases of arms from Japan, the extension of railway concessions in south China, and the "right of preaching in China."

Presented secretly, the terms of the Demands were leaked by Peking, and resulted in strong world reaction. But the European powers were engaged in a desperate conflict, and while the Chinese protested, they could only modify some of the demands. From Washington, Secretary of State William Jennings Bryan informed both Japan and China that the United States would not recognize any agreement that impaired United States treaty rights or the rights of its citizens in China, that impinged upon the political or territorial integrity of the Republic of China, or that abrogated the international policy relative to China commonly designated as the Open Door. Faced with some opposition in China and abroad, the Japanese in an agreement of May, 1915, received only part of their demands. Of these, the more important included the German leaseholds in Shantung, which were to be returned to China after the war but on the condition of the recognition of Shantung as a Japanese sphere of influence, the extension of Manchurian leaseholds to ninety years, and the right of Japan to be consulted first in case China required foreign capital to develop railways or harbors in Fukien province, located across the straits from the Japanese colony of Formosa. By pressing extreme demands and realizing only part of them, the Japanese lost face in China and redirected their efforts towards Manchuria. On the other hand, the Demands helped to crystallize Chinese national consciousness and sharpened Chinese distrust for Japan.

Buffeted in China, Japan pressed for advantages at the Versailles Conference after the war. There the Japanese delegation presented at least three items for the agenda which were of paramount importance to them: the cession of the former German islands in the Pacific which Japan was occupying (the Marianas, Carolines, and Marshalls), the confirmation of claims to the former German rights in Shantung, and a declaration of racial equality in the Covenant of the proposed League of Nations. In none of these areas did the Japanese wholly succeed. At Versailles, President Woodrow Wilson, unhappy over the necessity of granting Pacific islands to Japan, agreed to a mandate system, which gave Japan supervisory control, subject to League consent, over the islands but which was hardly distinguishable from annexation. Wilson compromised on mandates rather than colonies for Japan, because he had been forced by the insistence of Australia and New Zealand that they be awarded some of the German territories, which they occupied, preferably also as colonies. Japan's position was strengthened by the fact that in early 1917 she had concluded secret agreements (of which Wilson may not have had any knowledge) with Great Britain, France, Italy, and Russia, all of whom promised to support Japan's claims at the peace table. The administrative distinction was fine, but despite allied support, in the end Japan got mandates rather than colonies, with theoretical responsibility to the League for their administration.

Japan also wanted the former German rights in Shantung. The problem became complicated, for although Japan was determined to retain these rights, the Chinese were equally determined not to grant them. The Chinese delegation, while representing divided political factions at home, were united at Versailles on this issue. The members of the delegation, representing a young, progressive, idealistic, nationalistic, and revolutionary China, were adamant in opposing the Japanese claims. Japan's legal position in Shantung, on the other hand, had recently (September, 1918) been bolstered by an agreement, not concluded under duress, with the conservative warlord Peking government, which explicitly consented to the transfer of Kiaochow to Japan on the understanding that Japan would restore the leaseholds to China and would retain only certain rights. Caught between Chinese and Japanese adamance, Wilson took a middle stand on the issue. The Shantung properties were awarded to Japan, but, under Wilson's insistence, Japan declared that she would return them to China and would retain only certain of the rights. Japan remained unsatisfied and China, annoyed, refused to sign the Versailles Treaty and concluded a separate peace treaty with the Central powers.

Finally, Japan, a rising nonwhite world power, was sensitive to racial slights and asked that a declaration of racial equality among states be stated as a basic principle of the League of Nations. This proved to be a "hot potato." Japan did not get the declaration, and the rebuff struck deep resentment. Initially, Wilson appeared to favor this statement in the Covenant, as did France and Italy. But Australia, which excluded nonwhite immigration, vigorously opposed it. Britain, caught between ties of empire and the Japanese alliance, supported the former. Moreover, Wilson had second thoughts, for some state laws, such as those of California, forbade ownership of land by aliens ineligible for citizenship, who included the Japanese and other Asians. In Washington senatorial resistance to granting Japanese racial equality might defeat the Covenant, the president argued.

The Japanese, encountering a mixed response, then modified their request by asking for the endorsement of the principles of equality and just treatment of nations in the preamble, rather than in the operative text, of the Covenant. The amendment to effect this change was passed, 11 to 6, by the commission preparing the Covenant, but Wilson, the chairman, ruled that since the vote was not unanimous, the amendment did not carry. The Japanese had lost another round. Yet, despite setbacks, Japan gained appreciably from her participation in World War I. She expanded her territory and acquired more rights in China. With no great expenditure of troops or of armaments and with fighting confined to the Far East, gains had been achieved at slight cost.

As the war came to an end, international complications concurrently arose in Manchuria and in Siberia as a result of the Russian Revolution. In July, 1918, Japanese troops marched into north Manchuria to take over the Russian-administered Chinese Eastern Railroad on the pretext that peace of the region was threatened by the possible attempts of the Bolsheviks or Germans to enter the region in pursuit of anti-Bolshevik or White Russian forces that had fled there. The United States protested Japanese actions, but not desiring Chinese sovereignty over the railroad either, she solved the dilemma by participating in an interallied board, headed by a distinguished American engineer, to administer the railroad on an interim basis.

Siberia proved stickier. Several White Russian governments in exile, as well as self-appointed empire builders, operated independently in eastern Siberia. Into the political chaos came some fifty thousand Czech troops, who had been prisoners of the Russians or who were deserters from the Austrian armies, wending their way back to Europe via Siberia. On their retreat, they clashed with the Bolsheviks, and although they probably were never in danger of recapture by the Austrians or by the Germans, the Allies thought them endangered, and they tried to enlist them in the Allied side in the European war. In this confused state of affairs, in July, 1918, Wilson reluctantly permitted American participation in the Siberian intervention, ostensibly to save the Czechs but more realistically to prevent Japan from absorbing eastern Siberia. He disavowed intervention in internal Russian affairs.

Some 9000 American troops landed at Vladivostok, as well as a small number of British troops and some Annamese from Indochina under French command. The Japanese dispatched 72,000 men. The Allies took over the management of the Trans-Siberian Railroad, but the American attempts to stop effectively the build-up of Japanese troops failed. In the touch-and-go situation in chaotic Siberia, Japanese were killed by Russians in various incidents. The aftermath of one such incident resulted in the Japanese occupation of the northern half of Sakhalin and a demand for reparations from Russia. Gradually, the Bolsheviks consolidated their hold eastward in Siberia, and, in 1922, it was incorporated into the Soviet Union. By that time, the Americans had long since withdrawn (April, 1920), but the Japanese only left under pressures exerted that year at the Washington Conference.

The Washington Conference

By the time the Washington Conference was convoked in late 1921 to settle Pacific issues generally and to accommodate conflicting Japanese-American problems specifically, many sources of tension had arisen between the two countries. The immigration issue, commercial and naval rivalry, and political problems were the outstanding causes of conflict. In 1917 there had been momentary accommodation when Secretary of State Robert Lansing and the Japanese Ambassador Viscount Ishii Kikujiro, in a controversial exchange of notes in Washington, acknowledged that Japan had priorities in China, since "territorial propinquity creates special relations."

But the bulk of American policies in Asia seemed instead to aim at the containment of Japan. In 1910 Secretary of State Frank Knox had proposed the neutralization of Manchurian railroads. From 1911 to 1913 and again in 1920, the United States had joined multinational railroad consortiums in China to finance railways there and to block further Japanese commercial and financial programs. In 1915 Secretary of State Bryan had proclaimed the nonrecognition of the Twenty-One Demands. At Versailles Wilson did not fully endorse Japanese claims to racial equality, Shantung rights, or Pacific colonies. In 1918 the interallied board was created to manage Manchurian railroads, and the Siberian intervention was joined with the aim of containing Japan.

To resolve peacefully the conflicting national interests in east Asia, the Washington Conference, which met from November, 1921, to February, 1922, under the Harding administration, resulted in seven treaties and twelve resolutions relating to Pacific and Asian affairs. Three treaties were the more important. The Five Power Naval Treaty concerned itself with naval ratios for capital ships (battleships and aircraft carriers) among the leading naval powers of the world. Battleships were limited roughly to this 5:5:3:1.75:1.75 ratio for the powers concerned, respectively the United States, Great Britain, Japan, France, and Italy. Japan insisted that since her navy was especially reduced by this formula, the United States and Great Britain should join her in nonfortification programs to ensure Pacific security.

Accordingly, the three governments incorporated into the Five Power Treaty other provisions prohibiting construction of additional fortifications on certain island possessions. The relevant United States possessions included Wake, Midway, the Aleutians,

Guam, Pago-Pago, and the Philippines. The areas held by Great Britain which were covered by the treaty were Hong Kong and British insular possessions in the Pacific, east of the 110 east longitude, excepting the islands adjacent to Canada, Australia, and New Zealand. The Japanese islands included the Kuriles, Bonins, Ryukyus, Formosa, and the Pescadores. The United States and Great Britain could still fortify the major naval bastions of Hawaii and Singapore, but because of their distance from Japan, the arrangement practically insured Japanese security in the western Pacific.

Another agreement, the Four Power Treaty, replaced the Anglo-Japanese alliance. This alliance, initially aimed at Russia and then Germany, in 1921 could be interpreted as directed against the United States. Americans denounced the existence of the alliance, and strong Canadian protests were added to those of Americans. Canada feared both Japanese immigration and the spectre of involvement in war as a member of the empire on the side of Great Britain allied with Japan against the United States. Canada was not represented at the Conference, but the United States, Great Britain, Japan, and France signed the treaty. The signatories pledged to respect one another's rights in Pacific island possessions, to call joint conferences to solve area questions, and to take common action against any aggressive party. The Four Power Treaty endeavored to freeze the extent of colonial possessions as the Five Power Pact froze certain naval categories and fortifications.

Finally, the Nine Power Treaty, although relating primarily to China, affected Japan. The treaty internationalized the Open Door policy, which stood for equal rather than special treaty rights in China. Also signed by the four other parties with Asian interests at the Conference—China, Belgium, Netherlands, and Portugal—the nine powers agreed to respect the sovereignty, the independence, and the territorial and administrative integrity of China. This was as strong a statement as Japan would commit herself to. The Open Door, a traditional plank in United States foreign policy, was now written into international law.

Other miscellaneous agreements were concluded at the Washington Conference. The Shantung issue, not directly on the agenda, again cropped up. After three dozen Sino-Japanese meetings, at which American and British observers were present, a bilateral treaty between the two concerned powers signed in February, 1922, promised the return of Kiaochow to China, although Japan was to retain control of the Tsinan-Tsingtao railroad for another fifteen years. China got some territory back, but the Japanese retained a measure of economic and political control.

For a decade, the Washington Conference eased tensions in the Pacific and in Asia. However, the implementation of its terms was predicated on good faith, and it was only a matter of time until one party would first terminate the arrangements. As it turned out, Japan did end the agreements, but legally and correctly as provided for in their terms. The fact that Japan could agree to them at all in the early 1920's was a tribute to the statesmanship of the leaders of the political parties which now, for the first time, were beginning to exert influence and direction in foreign and domestic policy.

CHRONOLOGY

1912–1926	Emperor Taisho
1914–1918	Japan in World War I; acquires German Pacific and Chinese rights
1915	Twenty-One Demands presented to China; Bryan's non-recognition doctrine
1917	Lansing-Ishii notes
1918	Hara Kei (Takashi) as party prime minister; Siberian intervention; interallied board takes over Chinese Eastern Railroad; agreement with Peking to retain Shantung rights
1921–1922	Washington Conference: Four, Five, and Nine Power Treaties; Japan-China understanding on Shantung

XV

IMPERIAL JAPAN (1922–1937):
PEACE AND CONFLICT

After making necessary postwar readjustments, Japan experienced again new economic growth in the 1920's, which saw further advances in technology and diversification of industry. The renewed economic expansion permitted both military and industrial activities, and Japan became the third naval power in the world. Its industry was able to support a program of both "guns and butter." Japan recovered from the world depression fairly quickly, in part through the resumption and expansion of foreign trade, the acquisition of more Asian territory, and the increase of military expenditures. The zaibatsu as the handful of giant combines continued to dominate Japan's trade, industry, and commerce at home and abroad, but thousands of tiny workshops, grinding out traditional wares, undergirded what has been called the "double-structure" of the Japanese economy. As the country entered the latter years of the 1930's, the economy became more based on a war footing, and it came to fulfill the Meiji slogan of enriching the nation and strengthening its arms.

The 1920's: Domestic Developments

Paralleling political and economic changes in Japan were liberalizing and modernizing changes that were proceeding in society and in culture, particularly in urban areas, in the early decades of the

twentieth century. The great Tokyo earthquake and fire of September, 1923, abruptly quickened the rate of social and physical
change in the capital. A tremendous cataclysm, in three days of
destruction it exacted a hundred· thousand lives and obliterated
half of Tokyo and most of Yokohama. It helped to eradicate the old
urban areas and laid the groundwork for a new megalopolis. Central
Tokyo was transformed into a city of broad boulevards, flanked by
massive steel and reinforced concrete buildings. Other cities followed Tokyo's lead in a countrywide outburst of urban construction.

But despite modernization, in Japanese society, particularly in
rural areas, some old characteristics survived, such as the importance
of family ties, the exercise of paternal authority, and the dominance
of the male. Yet in increasing numbers, the younger generation in
the cities challenged these traditional social customs. Youth con-
tracted its own marriages rather than accepting those arranged by
families, and women joined the ranks of career workers. The *moga*
("modern girl") and *mobo* ("modern boy") enjoyed Hollywood
movies, jazz, and Western dancing. Western sports became the rage.
Tennis, track and field sports, swimming, and baseball, the great
national sport, became common in Japan.

City people began to share in new intellectual and cultural life,
but social currents in urban areas reflected the disruptive forces
of modernization. Neither completely traditional nor modernized,
the generation of the 1920's experienced the pangs of cultural
discontinuity. As the group most affected in the cultural conflict,
intellectuals tended to become alienated from society and from
contemporaneous political life. Naturalism, realism, socialism, and
anarchism were some of the philosophies of the day, and these were
reflected in literature. Soseki Natsume, probably the greatest of
Japan's modern novelists and professor of literature at Tokyo Imperial University, sought to blend Western ideas with indigenous
values. But few liberal, positive, and hopeful strains appeared in
his novels, as in those of other authors. The course of individual
action led not to freedom and to control of the forces of natural
desires but rather ended in fear, despair, and loneliness.

The politics of the 1920's revolved about the two conservative
parties, the Seiyukai and the Kenseikai, renamed the Minseito in
1927. Both represented identical interests, consisting of a fusion of
landlords, agrarian capitalists, big business, and the rising middle
class. The landlord class was probably somewhat stronger in the
latter, but fundamentally both parties were the same. The difference
lay in that each was composed of different factions within the same

classes. The Mitsui group was more pronounced in the Seiyukai, and the Mitsubishi dominated the Minseito. This period was the most democratic of Japanese political history to that time, but the degree of democracy should not be overrated. In 1925 suffrage was extended to all males twenty-five years of age and over, and no property tax was stipulated for the first time. The same year the Diet enacted the Peace Preservation Law that permitted the arrest of subversives and of radicals and that muzzled free speech. The relative freedoms of speech and of political activity that were extended were contained within orthodox bounds as defined by the government, for the parties and individuals could not be fundamentally critical of the Japanese economic, political, or social system.

The leftist movement, growing but illegal, was forced to operate outside the pale of the law. As noted, Marxist ideas had begun to percolate into Japan in the late nineteenth century. By the end of the Meiji period, some Japanese intellectuals were acquainted with the general outlines of Marxism. After the 1917 Russian Revolution and the establishment of the Comintern (Communist International) two years later, Communist ideas entered Japan. Japanese began to attend international conferences in Russia, and Japanese representatives, returning from one such conference, founded the Japanese Communist Party in July, 1922, the third oldest Communist party in Asia (after the Indonesian, established in 1920, and the Chinese, formed in 1921). The police acted quickly, and within a year there were only a small handful of party members.

In 1925, after a strategy conference in Shanghai with Comintern members, the party was reactivated and mass activity was emphasized. But few Japanese were attracted to the cause of militant Communism, and another meeting was called in 1927 to discuss the poor progress of the party. Members analyzed the nature of the class struggle and of the Japanese nation, and, operating rigidly within the prescribed Marxist interpretation of the historic evolution of man through five inevitable stages as determined by the economic modes of production (the primitive, slave, feudal, capitalistic, and socialistic), they placed their country, which contained both strong agrarian and industrial interests, between the feudal and the capitalistic Marxist eras. They proposed through a double revolution to destroy first the feudal elements, which they considered the weaker of the two, and then turn their attention to the capitalists.

Since the revitalized party was illegal, the Communists worked through the Farmers and Workers Party in the general election of 1928, the first one to be called after the new electoral laws of 1925.

Great progress was made, and the front party won a quarter of a million votes. In that same election year, however, the police embarked on another wave of arrests and drove party members into hiding. Police vigilance carried over into the depression years, and by the early thirties it was impossible for party members to operate politically. Prior to the disbanding of the party in 1932, the members reiterated the necessity of the double revolution on the road to socialism, or communism, but they now pronounced the feudal elements the stronger since these elements had not yet been eradicated. To gain their ends, the party also approved the policy of continued cooperation with all bourgeois parties. This Communist strategy was important since it re-emerged in party operations in postwar Japan.

The 1920's: Foreign Policies

Although a degree of liberalism existed at home, Japanese foreign policies were not basically altered abroad. After World War I, as in prewar times, liberals, or party men such as Hara Kei, tried to maintain the nation's privileged status on the Asian mainland, although they did give ground at the Washington Conference. Yet the goal remained the same—the maintenance of a paramount position in Manchuria and by extension, in north China. The means to the ends differed, for the military used direct action while the liberals advocated the use of diplomacy and of negotiation. The overall record of Japanese foreign policy in the decade of 1922 to 1932 compared favorably with that of other great powers. Secretary of State Henry Stimson of the Hoover administration declared that the Japanese government in that decade had an exceptional record of good citizenship in international affairs.

But the immigration issue with the United States continued to rankle. In 1924 the question of Asian immigration came up when the Congress debated a general immigration law. Some legislators, including senators from western states, voted for exclusion of Asians. Others opposed any type of discriminatory law. Secretary of State Charles Evans Hughes of the Harding administration pointed out that such a bill would undo much of the goodwill created by the Washington Conference (over which he had presided). He wrote to a congressman asking that the Congress not take any strong action. The Japanese ambassador in Washington added his protest, for he communicated to the Department of State that "grave consequences" would result should the bill pass. Mistakingly thinking that it would add to his cause, Hughes passed the note on to the Congress, which reacted adversely instead. In part because of Japanese interference in a domestic American issue (which had foreign policy ramifications), senators and congressmen voted for the immigration bill with its exclusion provisions. The House approved it, 308 to 62, and the Senate, 68 to 9. The reaction of the Japanese press was bitter but restrained. The Japanese foreign office sent along another note of protest. It was particularly difficult for Japan to accept the act in view of the extensive American aid rendered the year before during the Tokyo earthquake and fire. The fact that the immigration law, had the exclusion clause not been contained, would have provided for a total of only 250 Japanese under the national origins quota was also used by Japanese militarists to arouse anti-American hatred in years prior to World War II.

Accommodation was the keynote in Japan's relations with other countries. Toward Communist Russia, a rapprochement developed. In 1922 the last of the Japanese forces left Siberia, in part because of pressures generated at the Washington Conference and in part because of heavy occupation costs. In search of allies and friends, in the mid-1920's Japan in order to end her semi-isolated position turned to Russia. The United States immigration act had produced bitterness; no Chinese party or individual that Japan could decisively support had yet emerged on top of the muddled political situation in that country; the psychologically comforting alliance with Great Britain had terminated. Although Japan disliked Communists and their ideology that precluded emperor worship and private property, and although she cracked down on Communism at home, she began negotiations with Russia to normalize diplomatic relations, which had been cut off at the advent of the Russian Revolution. In 1925, after one and a half years of negotiations, Japan and Russia signed a treaty of recognition, pledged an exchange of diplomatic representation, and regulated matters of mutual concern, including the adjustment of fishing rights in contiguous waters. It was ironic that Japan, probably the most effective bulwark against Communism in prewar Asia, came to agreement with Russia and went to war with the United States, which also maintained a similar antipathy to Communism. Asian power politics proved stronger than international ideological affinities.

Toward a politically muddled China, both soft and hard approaches were advocated. The former was typified by Baron Shidehara Kijuro, the foreign minister between 1924–1927 and 1929–1931 in Kenseikai and Minseito cabinets. Related to the Mitsubishi family and supported by business interests that advocated peaceful measures in Manchuria and China, Shidehara outlined his accommodating policies before the Diet early in 1927. Japan was to respect the sovereignty and the territorial integrity of China, promote solidarity and economic relations between the two countries, help the just aspirations of the Chinese people, tolerate the China situation, and protect legitimate Japanese rights by reasonable means. The essence of his approach was to reconcile China's aspirations with Japan's interests. Yet in the course of his first term of office as foreign minister, he twice dispatched Japanese troops into both Manchuria and China to protect Japanese rights. On the other hand, in March, 1927, he did not commit Japan to the Anglo-American bombardment of Nanking on the lower Yangtze river in central China, where several Japanese nationals had been wounded by Chinese in anti-Western demonstrations and rioting in that city.

The so-called hard China policy was supported by a general, Baron Tanaka Giichi, prime minister between 1927 and 1929. He re-emphasized special Japanese interests in Manchuria and eastern Mongolia and deemed it his duty to protect those areas were they to be threatened by disturbances affecting Japan. He sent troops to Shantung to check the northern advance of the Chinese Nationalists under the young rising general, Chiang Kai-shek, who aspired to unify China, and who achieved some success when, in October, 1928, he proclaimed a reconstituted Republic of China at Nanking with himself as president. Tanaka, and some of his successors, began to fear the possibility of a reunified China under Chiang Kai-shek, a development that could presage the termination of special Japanese interests.

Adjusting its policies toward China and Russia, Japan expanded its role in international life as member of the League of Nations. A number of Japan's ablest statesmen, jurists, and diplomats served with the League, and two Japanese occupied the post of Under Secretary General. They were also active in the field of arbitration and in the adjudication of international disputes. They signed the Convention for Pacific Settlement of International Disputes, and a Japanese jurist helped to draft the statutes for the World Court (which the United States officially declined to join), of which a Japanese was one of the original eleven judges and of which one Japanese was later president.

The cooperative spirit carried on into further naval agreements. After the Washington Conference a naval race was possible in auxiliary ships, since the Washington ratios applied only to battle-ships and aircraft carriers. A naval race between Japan and Great Britain was already taking shape in categories of vessels not regulated by the Conference, and multilateral efforts were expended to solve the problem. In 1927 at Geneva, the United States, Great Britain, and Japan in preliminary conferences attempted to extend the Washington agreements on a 5:5:3 basis to other ships, but no agreement was reached. In 1930 another effort was made in London, in which France and Italy participated, though they did not ratify the resulting agreements. The presence of new men as national leaders who were more amenable to the settlement of the disputes, such as President Herbert Hoover, Prime Minister Ramsey McDonald of the British Labor Party, and Foreign Minister Shidehara, contributed to the agreement by the three main powers concerning maximum ratios for auxiliary naval vessels to be attained by the end of 1936.

Four types of vessels were affected by the London naval treaties. In regard to heavy cruisers the United States was allocated 18 ships, the British 15, and the Japanese 12. For light cruisers the overall limitations were respectively set at 143,500 tons, 192,200 tons, and 100,450 tons. Destroyers were allocated to United States and Great Britain on parity, each provided with a total tonnage of 150,000, with Japan limited to 105,500 tons. In submarines, all three parties achieved parity, with maximum tonnages set at 72,700. The Japanese insisted on a more favorable ratio in heavy cruisers, but the cabinet of Prime Minister Hamaguchi Osachi of the Minseito party compromised on the issue. The acceptance of the final London Naval Agreement in Japan, despite military objections to freezing long-range military programs, constituted a high point in Japan's march toward responsible government because it was a victory for the civilian and moderate point of view. But the victory proved short-lived in Japan, for there was no unified public opinion or popular backing for a government that was striving to maintain a responsible and viable parliamentary government.

The 1930's: Growth of Authoritarianism

The pattern of civilian ascendancy in politics and of international cooperation was reversed in the 1930's with the growth of militarism and of authoritarianism at home. Enjoying independent status since the turn of the century, the military by World War II had emerged as the key foreign policy maker. Even in politically

quiescent times, there had been precedents for military intervention in home and foreign affairs. In 1912, the minister of war
toppled Saionji's second cabinet. The army helped to commit the
country to the Siberian expedition and had prolonged its stay there.
Army leaders continually sought a greater portion of national budg-
ets for military expenditures. On occasion even its junior grade field
officers exercised independent action. They assumed initiative in
planning Japanese moves into Mongolia in 1915–1916, hatched plots
during the Siberian expedition with White Russian officers, and
propelled the army in taking over all of Manchuria in 1931–1932.
They, as did other political activists, purported to act in the name
of the emperor. Although foreign ministry officials and some high
army and navy figures at home questioned the feasibility of direct
military solutions to foreign policy issues, no top Japanese leader
disagreed with the basic foreign policy goal, which was Japanese
hegemony on the Asian mainland. Internal quarrels developed not
over policies but rather over the control and nature of policy-
making decisions.

Rightist groups, miltary and civilian, were in the background
ready to capitalize on opportunities for the advancement of their
views. These groups were successful in the 1930's, a period of the
gradual growth of totalitarianism in Japan. They took positive action
at home and abroad to destroy and to discredit representative
government. The spiral of events that consolidated authoritarianism
at home began abroad in south Manchuria, where young Japanese
army officers in the Kwantung army began to act independently of
both the military and the civilian authorities in Tokyo. The nature
of Manchurian affairs helped their cause. The nominal Chinese
ruler of Manchuria was a warlord, Chang Tso-lin. Known as the
"Old Marshal," he was assassinated in 1928 in a plot of young Japanese officers when he tried to cooperate with Chiang Kai-shek as
the latter moved north toward Peking in an effort to reunify China.
Upon his death, his son, Chang Hsüeh-liang, took the reins. The
"Young Marshal" proved even less satisfactory to the Japanese army
than his father had, for he recognized the Nationalist regime at Nanking under Chiang Kai-shek, who confirmed him as governor-general
of Manchuria. The many Chinese residents in Manchuria, who had
immigrated there in great numbers after the fall of the Manchu,
were becoming increasingly nationalistic and desired closer ties with
China. Moreover, the Chinese had built railroad lines parallel to
the South Manchurian Railroad, and the Japanese objected to this
competition. The Chinese in Manchuria also instigated effective boy-

cotts against Japanese goods. Against a background of growing Chinese restiveness, the Japanese army in Manchuria decided to act.

The Kwantung army forces had grown in numbers and independence over the years. Originating as troops to guard the South Manchurian Railroad, they became in time the Japanese army in south Manchuria. The general in charge of the army, moreover, since 1927 also had been the governor-general of the leased Kwantung territories. In this situation containing an independent-minded Chinese warlord, growing Chinese restlessness, and expanding Japanese military might and commitments, the incident of September 18, 1931, occurred. That evening at Mukden, the Manchurian capital, the tracks of the South Manchurian Railroad were blown up (by the Japanese themselves, as was later proved). Although the express train due in Mukden arrived on time in spite of the damaged tracks, the Japanese blamed the Chinese for the explosion. Using this as a pretext to commence large-scale military operations (and this was only one of any number of pretexts that might have been used), the Japanese troops clashed with Chinese troops under Chang Hsüeh-liang, who was pushed out of Manchuria into north China. Within several months the Kwantung army eventually took over all of Manchuria. In February, 1932, it promulgated the puppet state of Manchukuo with Henry Pu Yi, the last of the Manchu emperors, as the new chief of state.

Disapproving but not disavowing the acts that led to the formation of Manchukuo, the foreign office in Tokyo reluctantly recognized the new state eight months later. The commanding general of the Kwantung army, in addition to other duties, became the Japanese ambassador. In Tokyo tensions developed between the military and the foreign office as well as between the military and big business, who opposed the direct army action in Manchuria. In the spring of 1932 discontent among the younger and lower-ranking officers was reflected in a series of assassinations that included the governor of the Bank of Japan and the head of the gigantic Mitsui company. On May 15, 1932, young naval officers and army cadets, claiming to free from evil influences the emperor (now Hirohito, the Showa or "Enlightened Peace" emperor, who ascended the throne in 1926), killed the prime minister, Inukai Tsuyoshi. The army demanded the end of party government, and the bureaucrats tacitly went along. An admiral of moderate leanings was chosen prime minister in a compromise, nationalist cabinet. The balance of power was shifting in favor of the military, and the role of the political parties grew progressively weaker in the thirties.

The United States protested the unilateral Japanese takeover of Manchuria. Continuing the doctrine of nonrecognition of special Japanese interests, Secretary of State Stimson, like his predecessor Bryan on an earlier occasion, objected to violations of American treaty rights. The United States never recognized Manchukuo, although both Washington and Tokyo permitted American businessmen to operate there. The League of Nations dispatched a commission under Lord Lytton to Manchuria to investigate the train of events. Its report, in effect, blamed the Japanese for aggression. Japan's reply in March, 1933, was to walk out of the League when its members accepted the findings and report of the commission. Manchuria was swallowed up lock, stock, and barrel as a Japanese possession, and only the fiction of an independent state was maintained. But there were even further implications in the matter. The Chinese considered Manchuria a part of China, and while they were in no position to reconquer the region under Chiang Kai-shek, who had a multitude of problems to contend with closer at hand, they objected to Japanese domination there. By 1933 neither China nor Japan could separate Manchuria from China. Manchuria became the pivotal area in the foreign policy of both contending countries.

As Manchuria went into Japan's orbit, Japan moved toward becoming an autocratic state that sanctioned unilateral acts by the army. Support, tacit or overt, for militarism came not only from the bureaucracy and the middle classes, but from a growing group of rightist civilian societies. Reactionary factions were not new in Japan, but their doctrines at this time found a degree of intellectual acceptability. Right-wing civilian movements gathered strength in Japan shortly after World War I. A number of small but disorganized groups appeared, generally in reaction against postwar proletarian movements. Their names indicated their character—the Imperial Way Society, the Japanese National Essence Society, the Anti-Bolshevist Association, and the League of Blood Brothers. They propounded a fascistic way of life, with its connotations of the glorification of war, of extreme nationalism, and of a one-party government operating above and beyond the will of the people. Symptomatic of this postwar trend of thought was Kita Ikki, who has been termed the intellectual father of Japanese fascism. In 1919 his book, *The Reconstruction of Japan*, advocated, among other things, the dissolution of parliamentary parties, the enhancement of personal imperial rule, and the nationalization of the means of production.

Held in the background during the more liberal atmosphere of the 1920's, in the course of the 1930's the right-wing civilian movement joined forces with segments of the military, particularly those of junior rank, who became the motivating center for action. Agreeing with the civilian rightists, these younger officers proclaimed the so-called "Showa restoration," aimed at enhancing imperial rule and prestige. Propagating a violent brand of fascism, they performed terroristic acts and carried to an extreme a policy of radicalism, as they had in 1932. Anti-capitalistic as well as anti-Communist, they demanded the abolition of both capitalistic societies and left-wing movements. Their double attack attracted leaders from the middle class, which had been affected more by the depression than had the zaibatsu. By the mid-1930's, some of the middle class saw themselves as squeezed in between fancied or real oppressive Marxist and capitalist pressures. With new-found strength, a group of young officers from a Tokyo regiment took direct action on February 26, 1936. Leading enlisted men, the mutineers made attempts on the lives of leading statesmen. They tried to assassinate the premier and the aging genro, Saionji, and succeeded in murdering a former prime minister. Holding out for three days in downtown Tokyo, the rebels were eventually subdued, tried, and some executed. This time those around the throne and the elder military took decisive action against the younger rebels. But in the process of repressing extremism with forceful measures, they themselves contributed even further to the institution of dictatorial government in Japan. By 1936 fascism had become the form of the Japanese government.

Japanese fascism bore certain ideological similarities to the European brand as evidenced in prewar Germany, Italy, and Spain. These included the rejection of individualism and of representative government, the idealization of war, the disallowance of the class struggle concept, and the insistence on the unity and indivisibility of the nation. Yet the Japanese form had its own peculiarities. For one, the unitary society was based not so much on race as on the idea of the family. Japan was an extended, patriarchal family, the emperor was the father of the Japanese, and the individual was only a single element in the whole body politic. Secondly, agriculture assumed a mystical but leading role in society. European fascism emphasized state power to control modes of production, and while the same emphasis was found in Japan, it was effected with inconsistencies. State ownership was advocated in industry and commerce, but less control was placed in Japanese fascism on the peasants, who were to be respected and were not to be exploited at the expense of urban groups. The special role of agriculture in Japanese fascism arose in part because the young military leaders had a close affiliation with the countryside where many of them grew up, in part because Japan was still the most agrarian of all the highly industrial countries, and in part because rural interests had felt themselves sacrificed to industry ever since the Meiji restoration. Thirdly, Japanese fascism involved a Pan-Asian concept. It was Japan's sacred trust to free Asia from the West, to expel colonial powers, and to guide Asian countries to national and collective strength. The foreign policy calling for Asia for Asians, under Japanese hegemony, was the Japanese version of manifest destiny.

Those young military men who espoused Japanese fascism often turned to acts of heroism to promote their cause. Such a young man was termed a *soshi*, one who dedicated himself to the nation. In the tradition of Yoshida Shoin and of Saigo Takamori, the heroes of the right performed self-sacrifical, dramatic acts and offered themselves to the nation. In a peculiar psychology of heroism, as evidenced in the attempted Showa restoration, the young men believed themselves to be following in the footsteps of the leaders of the Meiji restoration. Yet there was a degree of irrationality involved in implementing their ends. They possessed no precisely outlined program of action nor did any blueprints exist on how to put an end to parliamentary government other than to assassinate persons considered unfriendly to the cause. Intuition, they argued, would outline definite plans and ends at a later time, for truth was not to be revealed by formal logic or through book-learning. Intuition and action were the limited sequence of reasoning.

By the late 1930's, the net result of a wider acceptance in Japan of the tenets of fascism had been to increase both authoritarianism and militarism in Japan. Each strain interacted with and enhanced the other. The reason for their growth—and, conversely, for the failure of parliamentary government—might be attributed to several factors. In Japan there had always existed a degree of government suppression of criticism, termed "dangerous thoughts," a tendency that was not conducive to a free exchange of ideas and philosophies. Dissent from the existing order was tolerated only within stipulated bonds, which were defined by the government. Moreover, Japan had no strong and deeply rooted tradition of democratic parliamentary government. By 1932, when nationalist, "transcendental" cabinets replaced party cabinets, the Meiji constitution had been operative for only forty-two years, and in this period there had been only one decade of a semblance of parliamentary responsibility. One generation had been too short a period to implant democratic procedures. The Japanese, strong traditionalists, probably understood the intellectual content of democracy but had little emotional attachment to it. When war came, Japan was still too close to authoritarianism for democracy to survive. Related to this lack of a liberal tradition was the structural weakness of the Diet, which could not control the government, although it tried, in the face of the military independence and the retention of the idea of imperial divinity. Lastly, the weakness, although temporary, of the economic base in early depression years acerbated social and political tensions. In the brittle domestic situation, rightist extremism was able to flourish.

Other economic developments of the mid-1930's contributed to the growth of centralized, militarized operations. Economic activity was increasingly oriented toward Manchuria and China. A new group of zaibatsu called the *shinko* developed, whose plants and wealth were located chiefly in Manchuria. Closely linked to Kwantung army interests, they were not so large as the traditional cartels, but they proved effective instruments in implementing military rule overseas. Raw materials from the Asian mainland, including coking coal, iron, and industrial salt, also flowed to home factories. More industries produced more goods and required more outlets, at home and abroad. The dependence on foreign trade, a necessary feature of Japan's economic structure, did not alter during this time.

Economic affairs were also characterized by increased state intervention. The government, now under greater military control, saw military expenditures as one solution to internal problems brought about by the depression. Military allocations went up from 31 per cent of the total budget in 1931 to 47 per cent in 1936. Deficit spending resulted in doubling of the government debt in the same five-year period. The economic and industrial consequences of government outlays for armaments were registered in an enormous expansion of heavy industry. By 1936 Japan was industrially self-sufficient and prepared for war. Control boards for each major industry were set up, and these boards fixed prices and allocated raw materials. Increased armaments put new strains on foreign relations, and the Washington and London naval agreements lapsed at the end of 1936.

Paralleling its role in domestic affairs, the army emerged as top policy maker in foreign relations. The Kwantung army controlled Manchuria, at home the fascist movement resulted in increased military control, and economic developments made industrialists and capitalists increasingly dependent on the military. Between 1932 and 1937, while busily consolidating gains in Manchuria, Japan pursued a generally quiescent policy toward China, and only gradually in those years did it extend its zone of control into north China. Japan began to ally herself with the European fascist powers, and she strove to secure her borders with Russia. But after 1937, when renewed aggression burst the dam in north China, Japan was placed in direct confrontation with Western powers in China, including the United States.

CHRONOLOGY

1919	Kita Ikki writes *The Reconstruction of Japan*
1922	Japanese Communist Party formed
1923	Japanese earthquake and fire, Tokyo-Yokohama area
1924	United States immigration law excludes Japanese
1925	Universal male suffrage; Peace Preservation Act; Russian treaty
1926	Emperor Showa (Hirohito) ascends throne
1927	Geneva Naval Conference
1930	London Naval Conference
1931–1933	Japanese army takes over Manchuria; puppet state of Manchukuo created
1932, May 15	Uprisings of young officers in Tokyo; nonrecognition doctrine reiterated by Stimson
1933	League condemns Japanese record in Manchuria; Japan walks out of League
1936	Army mutiny in Tokyo (February 26); end of Washington and London naval agreements

XVI

IMPERIAL JAPAN (1937–1945): WORLD WAR II

As Japan began to expand on the Asian continent, her leaders stepped up the diplomatic offensive after 1937. They buttressed their international position through treaties with the Axis powers and neutrality with Russia. They resumed extensive operations in a domestically weak China. By the end of 1941, they expanded their scope of operations through open conflict with the United States and the Western European powers. Spreading into southeast Asia and islands of the western Pacific, Japanese forces created temporarily one of the largest empires on record. But the imperial structure collapsed in a few years, and the political entity of Japan reverted essentially to the traditional four home islands after 1945.

Japan, the Axis Powers, and Russia

With a combination of political and economic factors at home and abroad favoring expansion, Japan moved towards total mobilization in the years immediately preceding World War II. She aligned herself with the Axis powers of Germany and Italy, who possessed similar ideology and expansionist tendencies. In the Anti-Comintern Pact of November, 1936, Japan and Germany pledged to counteract Soviet propaganda, and in an appended secret protocol, they promised not to help Russia if either signatory were attacked by the Soviets. The following year Italy joined the pact. In September, 1940, after the fall of France and fresh German successes in Europe, the three states concluded the Tripartite Pact. Its terms provided that if one of the three contracting states were to be attacked by a power not involved in the European war or the Chinese-Japanese conflict, the other two signatories would assist the partner with all political, economic, and military means. Since at the time only the United States and Soviet Russia, among the major states, were neutral, another article of the treaty stated that the terms did not affect the status then existing between each of the three parties and Soviet Russia. Despite these multilateral treaty arrangements, Japan's relationship with the Axis powers was not a happy one. They were never really united in common outlook and planning. The European and Asian parties went their respective, separate ways, and each neglected to inform the other of basic war plans and strategies.

Japan endeavored to secure its northern flank from Russian advances. In 1935 Russia sold the Chinese Eastern Railroad to Japan, and she kept out of Manchuria and of China. But time and again, large-scale military clashes erupted between Japan and Russia along Russia's Asian borders. Between 1937 and 1939, fighting broke out over islands in the Amur River that formed much of the Manchurian-Siberian border, at Changkufeng Hill near the Korean-Manchurian border, and in the Nomonhan border region in inner Mongolia. Tens of thousands of troops were employed in these campaigns by both sides, but war was not declared. With the conclusion of the surprising and unexpected German-Russian pact in July, 1939, Japan, fearing a Russian attack, halted her aggressive action. Two years later, when Hitler attacked Russia, Japan felt safer and redirected her efforts southward. Japanese military counsels decided against moving into eastern Siberia with its relative paucity of natural resources, including a lack of oil, essential for military and industrial operations. But to make doubly sure of Russian intentions, Japan concluded with Russia in April, 1941, a five-year neutrality pact in which each party pledged not to go to war with the other.

Japan in East Asia

Japan had meanwhile expanded its military operations into the Chinese heartland. On July 7, 1937, at the Marco Polo Bridge (Lukuochiao) near Peking, shots were exchanged between the Chinese garrison and Japanese forces on maneuvers there, where they had no right to be. Although the Chinese apologized, the tense situation persisted, and the Japanese military used the incident, one of any number in the area, as a pretext for further expansion.

There was now no stopping Japan. By the end of the month Japanese troops occupied Peking. They fanned out over north China until they were met and contained near the bend of the Yellow River by the independently operating Chinese Communist armies. In central China, along the broad Yangtze River, the Japanese in 1937 and 1938 also spread out from Shanghai where they, like other major Western powers, had extensive economic interests and troops protecting them. They captured Chiang Kai-shek's capital of Nanking and proceeded up the broad river valley. The Nationalist Chinese regime fled upstream to Chungking, located in the Yangtze river gorges which made it nearly impregnable to invading land forces. Chungking remained Chiang's capital throughout the war years. In south China, Japanese forces occupied the large city of Canton near Hong Kong and moved inland along river valleys and railroad lines. Several years prior to Pearl Harbor, the Japanese in China had absorbed most of the Chinese territory that they were ever to secure.

No formal declaration of war followed any of these Japanese military operations. As in the case of Manchuria, Japan tried to set up puppet governments in occupied China. In December, 1937, she established in Peking, a traditional capital in Chinese history, the Provisional Government of the Republic of China with elderly, experienced Chinese, hostile to Chiang Kai-shek's regime, as head officials. But the Japanese desired some outstanding Chinese to form a national government that could be recognized as legitimate for all China. They brought pressure to bear on a few warlords without success until they managed to obtain the services of Wang Ching-wei, who had held high positions under Chiang Kai-shek, but who had become dissatisfied with a perennially secondary position.

In March, 1940, the Japanese proclaimed the return of the national government to Nanking under Wang Ching-wei, who remained subservient to the Japanese until his death in 1944. The Japanese gave diplomatic recognition to his government and concluded a treaty with it, which was eventually recognized by Japan's totalitarian associates in Europe. Political reorganization was accompanied by a new economic plan, the "co-prosperity sphere," enunciated by the Japanese cabinet in 1938. Japanese companies and corporations controlled either directly or through subsidiaries the economic life of occupied China. Cultural redirection was also ordered.

Schools were reorganized and textbooks were revised. The Japanese attempted to impose total administration of subjugated areas. Through such wide-ranging policies, prior to the outbreak of the Pacific war Japan was well versed in the establishment and techniques of puppet governments.

Japanese expansion infringed on Western rights, particularly those of Great Britain, which retained strong economic interests in occupied China. The Japanese disliked the British, who through Hong Kong and Burma permitted aid, albeit a trickle, to flow to the capital of free China at Chungking. The British, walking a tightrope, under Japanese pressure closed the Burma road for three months in mid-1940, but then reopened it. In China, British subjects and diplomats suffered indignities and maltreatment. The Japanese seemed to delight in insulting the British in order to reveal the latter's impotence to take action. With comparatively few troops committed to Asia, particularly after the outbreak of the European war, the British were constricted in the possibilities of positive action, and the Japanese knew this.

Similarly, the Japanese pushed into Indochina after the fall of France and met with little resistance there. In 1940, with the conclusion of the Hanoi Convention, Japan received the right to station troops in northern Indochina. In the next year, her troops marched into Saigon. For all intents and purposes, Japan had also occupied Indochina prior to Pearl Harbor. Coveting the valuable oil, rubber, and tin of Indonesia, after the fall of the Netherlands to the Nazis, Japan sent delegations to Batavia, but the Dutch refused to extend any concessions until her Asian possessions were occupied by the Japanese after the advent of open hostilities there.

Japan and the United States

As she had done on previous occasions, the United States protested the infringement of her treaty rights in China. She refused to recognize the puppet Wang Ching-wei and for the record protested continually individual and collective private and official insults and attacks. America participated in attempted collective security measures to restore peace on the Asian mainland, and although not a member of the League, the United States cooperated unofficially with the Lytton Commission, on which she had an observer. In 1937 the Roosevelt administration participated in the Brussels Conference called by Belgium for the nine powers of the Washington Conference to deal with Japan's actions in China. Since Japan, the most directly affected foreign power, did not attend, the Conference was unsuccessful. Upon the termination of the Washington and of the London naval arrangements at the end of 1936, military escalation among Pacific powers became a reality.

The United States extended to Chiang Kai-shek air support and loans, but more effective were American economic sanctions against Japan. Although these sanctions were adopted to deal principally with the growing European embroilment, they affected American economic relations with Japan as well. To keep the United States out of potential foreign conflicts, in 1935 the Congress enacted a law to the effect that should the president declare the existence of a state of war, an embargo on the sale and transportation of arms would be imposed on the belligerents involved. The following year, provisions were enacted to forbid the extension of loans. In 1937 and in 1939 the Congress in effect reversed itself and repealed the embargo on arms, ammunitions, and implements of war to such foreign nationals, belligerents or neutral, as could cross the seas to buy for cash and take away anything they wanted. Meant to bolster the European position of the ally Great Britain, which possessed the ships and some funds, the laws paradoxically enhanced for the same reasons the position in the Pacific of a belligerent Japan.

The United States government in July, 1938, invoked an embargo on the sale of airplanes to Japanese parties, since these planes, it was argued, were used to bomb hapless Chinese civilians. In December, 1939, the embargoes were extended to cover shipments of oil and petroleum products to Japan. In July of that year, the United States also announced its intention to terminate the 1911 treaty of commerce. Japan's place in normal bilateral trade channels would then end, and legal obstacles would be removed should the United States desire to restrict further trade with Japan. Following this line, in July and December, 1940, effective export controls were imposed on scrap iron, aviation gas, munitions, and other items of war to Japan. After the movement of Japanese troops into Saigon following an American warning, the United States froze Japanese financial assets in July, 1941.

The American and Japanese positions had become irreconcilable. Yet the United States government was hard put to formulate a consistent China policy. She had to protect her nationals, but she did not wish to provoke war. She tried to restrain Japan but had to work for peace. She pledged to enforce orderly processes, but she could not tolerate shabby treatment. She continually protested Japanese actions but could not back the protests with force. Roosevelt's Secretary of State, Cordell Hull, continually enunciated like a litany the doctrines of faithful adherence to international agreements and the settlement of differences through peaceful negotiations. He sought negotiations with Japan on terms which the Japanese found unacceptable, such as the conclusion of a multilateral Asian non-aggression agreement, the complete withdrawal of Japanese troops from China and Indochina, and the recognition of Chiang Kai-shek as the legitimate head of the Chinese Republic. In return for such Japanese concessions, he promised that the United States would negotiate a new commercial treaty with Japan to restore normal economic relations. Japanese in Tokyo and their delegations in Washington rejected the basic American terms, for they desired the recognition of growing territorial and economic rights and free access to stocks of essential natural resources, which were now more than ever necessary for inflated military and industrial commitments. Against the backdrop of irreconcilable positions, Japan took the decision to go to war.

As early as July 2, 1941, an imperial conference decided on a drive into southeast Asia, where valuable natural resources could be obtained. Subsequent conferences reiterated the strategy. In October, General Tojo Hideki, as one of the top-ranking Japanese militarists, became prime minister of Japan, and expansionist plans swung into action. On November 1 Admiral Yamamoto Isoroku issued the orders for an attack on Pearl Harbor, which was meant to immobilize the United States navy temporarily while the Japanese could consolidate their gains in southeast Asia. On November 17 the admiral designated December 7 as the attack date. On November 26 under Vice-Admiral Nagumo Chuichi's command, the Pearl Harbor Striking Force, composed of six carriers protected by two battleships, three cruisers, and nine destroyers, sortied from Etorufu in the Kuriles. On the same day in Washington, Hull reiterated his final proposals for peace to a special Japanese delegation. On November 27, Washington, which had broken the secret Japanese code, sent war warnings to Pearl Harbor and to Manila, but these indicated possible aggression in the Philippines or in Malaya rather than in Hawaii. In the meantime, the Japanese striking force, undetected, approached Hawaii by a northern route. In the early hours of Sunday, December 7, despite the sinking of a small Japanese submarine and the fact that a United States army search radar picked up on its screen scouting planes from Japanese carriers, the first Japanese air attack at 7:55 A.M. caught Hawaiian forces unprepared. In two hours six United States battleships were sunk, 120 planes disabled, and 2400 persons killed.

The Pacific War

Pearl Harbor united a previously divided American people, but the first year of the Pacific War proved successful for the Japanese. Japan won all of her major objectives in Asia and the Pacific, and in the flush of "victory disease," she established control over land and maritime areas from the Aleutians in the north through Indonesia in the south, and from Burma in the west to the central Pacific archipelagos. Japan's initial successes made a great psychological impact on Asian peoples, for an Asian country had defeated Western nations. The myth of the invincibility of the white man had again been exploded (as in the Russo-Japanese War), and the white man was paraded through Asian streets as a prisoner of war. Colonial regimes in southeast Asia toppled and native nationalism was given impetus. The Japanese set up autonomous indigenous governments that claimed independence from the colonial powers. But as the war wore on, friction grew between the Japanese and their sponsored native governments. By the end of the war, the Japanese, because of their many brutal and tactless actions, became as discredited as the earlier colonial powers. "Asia for Asians" turned out to be more appropriately "Asia for the Japanese."

Despite extensive losses at Pearl Harbor, the United States recovered and made use of her remaining fleet until American industry could replace the military losses. The British fleet was decimated, for Singapore, the important naval base, had been taken and the British battleships sunk. On the other hand, the Japanese navy was in prime condition, but it began to receive setbacks after initial victories through a combination of second-rate strategy and some bad luck. In the Battle of Coral Sea, May 4–8, 1942, off Australia, the Japanese tried to secure Port Moresby, on the southern coast of New Guinea, as a southern anchor point. It was a unique battle for the time, since all fighting was done in the air by carrier planes against carrier planes. The Japanese failed to take the port.

In the Battle of Midway (June 4–6, 1942), conceived by Admiral Yamamoto as a frontal attack concealed by Japanese operations farther north in the Aleutians (where the United States temporarily lost Kiska and Attu Islands), Admiral Chester Nimitz saturated the Japanese navy with air attacks. The Japanese failed to gain Midway and in the battle, which constituted the first major defeat of the Japanese navy in modern times, Japan lost four of her best aircraft carriers. In the Guadalcanal operations of August, 1942, through February, 1943, the Japanese unsuccessfully continued their strategy to achieve a strong southern position. The tide of war was changing in the southwest Pacific. The Allied cause slowly advanced northward, island hopping under General Douglas MacArthur, who had withdrawn from the Philippines in mid-1942 to Australia, which became his headquarters and base of military operations.

Complementing MacArthur's military drive along the southwest Pacific island chain, which aimed at retaking the Philippines, were the naval and land engagements across the Pacific Ocean. In March, 1943, the two Aleutian islands of Attu and Kiska were retaken, and the Battle of Bismarck Sea, March 2–3, 1943, cleared the central Solomons. Within a year, intensive but costly operations regained the Gilberts including Makin and Tarawa, the Marshalls including Kwajalein and Eniwetok, and finally the Marianas among which were Guam, Saipan, and Tinian. The fall of Saipan in July, 1944, proved a turning point in the Pacific War. From the Marianas Japan could easily be reached in round-trip bombing raids (fields in China were too distant for the same purpose). Tojo's cabinet fell, and while no Japanese openly talked of defeat, some leaders were privately considering the possibility of a negotiated peace. The Allied troops recaptured the Philippines and took Okinawa, which was used as a staging area for the invasion of Japan.

By 1945, with tightened submarine warfare and air raids against the home islands themselves, the war had definitely turned against Japan. Japanese merchant ships had difficulty getting raw materials and importing food. Manpower was shifted from agriculture to military needs. The war effort was adversely affected by hasty reallocations of human resources. The conclusion of the war was hastened by the atomic bombs dropped on Hiroshima and Nagasaki on August 6 and 9 respectively, and the entrance of Russia in the Pacific War on August 8. The Japanese, despite last-ditch opposition from the army, followed an imperial rescript and surrendered on August 15. In the holocaust over the years 1937 to 1945, 3.1 million Japanese had lost their lives: 2.3 million soldiers died on the various fronts; 300,000 civilians were overseas casualties; and 500,000 others, including atomic bomb victims in Japan, perished.

During the war, military problems had taken precedence, for victory was the main objective. But international problems affecting Japan's postwar status persisted, and although they were temporarily subordinated to military concerns, they provided complications. Long-range diplomatic issues could not be separated from the immediate military considerations, and there were several Allied conferences held in the course of World War II to consider postwar problems relating to Japan.

In January, 1943, Roosevelt met with British Prime Minister Winston Churchill in Casablanca, where they issued the "unconditional surrender" statement. The Allies, they pledged, would fight until the unconditional surrender of their enemies in Asia and in Europe. There was to be no repetition of any of Wilson's Fourteen Points at Versailles implying accommodation of the enemy. The insistence on unconditional surrender was controversial, for it spurred the Japanese militarists to fight to the bitter end, in the absence of another alternative. The demand probably delayed the Japanese surrender, for the army used it in their arguments against the foreign office and the navy. In the case of Japan, unconditional surrender turned out to be conditional anyway, for the Japanese requested and received the right to retain the emperor, who, however, was made subject to the control of General MacArthur, who was designated by the Allies as the Supreme Commander of the Allied Powers (SCAP) in Japan.

In November, 1943, Roosevelt and Churchill met with Chiang Kai-shek at Cairo. There they agreed on the course of future operations against Japan and issued a joint statement of purpose. In the Cairo Declaration of November 26, four general areas of intent were announced. First, Japan was to be stripped of all islands in the Pacific seized or occupied since 1914. This essentially meant that the League mandates of the ex-German territories would be terminated. Second, all territories Japan had "stolen" from China were to be returned to the Republic of China. These included Manchuria, Formosa, and the Pescadores. Third, Japan was to be expelled from all other territories taken by "violence and greed." This meant much territory. It was understandable in terms of mainland and insular Asian holdings, but not in the case of South Sakhalin and the Kuriles which Japan had obtained from Russia in the course of legally concluded and internationally binding treaties. Finally, with reference to Korea, the Japanese colony "in due course" was to become free and independent. The Cairo Declaration meant to turn the clock back to pre-Perry times as far as Japanese territory was involved.

In February, 1945, at Yalta, in order to gain Russian support of the projected invasion of the Japanese homeland later that year, Roosevelt promised to restore to Russia its pre-1904 rights in Manchuria, and gave to Russia titles to the Kuriles and to South Sakhalin.

In July, 1945, at Potsdam, at the conclusion of the war in Europe, Harry S. Truman, the new American president, Clement Attlee, who had succeeded Churchill as the British prime minister, and Marshal Stalin reiterated the Yalta agreements. They outlined the zones of occupation in Asia. The Americans were to receive the Japanese surrender in the Philippines, Japan, the Pacific islands, and Korea south of the 38th parallel; the Russians in northern Japanese islands, north Korea, and Manchuria; the Chinese under Chiang Kai-shek in China and Indochina to the 16th parallel; and the British in southeast Asia. The Potsdam Declaration called for the elimination of militarism in Japan, the occupation of Japan, and the territorial limitations of Japan to its four main islands and some adjacent minor ones. After two atomic bombs and the Russian entry into war, which involved the unilateral scrapping of the neutrality pact with Japan, the Japanese surrendered in the emperor's name. At 9:08 A.M. on September 2, 1945, the instrument of surrender was signed on the United States battleship, the *Missouri,* in Tokyo Bay.

Japan was defeated, militarism was eradicated, and, for the first time in modern Asian history there was the spectacle of a weak, occupied Japan. A changed situation in Japan was matched by a changed situation throughout Asia. China was divided and weak, for though Chiang Kai-shek re-emerged in 1945 as the first among several Chinese leaders, the Chinese Communists, located in strength in north China, were contending for the mastery of the country. Colonial arrangements in south and southeast Asia were collapsing. Some metropolitan powers, as the United States and Great Britain, read the signs accurately and gave up their interests. Others, as the French and Dutch, retreated only after a show of force. The Pacific War had first resulted in great but transitory gains for Japan. No other power in world history had achieved in Asia precisely the same imperial stature and the same imperial bounds. However, Japan's temporary supremacy was achieved only at tremendous costs and was built on a hollow base. The sudden imperial collapse called for a complete rearrangement of the Asian power structure. In 1941 Japan's place in Asia was paramount; in 1945 it was conjectural. As postwar developments turned out, Japan re-emerged once again in new-found strength based on different policies.

CHRONOLOGY

1935	Russia sells Chinese Eastern Railroad to Japan; U.S. neutrality laws
1936	Anti-Comintern Pact
1937	Brussels Conference
1937–1938	Japan moves into north, central, and south China
1937–1939	Fighting with Russia on border areas; U.S. "cash and carry" laws
1938–1939	U.S. embargo laws
1939	Russian-German Treaty; U.S. declares intent to terminate Japanese trade treaty of 1911
1940	Axis or Tripartite Pact; puppet Chinese republic at Nanking; U.S. export controls; Japan in north Indochina
1941	Russian-Japanese neutrality pact; Hitler invades Russia; Japanese in Saigon; U.S. freezes Japanese assets; Japanese imperial conferences on war strategy; Pearl Harbor
1941–1945	Pacific War
1943	Casablanca and Cairo conferences
1945	Yalta and Potsdam conferences; atomic bombs on Hiroshima and Nagasaki (August 6 and 9); Russian entry into war (August 8); Japanese surrender (August 15); Instrument of Surrender signed (September 2).

PART FOUR

POSTWAR JAPAN

Defeated and shattered at the end of World War II, Japan experienced, for the first time in its history, the presence of a foreign power, that of the United States. During the seven years of occupation, measures of reform and recovery were effected, so that by the recovery of sovereignty in 1952, Japan once more came into its own political identity. However, despite the severance of formal bonds, the course of the rest of the decade was marked by continued Japanese dependence—economic, political, and military—on the United States. But then, as the 1960's progressed, the Japanese increasingly tapped their own sources of strength and independence. They achieved in the 1970's their position as a world power, one that had attained even greater heights than hitherto through peaceful means and international cooperation. Ironically, once again, the prewar historical pattern of isolation to involvement had been repeated, but this time predicated on differing grounds.

XVII

OCCUPIED JAPAN (1945–1952)

Japan, crushed at the conclusion of World War II, soon regained a sense of direction. In the remarkably short period of seven years of occupation, she recovered to a great extent economic productivity and political viability. This was due in part to the constructive and nonvindictive policies of the Occupation and in part to the remarkable ability, resilience, and creativity of the Japanese in adapting to changing conditions. As an attempt to transform Japan into a democratic society as defined by American norms, on the theory that democracies do not threaten the peace of the world, the Occupation was an ambitious undertaking.

Nature of the Occupation

The Occupation was not a complete break with the past. The Occupation might be viewed as a catalyst that speeded up certain limited prewar liberal trends such as universal male suffrage, the gradual emancipation of women, and the partial freedom of the press. Occupation reforms implemented by the United States that were favorable to concepts already initiated by the Japanese tended to be more enduring, while others were discarded. On the other hand, had Japan been occupied by an authoritarian regime, as Soviet Russia. its national life might have been redirected towards totalitarianism by following another set of prewar factors.

The chief planning for the Occupation, which was in essence an American operation, was done in Washington, for the United States alone possessed the military forces, the transportation facilities, and the economic assets to undertake the job. In early 1945, the United States government had already began to make concrete preparations for the occupation of Japan. By the end of August, 1945, a committee called the swncc (State-War-Navy-Coordinating Committee) drafted the *United States Initial Post-Surrender Policy for Japan*, which was sent to General MacArthur, the Supreme Commander of the Allied Powers, in Tokyo, as the overall guiding philosophy of the Occupation. The broad policy objectives were the demilitarization and democratization of Japan. To achieve these ends, more specific tactics were outlined, such as a purge of war criminals, encouragement of political parties, extension of civil liberties, and the break-up of the zaibatsu. With this directive as the overall blueprint for the remaking of Japan, the machinery of the Occupation swung into operation.

In contrast to its operations in Germany, the United States administrators in Japan utilized the Japanese as much as possible. The Japanese government was left in a position to implement American operations, although it was subordinated to MacArthur. This ambivalent approach was based on two sets of considerations: the prohibitively high costs of direct American government that would necessitate huge staffs, and the absence of sufficient Americans with a knowledge of Japan and the Japanese language. The Japanese state remained a constitutional monarchy, headed by the emperor, but he was stripped of his sanctified aura. In a rescript issued on New Year's Day, 1946, he himself renounced the idea of imperial divinity. The American decision to retain the emperor, strongly supported by the Japanese, was a wise one, for it left the country with an institution through which to implement change. Continuing in the native tradition of indirect rule, MacArthur simply acted as a twentieth-century shogun.

Yet because of the existence of double American and Japanese administrative machinery, a serious handicap in effecting reforms existed, the implementation of which had to be left to the Japanese themselves. The actual enforcement of the laws depended in the last analysis on the Japanese, and while there existed some procedures for evaluating results, these sometimes proved difficult. Until 1948 Occupation authorities worked through a Japanese liaison office, after which direct contact was substituted with individual branches of government.

The Occupation was run by predominantly military personnel. At the head was General MacArthur, responsible to the War Department in Washington, and not to the Department of State, which assumed a subordinate role in these years. He was the Supreme Commander of the Allied Powers (SCAP), a term that was variously used to designate the general himself, his headquarters in Tokyo, and the Occupation teams throughout the country. MacArthur performed in two capacities. As a military man, he endeavored to effect changes in civilian Japanese society. As indicated in the *Initial Post-war Surrender Policy,* these duties were clearly outlined for the reformation of Japanese society and government. He was, secondly, responsible for the various military commands of United States forces strung out throughout the Pacific and eastern Asia and for the United Nations forces in Korea after war broke out there. As commander of the American troops, his military duties were to safeguard American rights and to interpret the needs of American security, particularly after the noticeable eruption of the Cold War in 1948. With his sense of mission and his flair for destiny, he fitted the various posts admirably.

The Occupation was an overwhelmingly American affair, with some participation by the British Commonwealth. Yet the terminology of SCAP implied association with other concerned parties. The allies of the United States in the Pacific War operated through two nominal advisory multilateral agencies. Representing initially eleven and then thirteen countries which had participated in the war, the Far Eastern Commission (FEC) met in Washington to issue policy directives to MacArthur. Since the United States could veto any Commission directive, and since it could also issue interim directives pending any Commission action, the United States was guaranteed a primary position in deliberations of that organ. In Tokyo the Allied Council for Japan (ACJ), consisting of representatives of the United States, Soviet Russia, China, and the British Commonwealth, consulted with MacArthur on terms and implementation of policies. It was unsuccessful in its operations, and Council meetings degenerated into debates between the representatives of the United States and of Soviet Russia. Unlike the shared occupation of Germany and Austria but like the unilateral occupation of east European countries by Soviet Russia, the United States enjoyed on its own terms the luxury of relative lack of international problems in administering Japan.

The First Period: Reform

The Occupation may be conveniently divided into two periods, an initial one stressing reform between 1945 and 1948 and a subsequent one emphasizing recovery from 1948 to 1952. In the first period of reform, at least half a dozen basic sectors of Japanese life and society were affected by Occupation directives. First were the purges, military and civilian, of those high-ranking Japanese in official and private life who were associated with the prosecution of the war. An Allied International Military Tribunal for the Far East (IMTFE), representative of the powers involved in the Pacific War, was set up in Tokyo. For almost two years the tribunal tried top Japanese military and civilians on charges of conventional war crimes, crimes against peace, and crimes against humanity. Of the twenty-five tried, seven, including Tojo, were hanged. The rest were sentenced to imprisonment for terms varying between seven years and life, although these sentences were later commuted. In addition, individual Allied countries, in Japan or on their own soil, tried certain Japanese, whom they considered war criminals.

Although the international court was authorized by the Potsdam and other Allied agreements (which had also provided for the Nuremburg trials), its propriety aroused controversy and criticism because of its ex-post-facto nature and because only nationals from the country that lost were tried. Proceeding on the debatable assumption that some civilian economic and political interests were also automatically allied with prewar and wartime militaristic expansion, the Occupation purged by category, rather than by individual basis, some 200,000 bureaucrats from their jobs.

A second significant reform was the promulgation of the constitution of 1947, which replaced the Meiji constitution of 1889. In many ways written in terms similar to those of the United States constitution, the new document broadened the political life of Japan and provided for a parliamentary state. A draft prepared by the Japanese proved unsatisfactory to SCAP and was revised with American advice and then adopted by the Diet. The position of the emperor was transformed from divine ruler to symbol of the state. He continued to represent the unity of the people, but now he derived his position from the popular will, in which sovereign power resided. Although the emperor and royal family were kept, the peerage was abolished.

The constitution eliminated the predominance of the prewar elites over the cabinet, which now became, in true parliamentary form, a committee of the majority party or a coalition, from which the prime minister was selected. The Diet was made the highest and sole law-making organ of the state. Both houses of the Diet became fully elective, and the franchise was extended to all men and women over the age of twenty. The lower and more powerful House of Representatives consisted of 467 members elected to four-year terms, with three to five chosen from each of 118 electoral districts as in prewar days. The upper House of Councillors had 250 members sitting in six-year terms, of whom 100 were chosen at large and the rest in varying numbers from the 46 prefectures.

The judiciary, formerly subordinated to the Ministry of Justice, was made independent. A Supreme Court, like its counterpart in the United States, became the final adjudicator of constitutional matters. Approval of the membership of the Supreme Court was to be submitted every decade to popular vote. Local self-government was strengthened, for the constitution specified that the highest local officials, such as mayors, governors, and members of local assemblies, be elected by their respective constituencies. The constitution guaranteed the rights of life, liberty, and equality, as well as the more modern ones of academic freedom, collective bargaining, and higher standards of living.

The constitution was far-ranging, but it had some weak points. The document did not originate with the Japanese themselves. Conceivably, should occasion arise, they could claim its provisions as nonbinding or alterable. Moreover, troublesome Article Nine, insisted upon by SCAP, renounced war as an instrument of national policy, and it prohibited armed forces in the country. This constituted an idealistic and pacifistic proposition that appealed to many Japanese, but SCAP after the outbreak of the Korean War was to reverse itself on the question of Japanese defense forces.

In keeping with constitutional provisions to insure greater responsibility and more democratic procedures at the local level, another Occupation reform revised the highly centralized relations existing in Meiji and imperial Japan between Tokyo and subordinate political units. Local authorities were granted far greater powers of taxation, education, police, and legislation than they had previously enjoyed. Control of the police was transferred from the Home Ministry to the municipal and prefectural authorities. These local units hired educators, police, and bureaucrats, but problems soon arose from these decentralized patterns. The local administrative units had to tax themselves in order to discharge their functions, and they soon discovered that democracy required large funds and higher taxes. Tokyo stepped in with informal grants-in-aid, but with the extension of funds there returned a degree of centralized control. Because of the existence of multiple and confusing jurisdictions, the Japanese restored some measure of centralized control, particularly in police affairs. In their small and highly unified country, the Japanese preferred a pattern of political centralism.

SCAP reforms further emphasized the extension, the liberalization, and the equalization of educational opportunities for all. They stressed the importance of teaching students how to think rather than what to think. Textbooks were rewritten to eliminate nationalistic propaganda, and the traditional courses on ethics and morality were replaced by newer ones in the social sciences. In the prewar system students had been marked for either vocational or general training; postwar reforms standardized levels of education for all. Compulsory education of nine years was prescribed, and the academic structure came to resemble the American public school system—six years of primary school, three years of junior high school, three years of senior high, and then two years of junior college or four years of college. In the Occupation's zeal for extending the general educational level of the populace, which was presumed to be a prerequisite of democracy, educational facilities at higher levels particularly proliferated. A university, feasible or not, was established in every prefecture, and junior colleges blossomed. Japan experienced a proliferation of private and state-supported universities and junior colleges. The new system offered new educational opportunities, but many Japanese felt academic popularization was accompanied by deterioration in intellectual standards.

Occupation authorities devoted efforts to breaking up the great zaibatsu, on the debatable thesis that the cartels had been allied with Japan's military imperialists and on the more tenable proposition that such imbalanced accumulation of wealth in a country was detrimental to the development of a viable democracy. Besides purging members of zaibatsu families and their top-ranking managerial staffs, SCAP froze company accounts. It took over the greater bulk of financial holdings through capital levies, and it redistributed assets. In the first wave of reform, eighty-three holding companies were broken up into their components. An antimonopoly law was passed at the same time to preclude their recombination. In December, 1947, a law was enacted to provide for the further deconcentration of 1200 companies, but by that time the emphasis of Occupation policy had changed from reform to recovery, and only nine companies were affected.

As SCAP broke up the zaibatsu, so it encouraged labor organizations. It proceeded in the belief that the creation of bona fide labor unions would abet the process of democratization in Japan, that unions would tend to diminish the strength of the zaibatsu, and that unions would help lower urban income groups to participate in politics and mature through political experience. In December, 1945, a Trade Union Law gave workers the right to organize, bargain, and strike. A Labor Relations Board was created to enforce the Act. At the same time, SCAP ordered all political prisoners released, and these included labor leaders. Unionism experienced a phenomenal growth, and within a year of the passage of the law, union membership had jumped from a million to 4.5 million. But the movement was not so powerful as numbers indicated, since most Japanese were inexperienced in the matter, and employers set up unions with themselves as presidents and officials. Many workers joined unions without knowing their own rights and duties or the purposes for organization. The vigor of labor's response at first delighted Occupation reformers. However, their enthusiasm was soon dampened as the movement grew into a leftist political force, controlled in large measure by Communists.

Finally, a major achievement of the Occupation was land reform. At the end of the war, probably one-half to two-thirds of Japanese arable holdings was worked by tenants paying exorbitant rents in kind. On the assumption that an agrarian pattern structured on semi-feudal ownership of large holdings by a few landlords hindered democratization, land reforms were instituted. In 1946 legislation was passed, in part to check the evils of absentee land ownership as well as of tenancy, which set maximum ownership limits of two and a half acres for noncultivator owners and seven and a half acres for cultivator owners. The government purchased all remaining land at 1939 prices and sold it to former tenants at the same prices but at inflated 1947 rates. This was tantamount to expropriation, but by the end of the reform only 10 per cent of the land was worked by tenants, and rents in kind were virtually eliminated. Some five million acres of arable land were redistributed within two to three years. While the peasant enjoyed pride of ownership, the land reforms did not necessarily result in increased food production because of the continued utilization of uneconomical small plots, the marginal existence of many of the new owners, and the ever-recurring possibility of agrarian debt in the event of crop failure.

The Second Period: Recovery

Within the first few years of the Occupation, most of the basic reforms had been outlined and implemented. But a change of attitude in 1947 and 1948 occurred in SCAP which shifted emphasis from reform to recovery. Internal developments in Japan favored the tapering off of reform measures, and as early as 1947 MacArthur declared that Japan was ready for a peace treaty. Factors outside Japan affected the change in Occupation philosophy. Japan's role was reconsidered in the emerging Cold War situations, and the zealous reforms were slowed down. Tension was apparent in Europe and Asia, and the wartime alliance seemed to be splitting apart in the late 1940's. The Berlin airlift, the Trieste problem, Czechoslovakia's entrance into the Communist orbit, and the Marshall Plan were some of the major developments in the East-West conflict in Europe. Signs indicated that after the fall of Manchuria to the Communists in November, 1948, Chiang Kai-shek's regime on the China mainland was disintegrating in the face of stepped-up Chinese Communist activity. More than ever, the United States became concerned with the maintenance of political and economic stability in Japan and the necessity of Japan as an ally. The new emphasis on economic recovery sometimes conflicted with earlier SCAP policies of democratization.

Occupation authorities cracked down on left-wing radicals, including Communists, who had been released after the war. Labor union demands for higher wages and the right to strike were checked. In 1948 the Diet passed a no-strike law for both civil service and industrial workers. As a substitute for the lost right to strike, the government appointed an official employer-union Public Arbitration Board. The first important test of the Board was the case of a demand for higher pay by railroad workers on government lines. For six months the Board studied the case. After it decided to raise salaries by 25 per cent, the government refused to accept the recommendation and advocated instead a 3 per cent raise. The unions informed SCAP that the repeal of the right to strike was unfair; SCAP replied that the negotiations constituted a domestic affair. The railroad workers did not get the pay raise.

In 1949 the government embarked on a policy of fiscal retrenchment to cut the budget, a policy advocated by SCAP on the recommendation of an economic survey mission from the United States the year before. To reduce expenditures, the government laid off as many as 100,000 employees, including labor union leaders. On the other hand, the SCAP now permitted some purged economic leaders to return to their industrial and zaibatsu posts. The FEC stopped reparations shipments and the dismantling of plants, which it had permitted to a limited extent, although this action occasioned the particular wrath of the war-devastated Philippines, which felt entitled to extensive reparations. Lastly, the United States started preparations for a Japanese peace treaty to return full sovereignty to Japan as an ally of the United States, a matter of urgency particularly after the outbreak of the Korean War in June, 1950.

Peace Treaty Negotiations

As early as summer of 1947 the United States extended an invitation to the FEC powers to draft a peace treaty which would be accepted by majority rule. Stalin and Chiang Kai-shek objected, for they desired to retain the veto as stated in the provisions of the Potsdam Conference. Russia also pointed out that the United Nations Declaration of Janury 1, 1942, to which the United States had adhered, forbade any separate peace-making procedures. Finding it impossible to work through divided FEC councils, making no headway either on a German peace treaty, and deeming it imperative to strengthen Japan as early as possible, the United States began individual negotiations for a peace treaty with as many of the involved states as possible. In September, 1950, President Truman named a Republican, John Foster Dulles, who had an extensive background in procedures of international law and public conferences, as his special ambassador in charge of peacemaking with Japan. For almost a year, Dulles and his assistants, traveling to Tokyo and at least ten world capitals, worked at arriving at agreeable terms. In the course of negotiations for a peace treaty, in April, 1951, in a final lesson of democracy that impressed the Japanese, Truman fired MacArthur from all his posts because of the general's insubordination resulting from policy differences in the conduct of the Korean War, which MacArthur wanted to extend into Manchuria. Truman replaced him with General Matthew Ridgway, who served out the remainder of the Occupation as SCAP.

The initial United States proposals for peace were aimed at bringing a fully independent Japan back into the family of nations. Japan was to enter the United Nations, which was to establish a trusteeship for the Ryukyus and the Bonins. Japan was to recognize Korean independence and accept a later decision of the concerned powers regarding the disposition of Formosa, the Pescadores, South Sakhalin, and the Kuriles. In commercial agreements, Japan was to receive the usual most-favored-nation treatment. With respect to security measures, the United States advocated bilateral arrangements with Japan. The United States also pondered the advisability of including in the peace treaty clauses binding Japan to continue the Occupation reforms. This proposal was rejected, and it was hoped that the reforms would stick.

Reactions to the United States peace proposals varied. Soviet Russia continued to question the feasibility of a separate peace. She wanted Communist China to get Formosa and desired confirmation of titles to the Kuriles and South Sakhalin, which she was already occupying. The Russians advocated that all troops leave Japan and wished Communist China included as a party in all discussions. The Chinese Communists, not consulted, seconded the request for participation, and the British, who now recognized their regime, concurred. In reply, the United States, continuing to recognize Chiang Kai-shek, stated that no single nation through the exercise of the veto should hold up peace negotiations. She maintained that wartime agreements on dispositions of Japanese territory were not final and claimed that the trusteeship status advocated for the Ryukyus and the Bonins was not identical with territorial expansion.

From Formosa, where Chiang Kai-shek's regime had retired in December, 1949, after the fall of mainland China to the Communists, Nationalist China demanded foreign control of Japan for at least fifty years. Also with bitter memories of Japan, the Philippines and Australia wanted strong guarantees against possible resurgence of Japanese militarism, and they questioned the depth of Japanese democracy. Korea was not consulted on peace terms, since as a colony she was technically never at war with Japan. Japan had nothing to say. She objected to the terminology of certain wartime agreements and condemned Cairo's "violence and greed," but Prime Minister Yoshida Shigeru committed Japan "definitely and irrevocably" to the side of the free world. In an exchange of communications prior to the peace conference, Yoshida assured Dulles that Japan would recognize Chiang Kai-shek's government. Yet Yoshida claimed that Communist or not, mainland China remained Japan's next-door neighbor and that geography and economic laws would prevail in the long run over ideological differences and artificial trade barriers.

In August, 1951, the final text was drawn up by the British and the Americans, who served as co-hosts to the peace conference which met in San Francisco in September. The conference was unique, for the discussions of treaty terms had been essentially concluded prior to its convocation. The concerned parties were invited to come to sign the treaty as a take-it or leave-it proposition. Fifty-two countries attended, including the Soviets and two other Communist states. Not invited were neutrals such as Sweden and Switzerland and ex-enemies such as Italy and Germany. Burma was invited but did not attend because she believed that the treaty terms were too liberal. India declined to come for precisely the opposite reason. Neither rival Chinese government was represented, since the conference co-hosts each recognized a different China. Communist China stated that the treaty infringed upon Chinese interests and that it threatened the peace and security of Asia. Nationalist China approved generally the terms but felt that she should have been invited to sign.

President Truman opened the conference, Secretary of State Dean Acheson presided, and Dulles acted as peacemaker among the representatives. Endeavoring to confuse, disrupt, and divide the conference, the Soviet bloc offered nine objections and thirteen amendments to the treaty, none of which were adopted. In commenting on the terms, most delegations limited themselves to statements of special interest. Asian delegations generally welcomed Japan back into the family of nations, but Indonesia and the Philippines insisted adamantly on their right to reparations. On September 8, 1951, forty-nine of the fifty-two states signed the treaty. Yoshida complimented the "fair and generous treaty," but he pointedly recalled Japan's extensive territorial losses, the bleak international economic outlook, and the third of a million Japanese not yet repatriated from the Asian mainland. He apologized for Japan's prewar militaristic role, paid tribute to Generals MacArthur and Ridgway, and envisioned a reborn Japan.

Peace Treaty Settlement

The treaty of peace was a treaty of reconciliation. It was non-discriminatory, nonpunitive, and motivated by enlightened self-interest. The preamble contained a general statement of objectives and principles. Japan was to apply for United Nations membership (which she did, although Russian vetoes held up Japanese entrance until 1956), and she was to maintain the new ideals of human rights and freedoms expressed in the constitution. The treaty ended the state of war and recognized the full sovereignty of the Japanese people, but the terms relating to territorial dispositions were vague and unclear. As the Potsdam Declaration had provided, Japan was limited to the four main home islands and some minor islands. Japan renounced all rights, titles, and claims to Formosa, the

Pescadores, Kuriles, South Sakhalin, the former Pacific mandates, Antartic areas, and the Spratly and Paracel Islands in the South China Sea that she had occupied in the course of taking over Indochina. Yet the treaty remained silent on the new ownership for these territories for it did not provide for their disposition or the transfer of titles to any other parties. In the Ryukyus, Japan retained "residual sovereignty," but the United States administered the island chain which had been built up into a vast military complex.

Japan was to refrain from the use of force in international relations, but the treaty recognized that Japan, in keeping with the United Nations Charter, possessed the right of individual or collective self-defense. All Occupation forces were to be withdrawn within ninety days after the treaty went into effect, but the treaty provided that some of the forces might be retained and stationed in Japan according to special agreements between one or more of the Allied powers. Otherwise, the argument went, Japan would be defenseless in the face of aggression. In its economic and political clauses, the treaty provided for nondiscrimination in relations with Japan and pledged Japan to a free economy and an unlimited right to trade. Permanent agreements regarding specific issues were to be negotiated between interested parties. Japan renounced all her rights and privileges in China.

The issue of reparations proved sticky. The treaty implied that nations which suffered at the hands of the Japanese were to get reparations, but it stated that Japan at that time could not meet extensive reparations demands and still keep the economy going. Voluntary rather than mandatory reparations were implied. On this point, Indonesia and the Philippines signed the peace treaty with reservations, for they maintained that Japan had a legal as well as a moral obligation to pay reparations. Other treaty provisions related to Korea, which was treated as an Allied power rather than as an ex-colony of Japan, and to Nationalist China, which was given the right to conclude a separate peace treaty with Japan on the same terms as the general peace treaty.

When the final terms were released in Japan, the Japanese, a disciplined people, received them with great restraint. They feared the future with its imponderable economic and security problems. They simply wanted to be left alone, yet 85 million people could hardly enjoy the luxury of nonparticipation or noninvolvement in world affairs. They feared that too close ties with the United States could embroil them in a war with Russia or Communist China. They wanted a demilitarized utopia, and while Article Nine of the constitution might have provided this condition in Japan, strong neighboring countries did not have similar constitutional stipulations restraining the use of force.

Despite some qualms, both houses of the Diet approved the peace treaty by great majorities. The emperor ratified it, and the instrument of ratification was deposited in Washington. The United States Senate consented to the approval of the treaty with only a small negative vote. Other countries followed suit. On April 28, 1952, when the majority of signers, including the United States, had ratified it, Japan recovered her independence. On the same day, Chiang Kai-shek concluded a peace treaty with Japan, which recognized Nationalist China as sovereign authority in Formosa and the Pescadores. Other powers which did not sign the San Francisco peace treaty or which had signed it with reservations in subsequent years entered normal relations with Japan: India in 1952, Burma in 1954, Soviet Russia in 1956, and the Philippines and Indonesia in 1956 and 1958 respectively, after both countries had at the same time concluded reparations agreements.

To supplement idealism with practical security arrangements, the United States negotiated additional treaties with Japan. On the day that the peace treaty was signed in San Francisco, the United States and Japan also signed a Security Treaty. In this short but basic agreement, Japan granted to the United States the right to maintain forces in and about Japan. The forces were to guarantee peace and security in the Far East as well as to preserve the security of Japan both from external attacks and from internal subversion. This right to station forces, which was to continue indefinitely until other arrangements were made, was granted exclusively to the United States. To implement the details of the Security Treaty, the Administrative Agreement signed February 28, 1952, minutely stipulated for the disposition of such forces, the use of facilities, the sharing of costs, and the privileges and exemptions of, and jurisdiction over, American troops. The Diet approved the Security Treaty, but many Japanese worried about the dangers, costs, and extent of rearmament as well as its constitutionality.

In the wake of Japan's recovery of independence, the United States made other security arrangements with her uneasy allies to placate them in their fears of any possible resurgence of Japanese militarism. To smooth Philippine fears, the United States signed a mutual assistance treaty with the Philippines on August 30, 1951. To reassure Australia and New Zealand from a similar fear of future Japanese military strength, the ANZUS pact was concluded two days later. These arrangements, designed primarily for protection against Japan, later were to be the basis on which the United States was to build groupings against militant Communism in Asia. The Japanese peace settlement was comprehensive. It included not only the multilateral San Francisco peace treaty, but a series of other bilateral or multilateral arrangements with Japan and third countries. The settlement ended one era in Asia and anticipated another.

CHRONOLOGY

1945	MacArthur designated SCAP; *Initial Post-Surrender Policy*; Trade Union Law; purges commence in industry and military
1945–1948	First phase: reform
1946	Emperor renounces divinity; land reform law
1947	New constitution effected
1948	No-strike law
1948–1952	Second phase: recovery
1949	Fiscal retrenchment
1950	Korean war breaks out (June)
1951	MacArthur fired, replaced by Ridgway; signing of Peace Treaty at San Francisco and Japan-U.S. Security Treaty (September 8)
1952	Administration Agreement signed (February 28); Japan recovers independence (April 28); separate treaties with Nationalist China, India
1954	Peace treaty with Burma
1956	Peace treaty with Russia, Philippines
1958	Peace treaty with Indonesia

XVIII

CONTEMPORARY JAPAN (SINCE 1952): (1) DOMESTIC AFFAIRS

The Occupation of Japan was followed by a transitional phase of some eight years after the peace treaty in which many of the reforms of the Occupation persisted, but to a lessening degree. Then, particularly after the riots in the spring of 1960 and the revision of the United States Security Treaty at that time, Japan entered ino a period of a dozen years in which it began to initiate new programs and purposes in domestic and foreign affairs. By the end of 1972, with the return to the country of administrative control of Okinawa and the Ryukyus, with the normalization of relations with Communist China, and with the resolution of some other basic issues resulting from wartime conditions, Japan entered into yet another and greater degree of freedom of action and international standing.

Politics: The Right

After the initial political uncertainty that followed the surrender, conservative parties came to power in Japan and consistently remained in office. Usually receiving two-thirds of the popular vote, they were proportionately represented in the Diet. They constituted a permanent majority yet were periodically divided and reunited within the formal party organizations. Until 1950 there were two main streams of conservative parties. The Liberals built on the pre-war Seiyukai party and the Progressives and Democrats evolved from the Minseito. United in 1950 to form the Liberal Party, the factions coexisted uneasily until a split three years later. For another two years, the two conservative factions existed independently until they again reunited in 1955 to form the Liberal Democratic Party.

Factionalism continued and leadership proved unstable; as many as nine different groups existed in the nominally reunited conservative party. Consisting of multiple factions but having purported common programs, appeals, and slogans, the conservatives faced the dilemma of trying to satisfy all party leaders and yet distribute equitably positions of power. Unfortunately, there could be only one prime minister selected from the several party bidders. In order to stay in power, the one chosen had to enjoy the support of his own faction and work out a coalition among the others. Another basic dilemma of the conservatives was the problem of reconciling foreign and domestic policy planks, for their acceptance of American aid and trade ties went counter to strong Japanese wishes for neutrality in world affairs.

Supporters of the conservative cause included the older generation. Traditionally more conservative and adhering to old customs, and old family and political ties, this age group provided a solid basis for the conservative electorate. The upper and middle income urban groups, desiring economic and political stability, also tended to cast their votes for conservative candidates. The rural class overwhelmingly voted conservative. Constituting about two-fifths of the total electorate, it cast four-fifths of its votes for conservatives. There were several reasons for such strong agrarian conservatism. Tradition was a partial answer. In Japan, as in most societies, the agrarian sector has been conservative, and it adhered more strongly to concepts of hierarchy and of obedience to authority than inhabitants of urban areas. In the countryside conservatives had a heritage of local party organization that they maintained in spite of social and economic changes. Relatively satisfied with Japan's peace and prosperity, the farmers had shared in the unprecedented economic growth of Japan after the war. Since the opposition of the left, which was predominantly Socialist, was not able to formulate a program more appealing to rural voters, this group in society maintained its conservative political complexion.

The conservative postwar prime ministers, who worked up through party ranks, came principally from the bureaucracy, especially the Ministries of Finance and of Foreign Affairs. Yoshida, who held office over five cabinets for a seven and a half year period (1946–1947 and 1948–1954), presided over the transition stage from the Occupation to independence. Having opposed the war, he had not been purged and thus was eligible for office. Vigorous and competent, he controlled the party with a firm hand. Assailed as both a dictator of Japan and a puppet of SCAP, he followed a pro-Western foreign policy, although in his determination to modify Occupation reforms he showed his independence. Walking on a tightrope during the early years, he could not ignore either MacArthur's edicts or the Japanese people's feelings on any given issue. But he did modify some of the Occupation laws, and he regained Japanese sovereignty. Yoshida managed to have passed in the Diet a Subversive Activities Prevention program. He secured revision of labor laws to provide for compulsory arbitration of disputes that seemed to threaten the national economy. Despite Socialist opposition, he obtained more central control of the police force. He also helped to resurrect the zaibatsu.

The recovery of independence was followed by the United States Security Treaty, which required great skill and courage for Yoshida to accept and to implement because of the continued presence of American forces in the country. He pressed for United States trade ties, but he desired commercial relations with Communist China. In regard to rearmament, the prime minister was cautious. He refused to seek an amendment (which required a two-thirds majority in the Diet) to the constitution to permit Japan to rearm, but he had previously created the National Police Reserves during the Occupation to conform with MacArthur's interpretation that the constitution permitted self-defense measures.

Yoshida was succeeded by his most powerful rival, Hatoyama Ichiro, in three cabinets (1954–1956). A prewar legislator who opposed the militaristic policies of the Seiyukai and who then withdrew from politics, Hatoyama was nonetheless purged under the Occupation for having defended Japan's policy of expansion during the war. Before he was purged, he had formed the Liberal Party in an effort to unify antimilitarist conservatives. When he was purged in 1946, he turned over party leadership to Yoshida, who, by the time of Hatoyama's release in 1952, wanted to stay in office. Hatoyama promptly split the Liberals and formed his own party. With factionalism at its height in conservative circles, Hatoyama finally caused Yoshida's downfall and became the next prime minister.

Hatoyama followed a more independent nationalist line. Wanting a partial return to the old order, Hatoyama wished to revise the constitution to permit a more extensive program of rearmament and to re-establish the theory of imperial rule. He established a Council for Constitutional Research to suggest such changes. He wanted to hold down the budget but extended generous government aid to relieve the housing shortage. His desire to strengthen the control of the Ministry of Education over "subversives" led to the replacement of elected school boards by appointees of prefectural governors. To achieve a more independent foreign policy, he sought modifications in favor of Japan in the treaties with the United States. During his tenure, trade with Communist China increased, and Japan concluded peace with the Russians, who withdrew their opposition to Japan's entrance to the United Nations. Hatoyama presided over the birth of the united Liberal Democratic Party in November, 1955. Advancing in age, he lost his grip over the party, and the next year he surrendered the leadership.

After an interim of several months in which another conservative prime minister held office, Kishi Nobusuke, who presided over four cabinets from 1957 to 1960, took the helm. A strong personality, he had been a bureaucrat in Manchuria, and he had held a post in Tojo's cabinet. But he was not tried as a war criminal, and in time he emerged as leader of the Liberal Democrats. It was remarkable that he lasted as long as he did, since he did not personally endear himself to many of the Japanese, much less to conservative supporters. He sought to further the process of centralization in education and police matters. Despite great criticism for infringing on academic freedom, in 1958 he introduced a new efficiency rating scale for teachers administered by the Ministry of Education. The same year he pushed for the extension of centralized police power.

On other issues he went along with traditional conservative platforms, such as the recovery of Japanese administration of American-run Okinawa, the ending of nuclear weapons tests, and trade with Communist China. Kishi fell from office after ramming through the Diet the revised Security Treaty in spring, 1960, an act that caused the cancellation of President Dwight Eisenhower's imminent official visit to Japan after widespread leftist demonstrations in Tokyo. Since the press and many Japanese believed that the prime minister was utilizing the American president's visit for his own prestige and advancement, the resulting demonstrations were probably as much against Kishi as against the revised Security Treaty.

The next incumbent, Ikeda Hayato, in six cabinets (1960–1964), promised a "new forward" look. A career bureaucrat with homespun manners and down-to-earth speech, he entered politics comparatively late in life as Minister of Finance in one of Yoshida's cabinets. Leaving behind the controversies of the past, he refused to toy with Occupation reforms, and he closed that postwar chapter of Japan's history. Accepting the permanence of the reforms, he desired to build a new parliamentary framework within which both the conservatives and the Socialists could operate harmoniously. Concerned chiefly with economic progress, he advanced a ten-year program to double Japan's national income. On the foreign front, he practiced cautious conservatism and a "low posture," which to many Japanese meant the diminishing of newly earned prestige and gains abroad. Due to illness, he resigned in late 1964 after the Tokyo Olympiad.

His successor, Sato Eisaku (1964–1972), promised to display a higher posture and a more strident voice for Japan in world affairs. A younger brother of Kishi, the prime minister continued through the dominant right wing of the party a stronger defense pro-Western posture, oriented toward close United States ties. Yet he was also a nationalist and endeavored to follow an independent path by admitting that as "an Asian nation ourselves, we know the heart of Asia." But problems simmered. His party split over détente with China, the American role in the Vietnamese war, and growing economic pressures generated from inflation, pollution, and other industrial issues. A cautious administrator with little initiative, his position eroded in the last year, particularly through the "Nixon shocks" over China and American economic policies.

Assuming the premiership in mid-1972, Tanaka Kakuei was a departure from the usual mould of office. With not even a high school education, and as a one-time construction worker, he presaged a change in leadership style. As former secretary-general of the party, he maneuvered to defeat rivals for the top position. A man of action, he was faced, however, with spiraling problems resulting from Japanese affluence at home and involvement abroad. These issues forced his resignation from office in 1974 and replacement by a "low posture" party man, Miki Takeo.

The extreme right, which included the ultranationalists and the militarists, was relatively impotent in postwar Japan. It lacked sources of financial support, it could not advocate expansion on the Asian mainland where a strong Chinese Communist regime existed, and chauvinism was out of fashion even among the youth of Japan. Its proponents, like its prewar predecessors, lacked coherent programs. Rightist dissidents registered their protests through irrational assas-

'sination attempts on Japanese leaders and others. Within three months in 1960, they instigated three political stabbings—one of Prime Minister Kishi prior to his resignation and two on Socialist leaders, one of whom was killed. In 1964, an attempt was made on the American ambassador's life.

More important and in a different category was the rise of the Soka Gakkai ("Value Creating Association"), a modern-day variant of Nichiren Buddhism, which in the mid-1960's claimed over four million families as members. It appealed in its authoritarianism and discipline to certain economic and social groups that felt left out of Japan's rising prosperity. Its creed was utilitarian, and its goal was "to give absolute happiness to each individual." Politically active, the Soka Gakkai through its political arm the Komeito ("Clean Government Party") elected members first to local assemblies and then to the House of Councillors, where in the 1962 election it received over 11 per cent of the vote. Its political platform included such popular Japanese issues as peace, honest elections, and outlawing of nuclear weapons. But its dogmatic style of proselyting and electioneering left an adverse mark on subsequent elections.

Politics: The Left

The parties of the left, chiefly Socialist, commanded the support of a third of the Japanese voting strength. Like the conservative majority, Socialist groups in Japan were not united in outlook; as many as seven factions existed at a time. Though constituted of multiple factions, within the formal party structure of the Socialist movement there were, in general terms, a right and left wing. The former, constituting perhaps 30 per cent of the strength, was less disciplined, more opportunistic, and closer to the conservative cause. The latter, some 70 per cent, was the more vigorous and Marxist, with its extremist flank allied to Communism.

As in the conservative movement, in the postwar era there were phases of formal party cooperation and splits between the two main Socialist wings. Initially there was party unity (1945–1951). In this period Japan had her only Socialist prime minister, Katayama Tetsu, the Christian head of the Social Democrats (1947–1948), who derived power from a Socialist plurality within a coalition that included conservative Democrats and another minor party. The coalition was unworkable and fell apart, to be followed by a four-year period of party disunity. Reunited in forced companionship to contest elections in October, 1955 (a month before Hatoyama reunited the conservatives), the unstable cooperation endured from 1955 until 1960. Then another split occurred with the formation of the right-wing Democratic Socialist Party and the left-wing Social Democratic Party.

In their programs, the right-wing and left-wing streams of Japanese Socialism differed in point of degree rather than in principle. In domestic affairs, the left advocated a proletarian state and extensive nationalization. The right, in a type of evolutionary Christian or Fabian socialism, espoused popular democracy, a mixed economy of government and private interests, and civil liberties. But both desired the traditional Socialist program of more state control of industry and transport, strong local rather than national controls of police and education, and retention of land reforms to insure possession of land to peasants. In foreign affairs, Socialist views ranged from neutralistic to communistic extremes, but unlike the conservatives they did not favor the close military and economic ties with the United States. Supporting the strong feelings of neutralism and pacifism in Japan, the Socialists were in sympathy with popular causes.

Yet their political fortunes were not so high as those of the conservatives. In spite of their supporting of popular ideas, they contributed to their own weaknesses. Factionalism was prevalent, and although this was also the case among the conservatives, this made a weak movement weaker. Party organization was not uniformly strong, and it was represented in only one-third of Japan's four thousand political subdivisions. It was top heavy, for it tended to concentrate its greatest efforts at the national rather than local level. Socialists held about 30 per cent of the total seats in the Diet, but the percentage dropped precipitously at the prefectural, city, and district council levels, and in town and rural units. Moreover, their frequent parliamentary tactics of discourtesy, militancy, and volubility were not conducive to gaining support for them.

Despite its weaknesses, Socialism could count on certain sectors of Japanese life and society for support. Labor unions were traditionally allied with the Socialist cause, and they sponsored candidates who were expected if elected to further the program of trade unionism. Unions contributed funds to the party, and they campaigned in the hustings for Socialist candidates. Approximately half of the party members were from unions, and many Socialist members of the Diet rose through union channels. Some intellectuals also supported the party. The youth, a traditionally alienated group, perhaps more through emotion than reason, supported Socialist parties or causes. Finally, the urban lower classes, although assured of a degree of economic stability and job security, voted Socialist as a protest against their more fortunate city brothers in middle and higher income brackets.

The postwar Japanese Communist movement, despite its legalized status, was weak. When SCAP released political prisoners after the war or permitted their return from abroad, Japanese Communist leaders reactivated the party. Until 1950 their strategy was one of peaceful revolution, which followed from the 1932 thesis that called for the destruction of feudal elements through a democratic revolution in co-operation with bourgeois groups. Also, the presence of Occupation forces made this approach the only practical one. Invoking a policy of moderation, the Communists regarded the Occupation as an ally, since both aimed for a democratic, peaceful revolution at home. The party set out to win the allegiance of two particular groups of people, small business and the peasants, and it posed as their benefactor. During this period, there were parliamentary gains for the party, and in the early postwar years for the first time in Japanese history, Communists were elected to the Diet.

In 1950, the moderate and cooperative line changed because of outside pressures. The January issue that year of the journal of the Cominform violently attacked the theory of peaceful revolution and its Japanese proponents. The article declared that the Occupation was turning Japan into a military base. The moderate attitude of the party was, in effect, the article stated, collaboration with the United States, from which the party was to remove itself. The change in line advocated by the Cominform placed the Japanese Communist Party in a difficult position, since the party was not eager to resist the Occupation singlehandedly, and a program of violence would alienate many of the groups it was endeavoring to win over.

After secret meetings, the party issued a compromise statement. It acknowledged errors, but it claimed that it was not altogether wrong in its tactics. As a result of this clash between national and international Communist tactics and judgment, the party after 1950 entered a phase of direct action. Incidents, demonstrations, and riots were perpetrated during the last years of the Occupation and immediately afterwards. The Cominform advice proved harmful, for the militant policy failed. The acts of violence terrified elements who had previously been sympathetic to the Communist cause. The Japanese government cracked down on party activity, and it registered those leaders it could round up. By 1953 the party lost every one of its seats in Parliament and its membership fell off. In time, because of severe setbacks, the party reverted to peaceful procedures. Though continuing as a legal party, it remained weak, and it captured only 2 to 3 per cent of the popular vote in elections for seats in the lower house of the Diet. It was further debilitated when the Peking-Moscow differences in the mid-1960's caused a cleavage in international Communism.

The presence of ideological choice in Japanese political thought was a new phenomenon. The postwar political spectrum had broadened, and a radically different constitutional system was in operation. Increased mass participation in public affairs provided a greater base for a new political consciousness. More groups tended to support the democratic experiment, yet the voters continued to return to office conservative candidates. A perennial minority, the Socialists seldom enjoyed the highest offices. But on some basic issues such as neutralism, peace, and outlawing of nuclear weapons, the Japanese could unite. Political consensus of right and left on such fundamental points augured a reasonable degree of political stability in Japan.

Economics

A noticeable aspect of post-Occupation Japan was economic growth. Indices were impressive. Overall annual economic growth rates were 9.1 per cent between 1950 and 1955, 10 per cent between 1956 and 1962, a high of 12.1 per cent in 1963, followed by declines in the next two years to 9.4 and 7.5 per cent respectively. In spite of a decreasing proportion of the agrarian labor force, which fell to 30 per cent of the population, agricultural production because of increased commercialization and scientific practices kept pace with the growing economy and population. In the early 1960's per capita income in Japan went over $500, a remarkable figure for Asia, where some countries registered only a tenth of that figure.

Great economic progress in Japan can be attributed to several factors. As the state had previously been engaged in industrial activity for nearly a century, her people had acquired administrative skills and technical know-how over several generations. They had already made the psychological adjustment to industrialism, and they built on native techniques in modernizing. The government espoused the doctrine of free enterprise, but it did not hesitate to step in to shore up lagging segments of the private sector of the economy. Public industrial investment was heavy even during temporary recessions in order to spur greater increases in productivity.

As a pump-priming method, bank practices extended loans constituting an unusually great percentage of their assets to refinance and to expand industry.

Moreover, Japan shared, as the United States and Europe did, in the general postwar prosperity of the non-Communist world. This helped to account for growing Japanese markets overseas and expanded international trade. Massive direct American aid programs during the Occupation that amounted to $2 billion, as well as subsequent military procurements in Japan during the Korean War that totaled twice that amount, promoted the retooling of industry and aided the recovery from wartime destruction and immediate postwar doldrums. New-found prosperity resulted in a consumer revolution in city and countryside that spurred sales of household gadgets, electric hibachis, television sets, radios, and other material benefits of modern living.

For a non-Socialist state, Japan experienced a high degree of economic planning that resulted in controlled growth. The Prime Minister's Office was a prime factor in the formulation of economic policy, along with the Economic Planning Agency and highly qualified personnel particularly of the Ministry of Finance, the Ministry of International Trade and Industry, and the Bank of Japan. Experts in these governmental agencies continually analyzed domestic production figures and foreign market goals, and they projected national trends and formulated programs. Japan's industrial leaders gave support to the official economic decisions made. Government, finance, and private industry became meshed into a common outlook and purpose.

Despite the post-Occupation overall rise in prosperity, basic economic problems persisted. Millions of people did not share proportionately in the wealth. Riches and rewards were not evenly distributed, and intellectuals and white-collar workers particularly did not benefit from postwar economic gains. The government tended to relegate to a secondary role such public areas as housing, transportation, and social services. The Japanese standard of living rose to one of the highest in Asia, but it remained considerably behind that of economically advanced Western European states. Population growth appeared to negate some economic gains, but birth control measures were instituted as early as 1948 during the Occupation, when the Eugenics Protection Law was passed to legalize abortion. As a result of such measures, for a time the number of abortions exceeded births. The rate of natural increase declined to about 1 per cent, one of the lowest absolute population growth rates in the world outside of Western Europe.

Population might stabilize, but foreign economic relations had to expand. One perennial problem was to maintain a high volume of exports in order to meet obligations incurred by a high volume of imports. "Export or die" was a familiar slogan. Up to 80 per cent of Japan's raw materials for industry and up to 20 per cent of its foodstuffs were imported. Wheat, some rice, vegetable oils, and other edible commodities came from abroad. Another persisting economic problem was the double structure of the domestic economy, for while the zaibatsu might have dominated the economic scene, three-fifths of Japan's industry remained in the hands of relatively inefficient small or medium-scale operations. Underemployment was serious in the first years of the post-Occupation period, for there was no full-time utilization of much of the labor force. Japan's initial postwar labor surplus disappeared as the economy expanded, and a new fear arose instead of a labor shortage. As sources of labor grew shorter and as the birth rate declined, there arose the possibility of impediments to economic growth. Spiraling inflation in the 1970's, caused in part by the oil crisis, made the cost of living phenomenal. Tokyo became the most expensive world capital, according to United Nations sources.

Despite problems, the Japanese government planned for the future. In the early 1960's, Prime Minister Ikeda formulated a ten-year program to double national income; his successors equally concerned themselves with formulas for sustaining growth patterns.

Society

Economic growth accelerated social change, and Japanese conservatives were greatly alarmed at the degree to which the traditional positions of emperor, state, and family were altered. The concept of maintaining an emperor without emperor worship in postwar Japan was a new and unwelcomed phenomenon to them, for the imperial position became a mere symbol without sanction for its importance or its focus as a national institution. Emperor and state worship went out of fashion in widespread and prevalent postwar attitudes of pacifism, antimilitarism, and partial loss of national self-confidence. The Japanese flag was less frequently displayed in the early postwar decades, and the term Nihon came more into fashion to replace Nippon with its supposedly imperialistic connotations. Torn by the conflicting outlooks of the different generations within it, the family tended to break apart. The prewar positions of such conservative bulwarks as the bureaucracy and industrial classes were eroded. The peerage was abolished, the old militarist class was eradicated, and civil servants became responsive to public desires.

Having matured in a political environment different from that of their elders, younger Japanese officials pursued a tradition that included responses to, rather than insulation from, elections and public mandates. The old adage of "officials honored and people despised" lost its validity in modern Japan. Zaibatsu enterprises became more fluid, and a managerial system drawing upon young executives from among top college graduates emphasized merit and ability rather than family ties. Relations between big business and political parties broadened and diffused.

The postwar era also brought many changes to rural Japan. Land reform removed many inequities in agrarian society, and the new education attacked myths and institutions of the traditional social order, including state Shinto and the familial basis for the state. The Japanese farmer was better educated, lived better, and participated in a fuller political and cultural life than did his Asian counterparts. The legacy of conservatism lingered on in the farmer, yet his conservative vote was due in part to satisfaction with the material benefits that were brought about by his general economic advancement. Increased productivity and greater efficiency enhanced sources of farm income, which were further augmented, particularly in rural areas adjacent to towns or bordering on cities, by nonfarming jobs and activities. Japan's rural society was likely to be characterized by a further retreat from traditionalism, continued rising material aspirations, and increased political consciousness. Because of a greater degree of diffusion in the farmer's economic activity, his political response could well result in less uniformity in political patterns.

The urban working classes were no longer composed essentially of first generation peasants. The Japanese proletariat was becoming what was traditionally thought of in the West as a lower-middle class. With the introduction of the new education, unionization, and modern management, it grew in political influence. It was organized into labor unions that included about one-third, or nine million, of the total Japanese working force. The basic unit of unionism was the single enterprise or plant, federated into regional and national associations. The average number of workers per union was 180 (compared with 14,000 in Great Britain and 95,000 in the United States). Two national labor associations existed, the left-wing Sohyo (General Council of Japan Trade Unions) with about 45 per cent of the total union membership, and the moderate Zenro (Japan Trade

Union Congress), along with affiliated groups in the right collectively known as Domei Kaigi, with 13 per cent.

The rest were in independent unions or in ideologically neutral organizations, as the Shinsanbetsu (National Federation of Industrial Organizations). The unions of the left, which included government workers, in addition to the usual Communist causes, advocated direct political action. Although some of the Communist-leaning Sohyo-affiliated unions gave support to Communists, the majority supported the Socialists, while the minority Zenro-affiliated unions supported the Democratic Socialists. The growth of labor unionism in Japan was not deterred by the concurrent rise in national wealth, which might have reduced interest in union activity.

The younger generation, another major social group in postwar Japan, played a new role of prominence. Opposed to militarism and favoring neutrality in world affairs, it accepted many tenets of the Communist and Socialist political platforms. Youth groups participated in direct political action, but many students had to moderate their tactics, for the unemployed youth of Japan with socially unacceptable minority views had bleak employment prospects. The most extreme of the youth groups was the Zengakuren (National Federation of Student Self-Government Associations). Founded in 1948, it counted over 200,000 members from 266 college and university groups. Its initial aims were to improve student life and to safeguard academic freedom. In the 1950's it became involved in extremist political causes, a policy that estranged many of its followers. It became alienated from most students, and when it sought formal relations with the Japanese Communist Party, even the party found the student group too extreme. In 1960 its members spearheaded the spring demonstrations. By that time, when the group had reached its greatest notoriety, it had already entered into a period of decline, and the organization subsequently broke up into splinter groups which bitterly fought each other. The late 1960's was a particularly virulent time for student demonstrations over a variety of academic, professional, or foreign policy issues.

Another group, the intellectuals, were both liberated and frustrated in the new Japan. Certain prewar trends as nihilism and Marxism survived into the postwar era. These were augmented by a plethora of other *isms*, including an early vogue of existentialism. In the midst of a variety of ideologies, intellectuals served as the perennial opposition, for they continued to be strongly antagonistic to Japanese conservatism which they equated with basically antidemocratic regimes of the past. In general, Japanese intellectuals were leftist, but as more of them came in contact with Western democratic forces, they took a more flexible position. Japanese intellectuals saw much that was weak or negative in their own domestic milieu. But rather than point with pride to their country as superior to Asian neighbors in some respects, they decried in rather pessimistic terms her alleged intellectual subordination to Western countries. The rejection of old concepts accompanied by a lack of adequate new ideological substitutes left many in a state of aimlessness.

Literary figures wrestled with a myriad of themes. Some were swept up in international currents; others returned to traditional times for inspiration. In the latter category was Kawabata Yasunari (1899–1972), who, through his psychological novels that included *Snow Country* and *Thousand Cranes*, found stylistic precedent in Heian writing. In 1968, he was awarded the Nobel Prize for literature, the first Japanese writer so honored in the field (although other Japanese had already won similar prizes in physics).

Social realignments and flux suggested the dynamic changing life of modern Japan. After the pronounced emptiness and bleakness of immediate postwar years, education, economic progress, and mass communications opened new horizons. The new generation was taught to believe in democratic ideas, the equality of the sexes, and the rights of the individual. More young people went on to college in Japan than in any country excepting the United States and England. The extensive array of national publications, radio, and television programs disseminated new ideas quickly and thoroughly. Japan published more books than any other country but the Soviet Union and England. The Japanese read more newspapers per capita than any other people excepting the Swedes and the English. Three morning dailies alone enjoyed a total circulation of over ten million copies. Popular literature flourished, and young writers experimented with a variety of themes. As in the political and the economic spheres, more Japanese shared in the new possibilities in social, cultural, and intellectual life.

The new heights of affluence, particularly for an Asian power, that the Japanese attained contained, however, built-in paradoxes. Part of the overall prosperity was accounted for by the small proportion of the budget devoted, for a populous nation with international standing, to the military. Less than 1 per cent was allotted for the military establishment, which in the mid-1970's totaled an army of 180,000 men, a sea force of between 250,000 and 280,000 tons of four to five destroyer groups, and three aerial forces. The Japanese eschewed an atomic development program for military purposes but commenced in 1970 a scientific satellite landing program under the aegis of the Tokyo University Institute of Space and Aeronautical Science.

The highest wages in Asia did not get far in the spiraling inflationary life of Japan in the mid-1970's. Averaging a 34 per cent increase in 1973 alone in wholesale prices, urban workers witnessed salaries disappear rapidly in the rising cost of living, as well as in the paucity of adequate housing in urban areas for reasonable costs. Forty per cent of the population crowded into 2 per cent of the total land space; three-fifths of the some 100 million in Japan lived in six cities alone, mostly in the Pacific industrial belt, strung from Tokyo down to Kobe. The problems of industrialization and urbanization pressed in on the population, as the Japanese literally choked on their affluence; human, noise, air, food, and water pollution abounded. Despite tremendous material gains, the good life was not in sight for the majority of the Japanese.

XIX

CONTEMPORARY JAPAN:
(2) FOREIGN AFFAIRS

Upon recovery of independence, Japan hesitantly returned to the family of nations. With the passing of years, through the 1960's, it maintained a low posture in international affairs. By the early 1970's, however, with the rearranging multipolar world power structure and the numerous ramifications of the energy crisis, it assumed a more active role. Over time, it strongly advanced general policy objectives of increased participation in the United Nations and in international organs, the improvement of its position in the Afro-Asian world, and greater independence within the framework of cooperation with the West, particularly with the United States.

It particularly emphasized economic aspects of diplomacy. Industrial and commercial expansion at home called for an increased emphasis on heavy and chemical industrial exports, although no field was to be abandoned in the general effort to diversify Japanese products for foreign markets. Japan became more involved with the world economy, and it lifted export and import controls that dated back to 1932. It gave special attention to southeast Asian and Asian-African markets with emphasis upon reparations agreements, private investments, and technical assistance programs. Japan was committed to bilateral and multilateral economic arrangements with a number of Asian countries.

Of vital importance was Japanese-American trade, for Japan was America's biggest customer. It depended heavily on United States sources for important raw materials and foodstuffs, but in the United States trade problems arose in the wake of charges of dumped Japanese goods and unfair business practices. At the same time Japan was not reconciled to a policy of economic isolation from mainland China, and it traded with both Communist and Nationalist China. The vital need for foreign trade transcended ideology, and Japan's trading partners included nations, some not diplomatically recognized, of widely disparate ideologies.

Japan and the United States

After Japan's recovery of independence in 1952, it remained throughout the rest of the decade, in effect, a client state of the United States. But with the revision of the Security Treaty in 1960, more along lines conforming to majority opinion, at least in the ruling party, the country began to exert a degree of independence as a silent though junior member of the alliance in the course of the 1960's. With the reversion finally of the Ryukyus to Japanese administrative control in 1972, the last major postwar issue was settled, and Japanese-American relations took an added dimension of stature and counterbalance.

Two post-Occupation problems were resolved in the first decade following the re-entrance of Japan into international life. In 1960, the United States, as the final Allied power to do so, paroled the the last of the Japanese war criminals, about one hundred of them, held in Sugamo prison in Tokyo. The Japanese contended that their continued incarceration inflicted a "living stigma" on Japan for war guilt long since expiated.

On the other issue, that of the Japanese assumption of Occupation costs, the Americans insisted that they repay some of the obligation. Agreement was not reached on this issue until 1962, when the Japanese foreign minister and the American ambassador signed a memorandum that provided for Japanese repayment of $490 million (a fourth of estimated Occupation costs) over a fifteen-year period. Some of the funds were allocated to educational exchange, but the bulk was earmarked for economic assistance to underdeveloped countries of interest to both Japan and the United States. Advancing the argument that Japan's expanded economy could afford the costs, the United States advocated increasing Japanese participation in financial arrangements, especially in underwriting non-Communist Asian consortiums.

On another issue generated by the reaction to the nuclear holocausts ending the Pacific War, the Japanese in international and bilateral talks with concerned nations, including the United States, pushed for disarmament and outlawing of nuclear warfare. The Japanese objected to Pacific atomic testing by the United States, as they objected to nuclear testing by any power. They were particularly aggravated in 1954 when nuclear fallout in the Bikini atoll area on one of their fishing ships, the *Lucky Dragon,* affected twenty-three fishermen, some of whom died. After delays, the United States government extended $2 million compensation to families of the victims.

The revision in 1960 of the mutual Security Treaty heralded a new era of partnership in Japanese-American relations because the main Japanese objections to the 1951 original version had been largely overcome. In the amended version, Japan was recognized as an equal partner in the preservation of peace in the Far East. The terms of the latter document stated that an armed attack on either partner was to be regarded as a common danger and that the two signatories were to consult wherever Japanese security or Far Eastern peace was threatened. The pact was to last for ten years initially, with termination then subject to a year's notice. Japan was to be consulted on the movement of American military personnel within or from territories under her administration (which excluded Okinawa).

No nuclear weapons or implements of war were to be located in Japan without Japanese consent. Should Japan so desire, countries other than the United States could extend military assistance. Japan was relieved of financial obligation to contribute to the payment of American troops. The clause in the original treaty that provided for American troops to quell large-scale internal riots was eliminated. With these substantive changes made, the Diet ratified the new treaty, although the forced and hasty circumstances through which Prime Minister Kishi obtained ratification and the attendant demonstrations upon the eve of President Eisenhower's projected visit left a cloud on the legal procedures utilized.

The revised Security Treaty eliminated some problems but others remained. The status of American forces stationed in Japan and the jurisdictional rights over them remained unclear. Primary jurisdiction in disputes between Japanese nationals and American military, whether on-base or off-base, on duty or off duty, had not been precisely defined in the original Administrative Agreement or in its 1960 version amended. The possibility of dual American and Japanese jurisdiction resulted in unsatisfactory resolution of some infractions by nationals of both countries.

The gradual withdrawal of many American troops from Japan promised to ease the matter partially. Subsequent to a Kishi-Eisenhower agreement in 1957, some 35,000 United States ground troops were recalled from Japan, leaving about 50,000, mainly in the navy and air force contingents. Although the ground troops withdrew in appreciable numbers, the continued existence of a few large naval stations and air bases encroached on valuable land areas, some of which were used to accommodate expanded jet operations. Resistance to enlarged bases was encountered and was particularly strong in rural areas where it was fanned by Communist agitators, but United States facilities, again as a result of the 1957 agreement, were reduced by 60 per cent within three years. In the mid 1960's, Japan played host to some 36,000 United States servicemen (plus dependents) in 150 installations totaling 75,000 acres on Japanese home islands, with additional troops and bases on the Ryukyus. In late 1970, another 10,000 were withdrawn, and by early 1974 only 19,000 remained in Japan (plus 37,000 in Okinawa).

By the mid-1970's the main United States installations in Japan had been considerably reduced. The navy maintained Atsugi air facility in the Tokyo area; nearby Yokusuka, a repair base for the Seventh Fleet; and Sasebo supply depot in Kyushu. The marines used Iwakuni air station in southern Honshu. In the Tokyo area the army utilized Sagami depot, Camp Zama, Yokohama North Pier, the East Fuji firing range, and hospitals. The air force had Wakkanai air station in Hokkaido; Misawa, largely a standby base in north Honshu; Yokota and Tachikawa in the Tokyo area, the former with Japan's longest jet runway; and Itazuki air base near Fukuoka in Kyushu.

Territorial problems remained. The United States returned the Amami Islands south of Kyushu to Japanese jurisdiction on Christmas, 1953, but disputes continued over the Ryukyus and the Bonins, which the United States administered but over which Japan retained residual sovereignty. Japan desired greater control, but the United States. with over a billion dollars in military investment on Okinawa, a staging area for Asian military operations, was reluctant to diminish her position in any way. Sentiment in Japan, as well as among many Okinawans strongly favored the return of all control to Japan, but the Japanese government did not press the issue. Japanese and Okinawans criticized American policies in the island chain and raised charges of landgrabbing for bases and of dictatorial military policies.

Groups critical of American policy, including local Communist units, agitated for more autonomy for Okinawa. They desired the right to choose their own government, including a chief executive. In 1962, the Americans appointed a civil administrator for Okinawa, but they made it quite clear that they intended to retain bases in Okinawa as long as tensions existed in East Asia. The Bonins as well were retained, although the Congress in 1960 voted $6 million as compensation for Japanese residents earlier evacuated from the islands and prevented from returning to their homes. But by the end of the decade the Bonins were back in Japanese hands; a Sato-Johnson agreement in late 1967 stipulated their return, a promise effected in mid-1968 (along with Iwo Jima and Marcus Island). The return of Okinawa, the biggest stumbling block, was resolved in a Sato-Nixon communique in late 1969, wherein Okinawa was to revert to the Japanese by July 1, 1972. Some two weeks earlier, on June 17 of that year, the United States relinquished all rights and interests in Okinawa but were permitted to continue use of military installations (which covered one-fourth of the island chain), including the huge Kadena airfield.

As military and territorial issues fell into the background, that of economic relations remained a perennial problem. American trade complaints included sporadic Japanese flooding of American markets with certain items, although the Japanese attempted to impose export quota controls to moderate fluctuating volumes of goods. In 1961, Prime Minister Ikeda and President John F. Kennedy created the Joint United States-Japan Committee on Trade and Economic Affairs with representatives from cabinets of both countries that in annual meetings endeavored to solve economic issues of mutual concern. High on the agenda was the annual balance of payments. After enjoying an export surplus for several decades, the United States in the 1970's began to register trade imbalances; a high of over $4 billion was recorded in 1972 in favor of Japan. Japanese pledges to cut down its own export surpluses, as well as several devaluations of the United States dollar, helped to mitigate somewhat the adverse United States position in subsequent years.

Some issues remained as irritants; in part these were a matter of style rather than of substance. The Japanese, not used to bold strokes of diplomacy and shocks, were taken aback by the Nixon visit to mainland China in February, 1972, a move in which they were not previously consulted. Moreover, unilateral American trade moves, including temporary restrictions and quotas on needed Japanese imports, as soybeans, hit home in Tokyo. As the 1970's progressed, the changing, seemingly uncertain United States world moves went counter to Japanese desires for certainties and assurances. Continued consultation and mutual respect would be a partial resolution of conflicting views, as well as exchange of official missions. President Nixon met Emperor Hirohito and Empress Nagako at Anchorage in September, 1971, as the imperial party winged its way to Europe on an official visit (the first time in Japanese history that a reigning emperor left the country). President Gerald Ford journeyed to Japan in November, 1974, and the imperial couple repaid the visit with an official trip to the United States in October, 1975. Both occasions were historic precedents and indicative of the close bonds between the two countries and the two peoples.

Japan and Communist Countries

In her relations with Communist countries, Japan emphasized trade arrangements over ideologies, for she saw no necessary correlation between diplomatic and economic recognition. Soviet Russia did not sign the Japanese Peace Treaty at San Francisco, but agreement was reached between the two countries on a number of items. A treaty in 1956 ended the state of war, provided for the exchange of diplomatic and consular personnel, repatriated the remaining Japanese prisoners of war, waived reparations claims against each other, and agreed to effect further talks on trade agreements, fisheries conventions, and a formal peace treaty. Agreement on a number of issues seemed possible at the time because of the softening after 1953 of the Russian line under Khrushchev and the more neutralist policies of the independent-minded Prime Minister Hatoyama.

The agreement helped to smooth Russian-Japanese relations, and that year the Russians dropped their veto of Japanese entrance into the United Nations. But Japan protested Russian nuclear explosions and was disappointed when Russia refused to surrender to her some of the Kuriles, particularly the Habomai and Shikotan Islands that lay only a few miles off Hokkaido. Fishing rights in the Japan Sea constituted a perennial concern to Japan, which endeavored to regulate by agreement with the Soviet the catch in international waters. As anticipated, the Russians denounced the revised United States Security Treaty, but within a couple of weeks after the strongly worded denunciation, she signed a three-year commercial and trade agreement with Japan. Despite differences on some issues, the countries could periodically renew economic agreements. In 1966, a five-year trade agreement was initialed, and by the end of the period, trade had zoomed to a total annual figure of $1 billion. A Japan-Soviet Joint Economic Committee helped to iron out differences and trade issues. The Soviets also evidenced interest in having the Japanese participate in the development of Siberian natural resources, notably the Tyumen oil deposits, the Yakutsk coal and iron reserves, and the Sakhalin offshore oil and gas fields.

A major point of difference remained in the return of the Soviet-occupied Kuriles to Japan. The Russians pledged the return of Habomai and Shikotan Islands when a full-fledged peace treaty would be effected. In 1960, they qualified their stand by demanding also the abrogation of the United States-Japan Security Treaty before the return of the islands, although by late 1973 they had quietly dropped this proviso. With respect to Etorofu and Kunashiri, farther up the Kurile chain, the Soviets claimed the return of these islands as nonnegotiable issues. Prime Minister Tanaka, in the course of a European tour in October, 1973, in Moscow sought once again the return of all the islands in dispute. He further called for talks to resume to conclude a peace treaty and to settle all "outstanding" postwar questions. In the fluid Far Eastern political world, Japan was pressing its position on Soviet Russia.

Toward the People's Republic of China, or Communist China, trade was also a paramount consideration. Lack of de jure or diplomatic representation did not preclude de facto recognition. After the Occupation many Japanese traveled to Peking, and commercial relations were re-established. Between 1952 and 1958, four trade agreements were signed, although only the first three were implemented, and those imperfectly. The agreements were concluded between official Chinese Communist organs and unofficial, private Japanese trading associations. Each agreement was to last twelve to eighteen months, and each was to cover a total exchange of goods the equivalent of $100 million. Items of export and import were outlined in three categories. The most important one, Category A, constituted 40 per cent of the total trade, and Japan agreed to import, among other items, in this category coal, iron, and soybeans and to export strategic steel products on which the United States, for its part, had placed trade embargoes to Communist China. The fourth agreement was not implemented because in 1958 the Chinese Communists cancelled it after a rightist youth tore down a Chinese Communist flag flying over a Nagasaki department store. The Chinese Communists also endeavored, unsuccessfully, to interfere in national elections that year when they generated pressures to oust Kishi from office.

When China experienced agricultural difficulties in the early 1960's, Japan offered the sale of 400,000 tons of rice at reasonable rates, but the offer was not accepted. Japan's trade with China was only 3 percent of its total world trade at the time, and many Japanese nostalgically longed for their prewar stake in the old China trade, when it accounted for 40 per cent. In 1962, after a four-year trade hiatus, with Prime Minister Ikeda now in office and the Chinese more amenable, a fifth agreement was concluded that called for $100 million in trade each year for five years. In 1964, trade had already exceeded the figure by reaching $470 million. By 1970, it registered $820 million, which constituted one-fifth of Communist China's external trade; in the mid-1970's Japan was China's biggest trading partner. Further trade pacts were initialed to delineate the growing commercial relations.

Some other problems were resolved. As with the Soviets, fishing conventions were signed. The Chinese Communist repatriated some 30,000 prisoners of war and former Japanese residents in China. Japan did not initiate moves in the United Nations to consider the eligibility of Communist China as a member, but its spokesmen inferred that should majority sentiment favor such a move, Japan would join in voting for the admission of the Peking regime (which was admitted in late 1971).

On the question of formal diplomatic relations, no postwar Japanese prime minister in office raised its feasibility until 1972. Japan's ties with Taiwan complicated the issue, for neither China would historically accept a "two China" solution to diplomatic recognition. Prime ministers dating to Yoshida's time emphasized the close ties, however, with mainland China, based in great part on immutable geographic propinquity. But recognition was not achieved until after the Nixon visit to China, which started a chain reaction among American "allies" in Asia. In September, 1972, Prime Minister Tanaka journeyed to Peking, where he and Mao Tse-tung normalized

Sino-Japanese relations. According to the communique issued on the historic event, Japan "fully understands and respects" the Chinese view that Taiwan was an inalienable part of China. The two parties were to negotiate a treaty of peace and friendship as well as agreements relating to trade, civil aviation, navigation, and fisheries. The Japanese were not required to abrogate their 1952 peace treaty with the Republic of China on Taiwan, but they did anyway. Formal ties, as well as civil aviation connections, with Taiwan were cut as Japan embarked upon a reoriented course.

With or without diplomatic relations, Japan also traded with other Communist states as the Eastern European countries, Outer Mongolia, North Korea, and North Vietnam. Although Japan recognized the Republic of Korea, with its capital at Seoul, it permitted for eight years (1959–1967) some 87,000 Koreans to return from Japan to North Korea, the origin of their family ties. Japan maintained trade ties with North Vietnam throughout the course of the Vietnam war, but did not recognize the Hanoi-based Democratic Republic of Vietnam until 1973.

Japan and Rest of World

In the non-Communist world, Japan sought close relations, emphasizing once again economic ties, with Asian nations. But in dealing with South Korea, the Japanese ran into rough waters in their efforts to rebuild political fortunes in the former colony. When the Japanese were defeated, the Koreans insisted that their former overlords should leave and never return. During the Korean War, the Koreans resisted any idea of Japanese assistance to United Nations forces in their country. Although the Koreans were not present at the Japanese peace conference, the treaty stipulated that Japanese property in Korea and claims, including debts, should be the topic of bilateral talks between the two states. Since Japanese nationals had owned 80 per cent of the commercial and industrial property in Korea and over half the farmland, the economic stakes were large. Over the years the two parties argued ceaselessly over the nature of compensation to be accorded the Japanese. They also debated the rights of 600,000 Koreans living in Japan, who had emigrated before and during the Pacific War. The Japanese government declared that any Koreans who desired repatriation could go either to North or South Korea. Many Koreans, as noted above, chose the former destination.

An impasse was also reached over another problem, the so-called Rhee line, named after Syngman Rhee, president of the Republic of Korea, which controlled the southern half of the peninsula. Rhee extended Korea's offshore jurisdiction over the continental shelf up to two hundred miles out to sea, almost to Japan's shores. The president forbade all Japanese vessels within the waters, and he authorized the capture of those fishing ships that did enter the limits. Disliking the Japanese as much as the Communists, Rhee looked with disfavor upon United States efforts to rebuild Japan.

Korean-Japanese relations noticeably improved when Rhee left office. In 1965, agreement was finally reached on a number of points: the determination of fishing areas of the two states with their respective and now constricted twelve-mile limits; the provision for joint fishing operations outside these limits up to a catch of 150,000 tons a year for each of five years; the granting of permanent residence to Koreans in Japan who resided there prior to the termination of the Pacific War and their descendants born within five years after the conclusion of the agreement; a Japanese grant of $300 million in economic aid to Korea; a $200 million long-term low-interest loan; and private commercial loans of over $300 million. Despite minority opposition in both countries, the treaty re-established diplomatic relations between the two states for the first time in more than half a century, and it boded closer and friendlier ties.

In 1967, an additional $200 million loan was promised, and five years later $170 million was also pledged. But the implementation of economic aid programs was jeopardized when in 1973 a South Korean opposition leader was spirited away to Seoul from a Tokyo hotel room. As General Park Chung Hee, president of the Republic of Korea, cracked down on critics of his regime in the course of the next months, two Japanese were indicted for making financial contributions to rebellious students. The diplomatic situation clouded once again, although economic ties, on paper, remained extensive.

In 1952, upon the insistence of the United States, Japan recognized the Republic of China on Taiwan, where Chiang Kai-shek did not press reparations on the erstwhile enemy. The Japanese in the 1950's traded annually some $100 million worth of goods with the island (roughly the equivalent of the annual trade with Communist China), although in later years the amount spurted to the half-billion mark. So long as the United States had a vital security stake in the island, Japan went along with the interpretation that the defense of Taiwan was essential to that of Japan; in late 1969

Prime Minister Sato and President Nixon confirmed this under-standing. Yet within two-and-a-half years the situation had changed, for after the Nixon visit to China, a reordering of priorities came into being.

The re-establishment of normal diplomatic and economic rela-tions with southeast Asia states proved sticky, for reparations were a key issue. Not until some countries obtained reparations did they resume diplomatic ties. In 1955, Burma concluded the first repara-tions agreement with Japan. A ten-year arrangement, it called for total payments of $200 million. Since it was the first such agree-ment, the Burmese reserved the right to negotiate for additional reparations. They did so later and received the extension of an additional $140 million spread over twelve years.

In 1956, the Philippines, which originally demanded $8 billion, settled for $550 million over twenty years, plus $250 million in pri-vate loans. In 1958, the Indonesians, initially asking $18 billion, contented themselves with $223 million plus loans over twelve years. In 1960, the Republic of Vietnam (Japan refused to deal with the Hanoi regime on this matter) received $49 million with payments spread over five years. In addition, Japan extended small grants to Laos and Cambodia. Malaysia did not ask for reparations, for Prime Minister Churchill had earlier waived them, although demonstrations in Singapore from time to time demanded "blood money" from Japan. In 1966, Japan extended to Singapore $16.5 million, half in grants and half as reparations.

Japan augmented reparations arrangements with normal trade agreements with southeast Asian countries, which absorbed a third of Japanese exports. By the mid-1970's, Japan was the major trad-ing partner of all southeast Asian countries; trade imbalances with Japan ranged as high as 4 to 1 in the case of Thailand. From south-east Asia, Japan imported 93 per cent of its tin, 90 per cent of rubber, and 40 per cent of bauxite, copper, and timber. To selected southeast Asian countries, Japan provided for 35 per cent of Indo-nesian and Thai imports, 30 per cent of Philippine, and 20 per cent of Singapore's and Malaysia's. Aid and investment figures comple-mented those of normal trade channels. In the former category, Japan provided for almost half of Philippine foreign aid, and one-fifth of Indonesia's. In the latter, Japan had a sizeable stake par-ticularly in the Thai economy; in that country over seven hundred Japanese firms had invested some one-third billion dollars to pro-vide for over one-third of Thailand's total foreign investment. In Indonesia, of total investment figures, Japan's reached 15 per cent (most notably in joint ventures, especially in oil exploration), 11 per cent in Malaysia, and 2 per cent in the Philippines. With Manila, Tokyo had concluded in 1961 a trade treaty to regularize commercial ties, and while the Japanese Diet had long since ratified the agreement, it had been shelved by the Philippine Senate. Japan pledged subscriptions to regional developments in southeast Asia, but it generally held aloof from mediating between the conflicting states and issues in the region. While it appreciated the American position in the course of the Vietnam war in the late 1960's, it kept a low posture. But Tokyo pledged $200 million toward an Indochina Reconstruction and Development Fund for postwar aid.

Commercial stakes were similarly high in the Australasian region, where the Japanese purchased two-fifths of Australian wool and four-fifths of its mineral ores. In south Asia, Japan maintained normal but nominal connections. It extended financial aid to India and Pakistani development planning but avoided any involvement in political issues such as Kashmir, border disputes, or Communist Chinese military activities on the subcontinent.

Such a paramount role that Japan played in the economic life of the countries along the rim of Asia raised problems. To seal ties, in late 1967, Prime Minister Sato visited Taiwan, Indonesia, Australia, New Zealand, the Philippines, South Vietnam, Thailand, Singapore, Malaysia, and Burma. In early 1974, Prime Minister Tanaka ventured to the Philippines, Thailand, Singapore, Malaysia, and Indonesia, where in Bangkok and Jakarta his party met with violent anti-Japanese demonstrations. The conspicuous presence of Japanese nationals, companies, and wealth in less affluent neighbors rubbed nerves raw and initiated Japanese re-examination of their posture in non-Communist Asia.

Commercial relations were again stressed with non-Communist countries in the rest of the world. Oil diplomacy was paramount in the Middle East, and because of this Japan tended to support the Arab side in conflicts and issues with Israel. African interests were minimal, but in Latin America over two hundred Japanese companies operated and that continent provided some $2.5 billion annual trade in the early 1970's. Brazil emerged as a paramount consideration; the 700,000 nationals residing there provided the largest overseas Japanese community. The country, moreover, could be used as a further export base to the United States and Europe. In Europe itself, close Japanese ties were maintained with the European Economic Community (the Common Market), which, along with the United States and Japan was moving toward a strong tri-polar economic community of interests.

Japan also gained admittance into international economic organizations such as the General Agreement on Tariffs and Trade (GATT), and the Organization for Economic Cooperation and Development (OECD), Japan being the only non-European member besides the United States and Canada in this club of economically advanced nations. In September, 1964, Tokyo was the site for the largest international conference ever held in Japan to that time, the joint general meetings of the International Monetary Fund, the World Bank, the International Development Association, and the International Finance Corporation. Japan's successful mounting of the Tokyo Olympiad the following month enormously increased Japanese prestige and overseas awareness of its progress.

In its particular emphasis on Asian regionalism, it sponsored an array of conferences and ministerial meetings at home. It contributed one-fifth of the capital fund of the Asian Development Bank as well as the first two of its presidents. It supported other multilateral economic groups as the Colombo Plan and the aid consortia to several individual Asian countries. Because of its great dependence on imports of raw materials, it turned attention to a type of resources diplomacy through global investments (almost $7 billion in the mid-1970's) to assure access to required commodities. Commensurate with world status, it sought the location of the United Nations University in its home territory and a permanent seat on the United Nations Security Council. And as it became more involved in world affairs, it tried to improve its image in foreign lands through a well-concerted public relations program that included grants to universities to further Japanese studies and understanding.

In sum, Japan recorded remarkable postwar progress at home and abroad. Fewer nations, Communist or non-Communist, had greater obstacles to overcome at the end of World War II than a defeated Japan, but few accomplished more spectacular progress and recovery in economic life. As the only modern industrialized non-Western nation, Japan uniquely drew on native traditional and foreign-derived sources in shaping its national outlook and identity. Japan changed, but Japan could still remain distinctive and constant in spite of change. The complex Japanese society enjoyed both traditional culture and modern conveniences. With deep roots in the past, Japan was also very much a part of the dynamic contemporary world.

CHRONOLOGY

1952–1958	Four trade agreements with People's Republic of China
1954	*Lucky Dragon* incident
1955	Burma reparations agreement
1956	Philippine reparations agreement; Russian treaty; Japan in United Nations
1957	Kishi-Eisenhower agreement on reducing U.S. troops and facilities
1958	Indonesian reparations agreement
1960	Revised Japanese-U.S. Security Treaty and administrative agreement; Vietnam reparations agreement; U.S. paroles last POWs
1961	Ikeda and Kennedy create Joint U.S.-Japan Committee on Trade and Economic Affairs
1962	Japan-U.S. agreement on repayment of some Occupation costs
1964	Meetings of UN-affiliated international organs in Tokyo; Olympics
1965	Treaty with Korea; Japan joins Asian Development Bank
1966	Russian consular treaty; Singapore reparations
1967	Additional Japan loan to Korea; Prime Minister Sato tours Asian countries
1968	Bonins returned to Japanese administrative control
1969	Japanese-U.S. Security Treaty extended indefinitely
1971	Nixon meets Hirohito in Anchorage
1972	Ryukyus revert to Japanese administrative control; Japan recognizes People's Republic of China; additional loan to Korea
1973	Prime Minister Tanaka tours Europe
1974	Prime Minister Tanaka tours southeast Asian countries; Ford visits Japan (November)
1975	October. Imperial visit to the United States.

GLOSSARY

GLOSSARY

Bakufu	"Tent government"; the shogunate as established by Minamoto Yoritomo.
Be (or Tomo)	An ancient Yamato subsidiary work unit supporting the clans.
Bodhisattva	A Buddhist being of wisdom, who, in Mahayana Buddhism, could save supplicants.
Bonsai	Dwarf tree.
Buddha	"Enlightened one."
Bunraku (or Gidayu)	A puppet play.
Bushi	The mounted warrior-gentlemen who came into prominence in the late Heian and Kamakura period.
Bushido	The way, or code, of the warrior.
Cha-no-yu	Tea ceremony.
Chonin	Townspeople.
Chumon	Middle gate in Buddhist temple colonnade.
Daimyo	A great lord.
Dengaku	A Japanese harvest song, one source of *No* musical tradition.
Do	A circuit, or administrative unit created by the mid-seventh-century Taika reforms.
Dogu	Jomon clay figurines.
Dotaku	Ancient bronze bells dating to neolithic times and found in central Japan.
Eta	An outcast class in Japan.
Fudai	A Tokugawa "inside" lord; an ally of the shogun.
Fudoki	Provincial histories composed in early Japan.
Gagaku	Imperial musical tradition.
Geisha	Professional female entertainer.
Genro	Elder statesmen who presided over the destinies of Meiji Japan.
Giri	An individual's duty; often a theme in Japanese novels.
Gun	Early district administrative unit.
Haiku	A seventeen-syllable, three-line poem.
Han	A fief in feudal Japan.
Haniwa	Ancient clay figurines found in early Japanese tombs.
Harakiri	Ritual suicide.
Hibachi	Charcoal heating brazier.
Horo (or Kairo)	Covered colonnade in Buddhist temple complex.

Ikebana	Art of floral arrangement.
Ji	Suffix denoting a temple.
Joruri	The texts of puppet plays.
Kabuki	Late feudal dramatic tradition.
Kagami	Family histories or chronicles composed in aristocratic and feudal Japan.
Kami	A superior person or thing, worshipped in Shinto.
Kamikaze	A "divine wind," such as the typhoon that helped to repel the Mongol invasion of Japan in the late thirteenth century. Used in World War II for suicidal dive bombers.
Kampaku	A civil dictator, a title given to a regent over an adult emperor, generally reserved for the Fujiwara.
Kana	A Japanese phonetic syllabary based on Chinese characters.
Kanji	Chinese characters used for meaning.
Kinai (Kansai)	Home provinces around Nara/Kyoto.
Koan	An intellectual riddle posed by Zen masters to be worked out as a meditative exercise by their disciples.
Kodo	Lecture hall in Buddhist temple complex.
Koku	Unit of grain measurement.
Kokutai	National polity, or the essence of Japanese nationalism.
Kondo	Central Buddhist temple building housing deities.
Kuge	A court noble.
Kuni	Early provincial administrative unit.
Kyogen	"Crazy words"; interludes in No dramas.
Mandala	Buddhist paintings, symbolic in nature, mainly in Shingon sect.
Metsuke	The Tokugawa secret police.
Mingei	Folk art.
Mobo	Modern boy of 1920's.
Moga	Modern girl of 1920's.
Monogatari	Stories or tales (historical or fictional).
Mudra	Various hand positions in Buddhist art that denote aspects of doctrine.
Namban	Art portraying Western themes.
Nembutsu	The invocation of a buddha's name or a sutra for salvation, as found in some Mahayana sects.
Netsuke	Small ivory carvings worked during the Takugawa.
Nihon/Nippon	The Japanese name for Japan.
Ninjo	Passion or feeling; a theme often found in Japanese novels antagonistic to the individual's duty or obligations.
Nirvana	The extinction of self and desire; the goal of Buddhism.
Nise-e	"Likenesses" in scroll paintings.

No	Buddhist plays.
Nyorai	A buddha.
Renga	A chain poem consisting of an initial three-line, seventeen-syllable unit, followed by a two-line, fourteen-syllable unit, and so on alternately.
Ri	Early village administrative unit.
Ronin	A masterless or dispossessed samurai.
Ryubu Shinto	Dual Shinto; fusion with Buddhism.
Samisen	A three-stringed musical instrument.
Samurai	A military retainer of a feudal lord.
Sankin Kotai	The practice of alternate attendance at Edo required of the daimyo during the Tokugawa period.
Sarugako	"Monkey music," a source of No musical tradition.
Sengoku Jidai	Century of warring states during later Ashikaga.
Sessho	The regent for a child emperor.
Shiki	Rights based on land as they evolved in the practice of commendation and benefice during the feudal period.
Shinko	Zaibatsu generally connected with Manchurian economic development in the 1930's.
Shinto	The "Way of the Gods."
Shoen	Tax exempt private holdings which sprang up in aristocratic and feudal Japan and were held chiefly by monasteries and the nobility.
Shogun	"Barbarian subduing general"; after 1196 the title given to the indirect ruler behind the throne.
Shoji	Sliding wall paper panels in Japanese houses.
Soshi	A modern patriot; one who dedicated his life to his country.
Sumi-e	Monochromatic scroll ink painting.
Tanegashima	Firearms, after island where Portuguese first landed.
Tanka	A thirty-one-syllable, five-line poem.
Tatami	Straw mats on floors in Japanese homes.
Tenno	A term adopted by Japanese emperors from the Chinese signifying an omnipotent, divine ruler.
Tokonoma	An alcove in a Japanese home usually containing a flower arrangement or a hanging scroll.
Torii	A gateway, usually with two transverse bars.
Tozama	A Tokugawa "outside" lord, or traditional enemy of the shogun.
Ukiyo-e	Pictures of the "floating" or modern world, which were depicted on woodblock prints during the Tokugawa.
Uji	An ancient Yamato clan.
Wako	Japanese pirates who harrassed the Chinese coast during the Kamakura and Ashikaga periods.
Yamato-e	"Likenesses" (scrolls) depicting scenes of Yamato life.

Yang-yin	Chinese philosophic concept of necessary opposites, adopted by Japanese.
Za	Semiautonomous commercial guilds of feudal Japan.
Zaibatsu	Modern Japanese industrial cartels.
Zazen	The Zen practice of sitting in meditation.

BIBLIOGRAPHY

BIBLIOGRAPHY

References

American Universities Field Staff Reports from the Field. East Asia series. (New York, issued on an irregular basis).

Association for Asian Studies. *Bibliography* (annual September issue). 1956–

––––. *The Journal of Asian Studies*. Ann Arbor, quarterly, 1956–

BORTON, HUGH, ed. *Japan*. Ithaca, 1951.

BORTON, HUGH, et al. *A Selected List of Books and Articles on Japan in English, French, and German*. Cambridge, Mass., 1954.

Contemporary Japan. Tokyo, quarterly, 1932–

HALL, JOHN W. *Japanese History: New Dimensions of Approach and Understanding*. Washington, Service Center for Teachers of History, 2nd ed. 1966, paperback. A bibliographic essay.

HALL, JOHN W., and RICHARD K. BEARDSLEY. *Twelve Doors to Japan*. New York, 1965.

Japan, Consulate General, New York. *Japan Report*. Semimonthly.

Japan Quarterly. Tokyo, 1954.

Japan Times. Formerly *Nippon Times*.

Japan Tourist Bureau. *Japan Tourist Library*. Short volumes on various aspects of Japanese life and culture.

Oriental Economist. Tokyo, monthly, 1934–

SILBERMAN, BERNARD S. *Japan and Korea: A Critical Bibliography*. Tucson, 1962.

This Is Japan. The Asahi newspaper chain annual, 1954–

Transactions of the Asiatic Society of Japan. Tokyo, 1872–1922, 1924–1940, 1948 ff. Comprehensive index to all three series is found in issue of December, 1958 (Series 3, Vol. VI).

TSUNODA, RYUSAKU, et al., comps. *Sources of Japanese Tradition*. 2 vols. New York, 1961. Paperback.

United States Embassy, Tokyo. *Daily Summary of Japanese Press; Trend of Japanese Magazines; Summaries of Selected Japanese Magazines*. Mimeo.

VARLEY, H. PAUL. *A Syllabus of Japanese Civilization*. Rev. ed. New York, 1972.

WEBB, HERSCHEL. *An Introduction to Japan*. New York, 1960. Paperback.

General History

BEASLEY, WILLIAM G., and E. G. PULLEYBLANK. *Historians of China and Japan.* London, 1961.

BRINKLEY, FRANK. *A History of the Japanese People from the Earliest Times to the End of the Meiji Era.* New York, 1915.

FAIRBANK, JOHN, and EDWIN O. REISCHAUER. *A History of East Asian Civilization: Vol. I. East Asia: The Great Tradition.* Boston, 1960. Chapters on Japan, Korea, and China.

FAIRBANK, JOHN, EDWIN O. REISCHAUER, and ALBERT CRAIG. *A History of East Asian Civilization: Vol. II. The Modern Transformation,* Boston, 1965. A one-volume edition issued 1973.

HALL, JOHN W. *Japan: From Prehistory to Modern Times.* New York, 1970.

HANE, MISIKO. *Japan: A Historical Survey.* New York, 1972.

MURDOCH, JAMES. *A History of Japan.* 3 vol., Kobe and London, 1903, 1910, 1926. Reprint 1949. *Vol. I. From Origins to Arrival of Portugese in 1542* A.D. *Vol. II. Century of Early Foreign Intercourse, 1542–1651. Vol. III. Tokugawa Epoch, 1652–1868.*

REISCHAUER, EDWIN O. *Japan, Past and Present.* 3rd ed. New York, 1964. Later issued as *Japan: The Story of a Nation.* New York, 1970.

SANSOM, SIR GEORGE B. *A History of Japan.* 3 vol., Stanford, 1959–1963. *Vol. I. A History of Japan to 1334. Vol. II. A History of Japan, 1334–1615. Vol. III. A History of Japan, 1615–1895.*

———. *Japan, A Short Cultural History.* Rev. ed. New York, 1943.

VARLEY, H. PAUL. *Japanese Culture: A Short History.* New York, 1972.

Pre-1868 History

ASAKAWA, KANICHI. *The Early Institutional Life of the Japanese.* Tokyo, 1903. Reprint, New York, 1963.

ASTON, W. G. *Nihongi: Chronicles of Japan from the Earliest Times to* A.D. *679.* London, 1896. Reprint, 1956.

BEASLEY, WILLIAM G., ed. and trans. *Select Documents in Japanese Foreign Policy, 1853–1868.* London, 1955.

BELLAH, ROBERT N. *Tokugawa Religion: The Values of Pre-Industrial Japan.* Glencoe, Ill., 1957.

BOXER, CHARLES R. *The Christian Century in Japan, 1549–1650.* Berkeley, 1951.

BROWN, DELMAR M. *Money Economy in Medival Japan; A Study in the Use of Coins.* New Haven, 1951.

CHAMBERLAIN, BASIL H., trans. *The Kojiki, or Record of Ancient Matters.* 2nd ed. Kobe, 1932.

COSENZA, MARIO E., ed. *The Complete Journal of Townsend Harris.* New York, 1930.

DUUS, PETER. 2nd ed. *Feudalism in Japan.* New York, 1976.

GROOT, GERALD J. *The Prehistory of Japan.* New York, 1951.

HAWKS, FRANCIS L., comp. *Narrative of the Expedition of an American Squadron to the China Seas and Japan under the Command of Commodore M. C. Perry, U.S. Navy.* 3 vol., Washington, 1856.

KEENE, DONALD. *The Japanese Discovery of Europe.* London, 1950.

KIDDER, JOSEPH E. *Japan Before Buddhism.* New York, 1959.

MC CULLOUGH, C. *The Taiheiki: A Chronicle of Medieval Japan.* New York, 1959.

MIKI, FUMIO. *Haniwa: The Clay Sculpture of Protohistoric Japan.* Rutland, 1960.

MORRIS, IVAN I. *The World of the Shining Prince: Court Life in Ancient Japan.* New York, 1964.

MURASAKI, SHIKIBU. *The Tale of Genji.* Trans. by Arthur Waley. New York, Modern Library, 1960.

SANSOM, SIR GEORGE B. *The Western World and Japan.* New York, 1955. Emphasizes the period 1600–1895.

SEI, SHONAGON. *Notes from a Pillow Book.* Trans. by Arthur Waley. New York, 1960. Paperback.

SHELDON, CHARLES D. *The Rise of the Merchant Class in Tokugawa Japan, 1600–1868.* Locust Valley, New York, 1958.

SHINODA, MINORU. *The Founding of the Kamakura Shogunate, 1180–1185.* New York, 1960.

SMITH, THOMAS C. *The Agrarian Origins of Modern Japan.* Stanford, 1959.

TOTMAN, CONRAD D. *Politics in the Tokugawa Bakufu, 1600–1815.* Cambridge, 1967.

History: 1868 to 1945

ALLEN, GEORGE C. *A Short Economic History of Modern Japan.* London, 1946.

BORTON, HUGH. *Japan's Modern Century.* 2nd ed. New York, 1970.

BUTOW, ROBERT. *Japan's Decision to Surrender.* Stanford, 1954.
———. *Tojo and the Coming of the War.* Princeton, 1961.

Centenary Culture Council, ed. *Japanese Culture in the Meiji Period, 1868–1912.* 10 vol., Tokyo, 1955–1958.

COHEN, JEROME B. *The Japanese Economy in War and Reconstruction.* Minneapolis, 1949.

CRAIG, ALBERT M. *Choshu in the Meiji Restoration.* Cambridge, Mass., 1961.

DENNETT, TYLER. *Roosevelt and the Russo-Japanese War*. Garden City, New York, 1925.

FEIS, HERBERT. *Japan Subdued*. Princeton, 1961.

————. *The Road to Pearl Harbor*. Princeton, 1950.

FUKUZAWA, YUKICHI. *Autobiography*. Tokyo, 1940.

GREW, JOSEPH C. *Ten Years in Japan*. New York, 1944. American ambassador, 1931–1941.

HEARN, LAFCADIO. *Japan, An Attempt at Interpretation*. New York, 1904.

ISHII, KIKUJIRO, VISCOUNT. *Diplomatic Commentaries*. Trans. and ed. by William R. Langdon. Baltimore, 1936.

ITO HIROBUMI, PRINCE. *Commentaries on the Constitution of the Empire of Japan*. Tokyo, 1906.

JONES, F. C. *Japan's New Order in East Asia, Its Rise and Fall, 1937–1945*. London, 1954.

LOCKWOOD, WILLIAM W. *The Economic Development of Japan, Growth and Structural Change, 1868–1938*. Princeton, expanded edition, 1968.

MC LAREN, WALTER W. *A Political History of Japan during the Meiji Era, 1867–1912*. New York, 1916.

NORMAN, E. HERBERT. *Japan's Emergence as a Modern State: Political and Economic Problems of the Meiji Period*. New York, 1940.

OKUMA, COUNT SHIGENOBU, comp. *Fifty Years of New Japan*. 2 vol., London, 1910.

ORCHARD, JOHN C. *Japan's Economic Position, the Progress of Industrialization*. New York, 1930.

RAUCAT, T. *The Honorable Picnic*. New York, 1927.

REISCHAUER, ROBERT K. *Japan, Government-Politics*. New York, 1939.

SCALAPINO, ROBERT. *Democracy and the Party Movement in Pre-war Japan*. Berkeley, 1953.

SCHWANTES, ROBERT S. *Japanese and Americans, A Century of Cultural Relations*. New York, 1955.

SHIGEMITSU, MAMORU. *Japan and Her Destiny*. New York, 1958.

SMITH, THOMAS C. *Political Change and Industrial Development in Japan, Government Enterprise, 1868–1880*. Stanford, 1955.

SWEARINGER, ROGER, and PAUL LANGER. *Red Flag in Japan*. Cambridge, Mass., 1952. A study of the Japanese Communist movement, 1919–

TAKEUCHI, S. T. *War and Diplomacy in the Japanese Empire*. New York, 1935.

TREAT, PAYSON J. *Japan and the United States, 1853–1928*. Stanford, 1928.

WILLOUGHBY, W. W. *The Sino-Japanese Controversy and the League of Nations*. Baltimore, 1935.

YANAGA, CHITOSHI. *Japan Since Perry*. New York, 1949.

History Since 1945

BLAKESLEE, GEORGE H. *The Far Eastern Commission, A Study in International Cooperation, 1945 to 1953.* Washington, 1953.

FEARY, ROBERT A. *The Occupation of Japan, Second Phase, 1948–1950.* New York, 1950.

International Military Tribunal for the Far East. *Judgment. Documents. Evidence.* Mimeo. Tokyo, undated.

KAWAI, KAZUO. *Japan's American Interlude.* Chicago, 1960.

MARTIN, EDWIN M. *The Allied Occupation of Japan.* Stanford, 1948.

United States Department of State. *Record of Proceedings of the Conference for the Conclusion and Signature of the Treaty of Peace with Japan.* Washington, 1951.

Politics and Economics

ACKERMAN, E. A. *Japan's Natural Resources and Their Relation to Japan's Economic Future.* Chicago, 1953.

ALLEN, GEORGE C. *Japan's Economic Recovery.* New York, 1958.

——. *A Short Economic History of Modern Japan. Rev. ed.* London, 1963.

BEARDSLEY, RICHARD, JOHN W. HALL, and ROBERT WARD. *Village Japan.* Chicago, 1959.

BORTON, HUGH, ed. *Japan Between East and West.* New York, 1957.

BROWN, DELMER M. *Nationalism in Japan: An Introductory Historical Analysis.* Berkeley, 1955.

DORE, RONALD P. *City Life in Japan.* London, 1958.

——. *Land Reform in Japan.* London, 1958.

IKE, NOBUTAKI. *Japanese Politics.* New York, 1957.

REISCHAUER, EDWIN O. *The United States and Japan.* 3rd ed. Cambridge, Mass., 1965. Paperback.

SCALAPINO, ROBERT A., and MASUMI JUNNOSUKE. *Parties and Politics in Contemporary Japan.* Berkeley, 1962.

STORRY, RICHARD. *The Double Patriots.* Boston, 1958.

TAEUBER, IRENE B. *The Population of Japan.* Princeton, 1958.

TREWARTHA, GLENN T. *Japan: A Physical, Cultural, and Regional Geography.* 2nd ed. Madison, 1965.

YOSHIDA SHIGERU. *The Yoshida Memoirs.* Boston, 1962. Postwar Japanese prime minister.

Culture

AKUTAGAWA, RYUNOSUKE. *Rashomon and Other Stories.* Trans. Kojima Takashi. New York, 1952. Novellas.

ARMSTRONG, ROBERT C. *Light from the East: Studies in Japanese Confucianism.* Toronto, 1914.

ANESAKI, MASAHARU. *Religious Life of the Japanese People.* Tokyo, 1935.

BENEDICT, RUTH. *The Chrysanthemum and the Sword.* Boston, 1946.

BINYON, LAURENCE. *Painting in the Far East: An Introduction to the History of Pictorial Art in Asia, Especially China and Japan.* 4th ed., rev. London, 1934.

BOWERS, FAUBION. *Japanese Theater.* New York, 1952. Mainly Kabuki.

BROWER, ROBERT H., and EARL MINER. *Japanese Court Poetry.* Stanford, 1961.

CHIKAMATSU MONZAEMON. *The Major Plays of Chikamatsu.* Trans. Donald Keene. New York, 1961.

ELIOT, SIR CHARLES. *Japanese Buddhism.* London, 1936. Reprint, New York, 1960.

EMBREE, JOHN F. *A Japanese Nation: A Social Survey.* New York, 1945.

HOLTOM, DANIEL C. *Modern Japan and Shinto Nationalism.* Rev. ed. Chicago, 1947.

KAWABATA YASUNARI. *Snow Country.* Trans. Edward G. Seidensticker. New York, 1957. Novel.

KEENE, DONALD, ed. *Anthology of Japanese Literature from the Earliest Era to the Mid-19th Century.* New York, 1955. Paperback.

———. *Japanese Literature.* New York, 1955. Paperback.

———. *Living Japan.* New York, 1959.

———. *Modern Japanese Literature, an Anthology.* New York, 1956. Paperback.

MALM, WILLIAM P. *Japanese Music and Musical Instruments.* Tokyo, 1959.

MICHENER, JAMES A. *The Floating World: The Story of Japanese Prints.* New York, 1956.

MISHIMA, YUKIO. *The Sound of the Waves.* Trans. Meredith Weatherby. New York, 1956. Novel.

MITSUOKA, TADANARI. *Ceramic Art of Japan.* 5th ed. Tokyo, 1960.

MUNSTERBERG, HUGO. *The Arts of Japan: An Illustrated History.* Rutland, 1957.

PAINE, ROBERT T., and ALEXANDER C. SOPER. *The Art and Architecture of Japan.* Rev. ed. Baltimore, 1960.

SILBERMAN, BERNARD S., ed. *Japanese Character and Culture: Selected Readings.* Tucson, 1962.

SOSEKI, NATSUME. *Kokoro.* Trans. Edwin McClellan. Chicago, 1957. Novel.

STATLER, OLIVER. *Japanese Inn.* New York, 1962. Paperback.

SUZUKI, DAISETZ T. *Introduction to Zen Buddhism.* New York, 1949.
——. *Zen Buddhism and Its Influence on Japanese Culture.* Kyoto, 1938.

TANIZAKI, JUNICHIRO. *The Makioka Sisters.* Trans. Edward G. Seidensticker. New York, 1957. Novel.

Tokyo National Museum. *Pageant of Japanese Art.* 6 vol., Tokyo, 1952–1954.

WALEY, ARTHUR, trans. *The No Plays of Japan.* London, 1921.

WARNER, LANGDON. *The Craft of the Japanese Sculptor.* New York, 1936.
——. *The Enduring Art of Japan.* New York, 1958. Paperback.

JAPAN'S CHIEF POSTWAR POLITICAL PARTIES

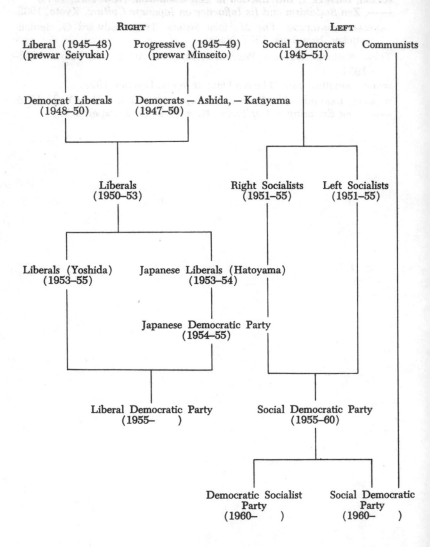

RIGHT   LEFT

Liberal (1945–48)
(prewar Seiyukai)

Progressive (1945–49)
(prewar Minseito)

Social Democrats
(1945–51)

Communists

Democrat Liberals
(1948–50)

Democrats — Ashida, — Katayama
(1947–50)

Liberals
(1950–53)

Right Socialists
(1951–55)

Left Socialists
(1951–55)

Liberals (Yoshida)
(1953–55)

Japanese Liberals (Hatoyama)
(1953–54)

Japanese Democratic Party
(1954–55)

Liberal Democratic Party
(1955–   )

Social Democratic Party
(1955–60)

Democratic Socialist
Party
(1960–   )

Social Democratic
Party
(1960–   )

ELECTION RETURNS BY MAIN PARTIES:
(1) HOUSE OF REPRESENTATIVES

Date	Progressive	Liberal	Socialist		Communist	Komeito	Total*
4/10/46	94	140	92		5		464
	Democratic						
4/25/47	121	131	143		4		466
		Democratic-Liberal					
1/23/49	69	264	48		35		466
			Socialist				
	Reform		Left	Right			
10/1/52	85	240	54	57	0		466
		Hato-yama · Yoshi-da					
4/19/53	76	35 · 199	72	66	1		466
	Democratic · Liberal						
2/27/55	185 · 112		89	67	2		467
	Liberal-Democratic		Socialist				
5/22/58	287		166		1		467
			Socialist	Democratic Socialist			
11/20/60	296		145	17	3		467
11/21/63	283		144	23	5		467
1/29/67	277		140	30	5	25	486
12/27/69	288		90	31	14	47	486
12/10/72	282		118	19	38	29	491

* Total figures include other minor parties and independents.

ELECTION RETURNS BY MAIN PARTIES: (2) HOUSE OF COUNCILLORS

Year	Liberal	Democratic-Progressive		Socialist		Communist	Komeito	Total[*] (national/ local)
1947	38	28		47		4		250 (110/150)
1950	52	9		36		2		132 (56/76)
			Right	Left				
1953	46	8	10	18		0		128 (53/75)
	Liberal-Democratic			Socialist				
1956	61			49		2		127 (52/75)
1959	71			38		1		127 (52/75)
		Democratic-Socialist						
1962	69	4		37		3	9	127 (51/76)
1965	71	3		36		3	11	127 (52/75)
1968	69	7		28		4	13	126 (51/75)
1971	63	6		39		6	10	126 (50/76)
1974	62	5		28		13	14	130 (54/76)

[*] Total figures include other minor parties and independents.

JAPANESE CABINETS

(Pre-constitution prime ministers: Ito Hirobumi, 1885–1888; Kuroda Kiyotaka, 1888–1889)

Yamagata Aritomo, 1889–1891
Matsukata Masayoshi, 1891–1892
Ito Hirobumi, 1892–1896
Matsukata Masayoshi, 1896–1898
Ito Hirobumi, 1898
Okuma Shigenobu, 1898
Yamagata Aritomo, 1898–1900
Ito Hirobumi, 1900–1901
Katsura Taro, 1901–1906
Saionji Kimmochi, 1906–1908
Katsura Taro, 1908–1911
Saionji Kimmochi, 1911–1912
Katsura Taro, 1912–1913
Yamamoto Gonnohyoe, 1913–1914
Okuma Shigenobu, 1914–1916
Terauchi Masataki, 1916–1918
Hara Kei, 1918–1921 (Seiyukai)
Takahashi Korekiyo, 1921–1922 (Seiyukai)
Kato Tomosaburo, 1922–1923
Yamamoto Gonnohyoe, 1923–1924
Kiyoura Keigo, 1924
Kato Komei, 1924–1926 (Kenseikai)
Wakatsuki Reijiro, 1926–1927 (Kenseikai)
Tanaka Giichi, 1927–1929 (Seiyukai)

Hamaguchi Yuko, 1929–1931 (Minseito)
Wakatsuki Reijiro, 1931 (Minseito)
Inukai Tsuyoshi, 1931 (Seiyukai)
Saito Makoto, 1932–1934
Okada Keisuke, 1934–1936
Hirota Koki, 1936–1937
Hayashi Senjuro, 1937
Konoye Fumimaro, 1937–1938
Hiranuma Kiichiro, 1938–1939
Abe Nobuyuki, 1939–1940
Yonai Mitsumasa, 1940
Konoye Fumimaro, 1940, 1941
Tojo Hideki, 1941–1944
Koiso Kuniaki, 1944
Suzuki Kantaro, 1945 (April)
Higashikuni, Prince, 1945 (August)
Shidehara Kijuro, 1945 (October)
Yoshida Shigeru, 1946–1947
Katayama Tetsu, 1947
Ashida Hitoshi, 1948
Yoshida Shigeru, 1948–1954
Hatoyama Ichiro, 1954–1956
Ishibashi Tanzan, 1956
Kishi Nobosuke, 1957–1960
Ikeda Hayato, 1960–1964
Sato Eisaku, 1964–1972
Tanaka Kakuei, 1972–1974
Miki Takeo, 1974–

INDEX

INDEX